DEPARTMENT OF THE NAVY
OFFICE OF THE CHIEF OF NAVAL OPERATIONS
WASHINGTON, DC 20350-2000

IN REPLY REFER TO

Ser: 00/1U500179
15 May 1991

Subj: **THE UNITED STATES NAVY IN "DESERT SHIELD" / "DESERT STORM"**

Encl: (1) Summary Report

1. This summary of the role of the United States Navy in Operations DESERT SHIELD and DESERT STORM was compiled from the reports of operational commanders and supporting commands, and information gathered at headquarters. It provides a ready reference of Navy participation in DESERT SHIELD/STORM with the objective of making accurate, useful information available as quickly as possible.

2. The significance of the Navy's role in Operations DESERT SHIELD and DESERT STORM is clear. Forward deployed naval forces provided protection for early introduction of land-based ground and air assets, and may well have deterred further aggression by Iraq. Maritime superiority and unchallenged control of the sea enabled the safe and timely delivery of equipment, supplies and spare parts necessary to support the allied campaign. Interdiction of Iraqi seaborne trade, an ongoing operation, cut enemy resupply, dampened their will to fight and significantly impacted Iraq's economic health. More than 90% of material to support the campaign was delivered by sealift, and the majority of medical assets in the early months were provided by Navy. The presence of Middle East Force ships deterred Iraqi mine laying in the southern Persian Gulf. Naval aviation complemented allied air operations, added flexibility to the air campaign and deterred reintroduction of Iraqi aircraft from Iran into the conflict. Tomahawk cruise missiles took out heavily defended targets in Iraq and significantly degraded enemy air defenses.

3. The most significant contributor to our decisive victory was our motivated, dedicated, well-trained volunteers. Our people performed superbly, and validated the investments made in them over the past decades. Their courage, commitment and professionalism inspired unprecedented and well-deserved support from the American public and national leadership. Their compassion and generosity in the war's aftermath inspired the world. The men and women of the U.S. Armed Forces gave us victory, and America's sailors were a crucial part of that victory. This report documents the contributions of the men and women who wear the uniform of the United States Navy.

F. B. KELSO, II

- ii -

THE UNITED STATES NAVY IN "DESERT SHIELD" / "DESERT STORM"

TABLE OF CONTENTS

	EXECUTIVE SUMMARY. v	
	The Role of the Navy v	
	Lessons Learned vi	
I.	OVERVIEW — The Role of the Navy 1	
	Overview 1	
	A Short History of the United States Navy in the Persian Gulf 2	
	The Role of the Navy in Joint Operations 5	
	Flexible Response: The Navy Marine Team in Action 8	
II.	"THE GATHERING STORM" — The Build-up of U.S. Forces. 11	
	Introduction 11	
	The Buildup of U.S. Navy Forces 11	
	The Buildup of Airpower 12	
	The Buildup of Ground Forces 13	
	Navy Medical Buildup and Follow-Through 15	
	Naval Reserve Support 16	
III.	"A COMMON GOAL" — Joint and Multinational Operations 19	
	Introduction 19	
	Joint Operations During DESERT SHIELD/STORM 20	
	The Maritime Inerception Campaign 20	
IV.	"BULLETS, BANDAGES AND BEANS" — Logistic Operations 27	
	Sealift Investments of the 1980s 27	
	Sealift During DESERT SHIELD/STORM 28	
	Maintaining Combat Readiness 30	
	Navy Combat Logistics 30	
	Navy SEABEES — "Can Do" in Action 32	
V.	"THUNDER AND LIGHTNING" — The War with Iraq 35	
	Introduction and Overview 35	
	The Air War 36	
	The War at Sea 39	
	Amphibious Operations 44	
	Support for the Troops: The Ground War 45	
	The Weapons of War 47	
	The Post-War Period 49	
VI.	LESSONS LEARNED AND SUMMARY 51	
	Introduction 51	
	Areas Not Tested 52	
	Old Lessons Revalidated 54	
	The Lessons of DESERT SHIELD/STORM 54	
	Summary 63	

EPILOGUE 65

APPENDICES

APPENDIX A: CHRONOLOGY A-1
APPENDIX B: ALLIED PARTICIPATION AND CONTRIBUTIONS B-1
APPENDIX C: PARTICIPATING NAVAL UNITS C-1
APPENDIX D: AIRCRAFT SORTIE COUNT D-1
APPENDIX E: AIRCRAFT READINESS RATES...E-1
APPENDIX F: AIRCRAFT AND PERSONNEL LOSSES F-1
APPENDIX G: NAVAL GUNFIRE SUPPORT G-1
APPENDIX H: SURFACE WARFARE H-1
APPENDIX I: UNMANNED AERIAL VEHICLES I-1
APPENDIX J: MARITIME INTERCEPTION OPERATIONS J-1
APPENDIX K: SEALIFT K-1
APPENDIX L: AIRLIFT L-1
APPENDIX M: MISCELLANEOUS PERSONNEL DATA M-1
APPENDIX N: NAVAL RESERVE N-1
APPENDIX O: MEDICAL SUPPORT O-1
APPENDIX P: MEDIA POOLS P-1

THE UNITED STATES NAVY IN "DESERT SHIELD" / "DESERT STORM"

EXECUTIVE SUMMARY

THE ROLE OF THE NAVY

This report highlights the role of the U.S. Navy in conjunction with the nation's other maritime forces — the Marine Corps and Coast Guard — in DESERT SHIELD/STORM. But neither of those operations could have been accomplished without the full participation of all services. Each service brought its strengths and special operational capabilities to bear as the situation required. The result was the most complex, fast-moving, successful, major joint power projection operation in history.

The six ships of the Middle East Force were on station in the Persian Gulf when the President decided to deploy additional forces to Southwest Asia beginning 7 August. The INDEPENDENCE battle group had steamed into strike range in the North Arabian Sea, and the EISENHOWER battle group was transiting the Suez Canal to the Red Sea within strike range of Iraq. When United Nations sanctions were imposed, the U.S. Navy immediately commenced interception operations against ships headed to and from Iraq and Kuwait.

We may never learn the extent to which on-scene naval forces influenced Saddam Hussein to stop short of invading Saudi Arabia. We do know that the sustainable combat capability and control of the sea provided by those naval forces afforded protection for the introduction of ground and air forces arriving in theater in response to deployment orders.

The Navy's ability to control the seas was taken for granted, as it has been since 1945. That control makes it possible for us to deliver our troops and supplies safely to any area of conflict. The maritime superiority which enabled our victory was made possible by earlier sound investments in people, ships, aircraft and weapons systems. DESERT SHIELD/STORM demonstrated again that sea control is fundamental to successful power projection. Because naval forces were on station and ready, we were never seriously challenged, and sea control was assured from the outset.

Maritime superiority and forward deployment gave us another edge in DESERT SHIELD/STORM. Only a nation possessing both unquestioned control of the seas and significant experience operating in forward areas in close cooperation with the naval forces of our coalition partners could have provided the leadership for 23 nations whose naval forces participated. The ability of the U.S. Navy to operate effectively with so many other navies did not come quickly or easily. It was built over forty years of close cooperation with the navies of NATO and other allies. Familiarity with the geography and local navies was gained through a continuous presence in the Gulf since 1949. During the Persian Gulf "Tanker War" of 1987-88, the U.S. vividly demonstrated its military and political staying power to even the most skeptical critics within the Arab world. Operation EARNEST WILL laid the foundation for DESERT SHIELD/STORM.

Multinational naval cooperation was

demonstrated in many warfare areas but was most evident in the maritime interception campaign. Maritime interception was an important military and political tool from the outset. Enforcement of the U.N. sanctions weakened Iraqi forces prior to the conflict and imposed a heavy burden on Iraq's economy. Through April 1991, over 9200 merchant ships had been challenged, more than 1200 boarded for inspection, and at least 67 diverted for carrying prohibited cargo. Countless ships were deterred from on-loading Iraqi oil and other products for export. Iraq's GNP was reduced by half. The impact of the embargo was clearly felt by Iraqi soldiers in the trenches. The eroding effect on their morale and will to fight undoubtedly saved many coalition lives. The maritime interception effort continued even after cessation of offensive operations as a guarantee of Iraq's compliance with U.N. resolutions.

The contribution of strategic sealift was one of the major success stories of DESERT SHIELD/STORM. Sealift investments of the 1980s paid great dividends. The early force arrival dates achieved by maritime prepositioning and fast sealift ships met or exceeded our most optimistic projections. Military Sealift Command (MSC) controlled ships delivered 3.4 million tons of cargo and 6.8 million tons of fuels — much of it moved half-way around the world. Over 90% of all cargo was transported into theater via sealift; more than 95% will return the same way.

The five month build-up period during DESERT SHIELD allowed the Navy to overcome obstacles and build teamwork with the other services and our coalition partners required to meet the challenges which arose during combat. Once unleashed, a massive joint and combined force acted in unison to quickly eject Iraqi forces from Kuwait. Naval forces played an essential role. For example, about one third of all strike sorties were flown by Navy and Marine Corps aircraft. Six aircraft carrier battle groups and two battleships were simultaneously engaged. Cruisers, destroyers, battleships and submarines launched a combined total of 288 Tomahawk cruise missiles from the Red Sea and Persian Gulf against heavily defended key Iraqi facilities. About 85% of those missiles hit their targets with pin point accuracy, contributing to the early neutralization of Iraqi air defenses and reducing the risks for American aircrews.

Naval forces literally eliminated the Iraqi Navy and projected power ashore. Surface combatants, helicopters, carrier-based aircraft, land-based P-3s, and our multinational naval partners all contributed to the destruction of more than 100 Iraqi vessels. Amphibious forces conducted an impressive series of raids, feints and rehearsals which highlighted their exceptional responsiveness and flexibility and paved the way for a most successful deception operation.

DESERT STORM once again illustrated the challenge of mine countermeasures, especially in a confined area like the Northern Persian Gulf. Finding and neutralizing mines is difficult under any circumstances. We cannot always afford to allow minelaying in international waters to go unopposed as we did in this case. There is no capability, either existing or projected, which could quickly neutralize over 1000 mines once laid. The U.S. Navy must possess the best mine countermeasures capability available.

LESSONS LEARNED

The lessons of DESERT SHIELD/STORM might usefully be separated into three broad categories: areas not tested, old lessons revalidated, and new lessons learned. Areas not tested encompass those systems and capabilities which, because of the special circumstances of these operations, were not realistically stressed, tested or evaluated. Reviewing the areas not tested helps avoid learning the wrong lessons.

AREAS NOT TESTED. Nearly every early attempt to extract the lessons of DESERT SHIELD/STORM has begun with a cautionary note concerning the "unique aspects" of those operations and the "lessons not learned." This assessment reviews those "areas not tested" in context with the old and new lessons to foster critical examination of the entire range of naval warfare capabilities and their applicability to future scenarios. Specific areas not tested by DESERT SHIELD/STORM include:

- Limited access to critical enroute support bases, aircraft refueling facilities and overflight rights.

- Non-availability of overseas bases from which to conduct offensive or support operations.

- Force and mobility requirements for a second major simultaneous crisis in another region.

- An opponent who receives support from allies with significant capabilities such as the USSR or China.

- U.S. action without strong regional or international support.

- Rapid transition to hostilities.

- Significant naval opposition, antisubmarine warfare, or a requirement for forcible entry. Amphibious assault was not fully tested.

- Confrontation by an integrated defense and strong resistance from a capable adversary with modern high-tech weapons. Neither close air support nor anti-air warfare were fully tested by this conflict.

- Limited host-nation support and infrastructure.

- While the extreme and unique topographical and climatological conditions of Southwest Asia posed special challenges, DESERT SHIELD/STORM only tested our capabilities to operate in one of many possible environments.

OLD LESSONS REVALIDATED. DESERT SHIELD/STORM reaffirmed the importance of clear-cut military objectives, political cohesion and popular support. Established principles of war such as concentration of force, unity of command, effective leadership, the will to fight, and detailed planning were also reaffirmed. Other lessons revalidated include:

- The value and effectiveness of joint and combined military operations.

- The importance of control of the sea for successful power-projection.

- The importance of maritime superiority in affording the United States a position of leadership.

- The vital role of sealift in moving heavy equipment and supplies into the theater.

- The strategic and tactical advantages of high technology.
- The challenge of finding and neutralizing naval mines.

THE LESSONS OF DESERT SHIELD/STORM. This initial review of lessons learned underscores keys to victory which must be nurtured and reinforced. It also highlights areas for improvement.

QUALITY PEOPLE AND REALISTIC TRAINING. The outstanding quality of our people, and their high state of training, were fundamental to success. The all-volunteer force worked and worked well. Our men and women knew their jobs, knew their equipment, and knew how to fight. Naval forces arrived in theater trained and ready. We must continue to emphasize:

- People programs — the foundation of the all-volunteer force.
- High quality, realistic training — including joint operational training — which is fundamental to success in combat.

JOINT OPERATIONS. DESERT SHIELD/STORM illustrated the importance and benefits of joint and combined operations. While some problems were encountered — particularly in command and control, communications, interoperability, and matters of joint doctrine — the significant progress made in joint operations over the past several years was reflected in success on the battlefield. That success firmly cemented the Navy's commitment to joint operations.

WARFIGHTING. Conducting complex joint operations in an environment like Southwest Asia poses special challenges for the Navy. While not every naval warfare area was stressed or even tested, naval forces participated in virtually every aspect of the campaign. Multi-mission platforms proved especially valuable.

- **COMMAND RELATIONSHIPS.** DESERT SHIELD/STORM highlighted the importance of establishing peacetime planning relationships and staffs which parallel wartime responsibilities and requirements.

- **ANTISUBMARINE WARFARE.** ASW was not tested as there was no threat, but primary ASW systems such as P-3s, S-3s and LAMPS helicopters used multi-mission capabilities to good advantage.

- **ANTI-AIR WARFARE.** DESERT SHIELD/STORM presented a complex AAW challenge. All operations were conducted safely and successfully from pre-hostilities through redeployment. There were no "blue-on-blue" air engagements.

- **STRIKE WARFARE.** The Joint Force Air Component Commander (JFACC) used the air tasking order (ATO) as a centralized planning and execution tool to effectively manage the unprecedented volume of sorties, especially during the preplanned, structured stages of the campaign.

  - **STRIKE AIRCRAFT.** The A-6 aircraft was the workhorse for long range strike and performed extremely well in an environment of established air superiority. However, it was also apparent the

A-6's advanced age necessitates both upgrades and eventual replacement. The performance of the F-117 demonstrated the value of stealth and validated the requirement for a follow-on, long range, all weather, stealthy strike aircraft (AX) as a replacement for the A-6. In addition, the excellent performance of the F/A-18 confirmed the validity of the multimission strike/fighter concept.

- **TOMAHAWK CRUISE MISSILE.** Tomahawk was a tremendous success, and its first use in combat fully confirmed the results of previous extensive operational testing.

- **DEFENSE SUPPRESSION.** The outstanding performance of the EA-6B and other Navy defense suppression aircraft and weapon systems placed these platforms in high demand.

- **SMART WEAPONS.** "Smart" or precision weapons clearly demonstrated their capabilities against point targets. The requirement for highly accurate penetrating weapons for use against heavily bunkered or hardened structures was reaffirmed.

- **TACTICAL RECONNAISSANCE.** The importance of real-time and near-real-time tactical reconnaissance in support of strike planning, naval gunfire support (NGFS), and battle damage assessment (BDA) was clearly demonstrated.

- **AIRBORNE TANKING.** Geography dictated extensive land-based tanking support for both USAF and naval air strikes. Tanker coordination went extremely well. But tankers were stretched thin, and their apportionment necessarily limited the Navy's long-range strike contribution.

• **SURFACE WARFARE.** DESERT STORM demonstrated the enduring value of long range naval gunfire support. Unmanned aerial vehicles (UAVs) were effective in target selection, spotting naval gunfire and damage assessment. The firepower of surface action groups was augmented with attack helicopters, effectively enhancing offensive/reconnaissance capability. The offensive firepower of strike aircraft (A-6s and F/A-18s) and surface combatants destroyed the Iraqi navy.

• **AMPHIBIOUS WARFARE.** Amphibious operations focused enemy attention on the threat from seaward and tied down at least seven Iraqi divisions, even after the coalition ground campaign was well underway. The responsiveness and flexibility of amphibious forces was highlighted by successful raids, rehearsals and feints.

• **MINE WARFARE.** DESERT STORM again illustrated the challenge of mine countermeasures (MCM) and how quickly mines can become a concern. Because of the difficulty of locating and neutralizing mines, we cannot always afford to give the minelayer free rein. Operation EARNEST WILL (during the Iran-Iraq war) and DESERT STORM both highlighted the need for a robust, deployable U.S. Navy MCM capability.

INTELLIGENCE. Intelligence support reflected application of proven principles coupled with outstanding innovation. A joint intelligence doctrine and architecture are needed to support both joint and component commanders. More interoperable intelligence systems are also required.

COMMUNICATIONS. Almost every aspect of naval command and control communications capability was stressed to the limit during DESERT SHIELD/STORM. Problems were solved through aggressive management, work-arounds, innovation, close cooperation and coordination, equipment upgrades and new installations. The Navy is focusing attention on improving our ability to communicate with other services and nations, strengthening jam-resistant communications, and using high speed computer networks to increase capacity.

LOGISTICS. Naval forces arrived in theater with full sea-based, self-sustained logistic support capability. Naval forces required minimum airlift and sealift for deployment and support. Aircraft readiness averaged nearly 90%. The readiness of our ships was equally impressive and reflects a high degree of unit self-sufficiency. The combat logistics force (CLF) performed superbly, meeting all requirements. There were ample supplies of fuel and ammunition.

STRATEGIC SEALIFT. The contribution of strategic sealift was a major success. World-wide sea control afforded by our naval forces clearly contributed to a responsive charter market. Early, accurate identification of lift requirements was difficult and changed often. DESERT SHIELD/STORM identified a need for more roll-on/roll-off (RO/RO) ships to meet unit equipment surge requirements.

MARITIME PREPOSITIONING. The afloat prepositioning concept was validated. No other alternative could have achieved the early force closure dates witnessed during DESERT SHIELD. Beginning 15 August, two squadrons of Maritime Prepositioning Ships (MPS) delivered unit equipment and 30 days supplies for two Marine Expeditionary Brigades (MEBs) totaling nearly 45,000 men -- the first heavy ground combat capability in theater.

MEDICAL SUPPORT. Navy ships and fleet hospitals provided well over two-thirds of in-theater medical capability during the first four months of the operation. In accordance with plans, the hospital ships MERCY and COMFORT were activated and deployed on five days notice. Together with the Fleet Hospitals, they provided the most comprehensive medical care facilities in theater and the capability to deal with a major influx of combat casualties.

TOTAL FORCE CONCEPT. DESERT SHIELD/STORM validated significant aspects of the Navy's Total Force concept.

FUTURE FORCE STRUCTURE. To defend America's interests around the world, future force structure must enable us to continue to employ the winning strategy of concentrating superior force anywhere rapidly enough to deter aggression or achieve quick success in combat.

SUMMARY

While there were problems encountered, the outstanding first impression generated by the performance of our forces in DESERT SHIELD/STORM is being reinforced as we review the after action reports. The success of our forces provides a solid foundation for continued progress. The challenge is to translate the lessons of DESERT SHIELD/STORM into decisions, programs, and actions which will shape our forces, guide our training and ensure our continued readiness to forcefully defend America's interests whenever and wherever required.

THE UNITED STATES NAVY IN "DESERT SHIELD" / "DESERT STORM"

I: OVERVIEW -- THE ROLE OF THE NAVY

"...My administration, as has been the case with every President from President Roosevelt to President Reagan, is committed to the security and stability of the Persian Gulf."

-- **President George Bush**
   Address to the Nation
   8 August 1990

"Our action in the Gulf is about fighting aggression and preserving the sovereignty of nations. It is about keeping our word, our solemn word of honor, and standing by old friends. It is about our own national security interests and ensuring the peace and stability of the entire world."

-- **President George Bush**
   Remarks to Pentagon Employees
   15 August 1990

"When a crisis confronts the nation, the first question often asked by policymakers is: What naval forces are available and how fast can they be on station?"

-- **Admiral C.A.H. Trost, USN**
   Chief of Naval Operations
   Proceedings, May 1990

OVERVIEW. After the world's fourth largest army poured across the border into Kuwait on 2 August 1990, the United States deployed a major joint force which served as the foundation for a powerful 33-nation military coalition to stem Iraq's brutal aggression. The United States Navy provided the sea control and maritime superiority which paved the way for the introduction of U.S. and allied air and ground forces, and offered strong leadership for the multinational naval force.

At the time of the invasion, the Navy was already on station in the region. The ships of Joint Task Force Middle East, a legacy of U.S. Navy presence in the Persian Gulf since 1949, were immediately placed on alert. Battle groups led by USS INDEPENDENCE (CV 62) and USS DWIGHT D. EISENHOWER (CVN 69) sped from the Indian Ocean and Eastern

Mediterranean to take up positions in the Gulf of Oman and Red Sea, respectively — ready to commence sustained combat operations on arrival.

When President Bush ordered the deployment of troops and equipment to defend Saudi Arabia, long-established maritime superiority facilitated the largest, fastest strategic sealift in history, with more than 240 ships carrying more than 18.3 billion pounds of equipment and supplies to sustain the forces of DESERT SHIELD/STORM. Maritime superiority also allowed allied naval forces to implement and sustain United Nations trade sanctions against Iraq immediately after they were imposed severing Saddam Hussein's economic lifeline.

Low-key but close military ties with friendly Arab states, developed during 40-plus-years of naval operations in the region, helped pave the way for the quick introduction of U.S. ground and air forces into Saudi Arabia and other Gulf states. When U.S. Marines began arriving in Saudi Arabia, their supplies and equipment were close at hand. Maritime Prepositioning Ships based at Diego Garcia and Guam carried enough tanks, artillery and ammunition to sustain the Marines for 30 days. The MPS ships' proximity to the theater of operations allowed Marines to begin marrying up with their supplies in Saudi Arabia less than two weeks after the invasion of Kuwait.

Under the Navy's Total Force concept more than 21,000 naval reservists were called to active duty in support of DESERT SHIELD/STORM. Serving in specialties from medicine to mine warfare, reservists worked alongside their active duty counterparts in the Persian Gulf. Others filled critical vacancies on the home front.

Saddam Hussein's rejection of diplomatic efforts to solve the crisis led to the final decision to restore Kuwait's sovereignty by military force. The ensuing air war and the effects of the economic embargo decimated Iraq's military infrastructure, severed communication and supply lines, smashed weapons arsenals, and destroyed morale. Some of the first shots fired were from Navy ships in the Persian Gulf and Red Sea, as they launched salvos of Tomahawk cruise missiles against pre-programmed targets in Iraq.

After an impressive 38-day air campaign, the ground offensive began with allied forces sweeping through Iraqi defenses in blitzkrieg fashion. The allied push into Kuwait and southern Iraq was made easier by the amphibious forces on station in the Persian Gulf. The threat they posed forced tens of thousands of Iraqi troops to maintain positions along the Kuwaiti coastline to defend against attack from the sea. The Iraqi army was crushed after a mere 100 hours. Iraqi troops — tired, hungry and war-weary from six months of economic blockade and more than a month of relentless allied bombing — surrendered by the thousands. Less than seven months after the Iraqi invasion, Kuwait was once again free.

A SHORT HISTORY OF THE UNITED STATES NAVY IN THE PERSIAN GULF. DESERT SHIELD/STORM brought together the largest force of Navy warships assembled in a single theater since World War II, adding a powerful punch to Navy forces already on-scene the night of Iraq's invasion of Kuwait. The Persian Gulf and Southwest Asia are familiar territory to the United States Navy. U.S. naval forces have been operating in the region since 1801 and have maintained a continuous presence there for over 40 years. It is likely that Navy ships will continue to represent and protect U.S. interests in the region for the foreseeable future.

The American response to the Iraqi invasion of Kuwait and the threat against Saudi Arabia was a logical extension of the United States' post World War II Persian Gulf policy. Saudi Arabia, with its enormous petroleum reserves, has long had a special relationship with the United States, symbolized by President Franklin Roosevelt's meeting with King Ibn Saud in February 1945. The present Saudi monarch, King Fahd, recalled that meeting when he met with Secretary of Defense Dick Cheney in Jidda on 6 August 1990. Planning for the huge air base at Dhahran, which figured so prominently in DESERT SHIELD/STORM, began in 1944 and continued after the war as a symbol of American commitment to the Saudi monarchy. The U.S. Navy has maintained a permanent presence in the Gulf since the establishment of the Middle East Force in 1949.

Navy presence was embodied in the "little white fleet" of USS DUXBURY BAY (AVP 38), USS GREENWICH BAY (AVP 41) and USS VALCOUR (AVP 55) — former seaplane tenders — which rotated duties as flagship for Commander Middle East Force and his staff. All three ships were painted white to counter the region's extreme heat. The flagship served as the primary protocol platform of the United States throughout the region. Accompanied by one or two other rotationally deployed warships, the Middle East Force (MIDEASTFOR) provided the initial U.S. military response to any crisis in the region, as well as humanitarian and emergency assistance.

For the next 20 years, three or four ships at a time were assigned to MIDEASTFOR — generally a command ship and two or three small combatants such as destroyers or frigates. Because temperatures in the Persian Gulf, Red Sea and Indian Ocean reached as high as 130 degrees, the non-air-conditioned ships rotated every few months — a practice still followed today, with the exception of the single forward-deployed command ship.

American political involvement in the Persian Gulf after the end of World War II deepened with successive crises. For three decades we depended on others to provide for the defense of the region. The United States first looked to the British, who withdrew from the Gulf in the late 1960s. In the 1970s we turned to Iran and Saudi Arabia to act as "twin pillars" in the region. When Bahrain became a sovereign state in 1971, the U.S. Navy worked out an agreement to take over piers, radio transmitters, warehouses, and other facilities left vacant by the departing British. USS LASALLE (AGF 3), an amphibious transport ship converted for Gulf duty, began to serve as the permanent MIDEASTFOR flagship 24 August 1972.

LASALLE became a familiar site in the Middle East. LASALLE and the small MIDEASTFOR's peacetime mission has focused on building good relations — "showing the flag" to generate goodwill and promote mutual understanding, while providing a counterweight to aggressive Soviet Navy expansion in the region.

After the fall of the Shah of Iran in 1979, the United States assumed greater responsibility for the security of the Gulf. During the 1979-1981 Iranian hostage crisis, nearly 30 Navy ships were on constant patrol in the region, including one carrier battle group in the Indian Ocean or North Arabian Sea. In April 1980, the USS NIMITZ (CVN 68) battlegroup served as a jumping off point for the joint-service rescue attempt of the 52 American hostages.

In 1980, the Carter Doctrine declared the Persian Gulf region to be a "vital" interest to the United States — one for which we were willing to fight. Events in the Middle East convinced President Carter that the United States required a means of rapid response to regional crises. In October 1980, a new unified Rapid Deployment Force (RDF) was created to meet that need. The RDF later evolved into Central Command, which marked the beginning of the capability to move large military forces into the Persian Gulf, the sine qua non of DESERT SHIELD/STORM.

The political situation in Southwest Asia continued to deteriorate. After 10 months of intermittent skirmishes over the Shatt-al-Arab waterway, Iraq attacked Iran in September 1980, launching a war that would last eight years. By 1982, more than 100,000 people had died. The war was costing each side $1 billion a month and devastated both countries' oil industries. In the so-called "tanker war", both belligerents launched attacks on neutral merchant vessels transiting the Gulf, prompting several Gulf states to seek protection from foreign navies.

On 1 November 1986, Kuwait, a non-belligerent, announced it would seek international protection for its ships. On 7 March 1987, the United States offered to reflag 11 Kuwaiti tankers and provide U.S. Navy protection. Kuwait accepted.

On 17 May 1987, an Iraqi attack aircraft fired two Exocet missiles, killing 37 sailors and wounding 21 others aboard USS STARK (FFG 31). Iraq apologized, claiming "pilot error."

American units had already found a dozen mines in Persian Gulf shipping lanes when the Navy began escorting re-flagged Kuwaiti tankers during Operation EARNEST WILL in July 1987. During the very first escort mission, a mine ripped into the re-flagged supertanker BRIDGETON. That first month, three tankers hit mines and minesweeping operations by Navy helicopters began.

Later that summer, U.S. forces captured the Iranian minelayer Iran Ajr while it was deploying mines in international shipping lanes and U.S. helicopters repelled an attack by Iranian speedboats. In October 1987, U.S. surface forces destroyed an armed Iranian oil complex in retaliation for an Iranian missile attack on a U.S.-flagged tanker.

On 14 April 1988, watchstanders aboard USS SAMUEL B. ROBERTS (FFG 58) sighted three mines floating approximately one-half mile from the ship. Twenty minutes after the first sighting, as ROBERTS was backing clear of the minefield, she struck a submerged mine nearly ripping the warship in half. Working feverishly for seven hours, the crew stabilized the ship. ROBERTS was sent back to the United States for repair and later returned to the region to serve with the Maritime Interception Force during DESERT SHIELD.

Three days after the mine blast, forces of the now-Joint Task Force Middle East executed the American response — Operation PRAYING MANTIS. During a two-day period, the Navy, Marine Corps, Army and Air Force units of Joint Task Force Middle East destroyed two oil platforms being used by Iran to coordinate attacks on merchant shipping, sank or destroyed three Iranian warships and neutralized at least six Iranian speedboats. The success of PRAYING MANTIS — and broad-based allied naval cooperation during Operation EARNEST WILL — proved the value of joint and combined operations in the Gulf and paved the way for the massive joint/coalition effort during DESERT SHIELD/STORM.

It was during these operations that USS VINCENNES (CG 49) shot down an Iranian commercial airliner after mistaking it for an Iranian F-14. Within two months, Iran and Iraq reached a fragile agreement to end hostilities.

At the height of the Iran-Iraq war, MIDEASTFOR was composed of 12 or more ships. That force, along with mine countermeasures teams, special warfare units, and rotating carrier battle groups deployed to the North Arabian Sea, made up America's largest deployed naval force since the Vietnam era. The Navy's Administrative Support Unit contingent in Bahrain grew to over 800 personnel. By the end of 1989, however, U.S. Navy presence in the Gulf had drawn down to the normal flagship and four or five other ships, monitoring the again-busy transit lanes. That force was often augmented by a carrier battle group in the Indian Ocean.

The Navy benefited from years of experience in the harsh operating environment of the Middle East, and the requirement to conduct those operations independent of major support bases. With no permanent U.S. bases in the area, forward-deployed ships became increasingly important as the United States worked to demonstrate the continuity of American commitments and maintain stability in the region.

THE ROLE OF THE NAVY IN JOINT OPERATIONS. The United States Navy is structured to provide four fundamental military capabilities. First is control of the sea to assure the U.S. can use the oceans for economic and military purposes while denying such access to opponents in time of crisis or war. Second, the Navy projects power ashore — with air power, naval gunfire, cruise missiles, and Marine forces — either in support of sea-control or to support a joint campaign ashore. Third, the Navy provides nuclear deterrence. Finally, the Navy and the Maritime Administration provide strategic sealift to support joint military operations.

The Navy applies the concept of combined arms operations at several levels. The Navy-Marine Corps team synergistically combines land, sea, and air capabilities and exemplifies the combined arms concept. In recent years, the Navy has also operated extensively with the Army and Air Force, which proved to be valuable preparation for DESERT SHIELD/STORM. The fundamental role of the Navy in joint power projection operations is to gain control of the sea. Sea control is an essential prerequisite for introduction of joint power projection forces.

As an integral part of the U.S. military strategy of forward defense, the Navy has maintained a significant forward presence since World War II. Forward deployments promote regional stability and maintain readiness for crisis response. President Bush reaffirmed forward presence and crisis response as fundamental pillars of U.S. strategy in a speech at Aspen, Colorado on 2 August, the day Iraq invaded Kuwait.

Like forward-deployed Navy forces everywhere, the forces on station in the Persian Gulf, Indian Ocean and Eastern Mediterranean on 2 August were self-sufficient and combat ready, capable of remaining on station for months independent of infrastructure ashore. The unique character of naval forces gave President Bush and his advisors a number of immediate options for responding to the crisis:

- Ready forces to operate from over the horizon, independent of politically sensitive operating bases ashore.

- A mechanism for allied involvement by nations unable or unwilling to commit land-based forces.

- A ready capability to enforce U.N. economic sanctions.

- And, as we saw in Operation DESERT STORM, an effective force, ready to fight and win.

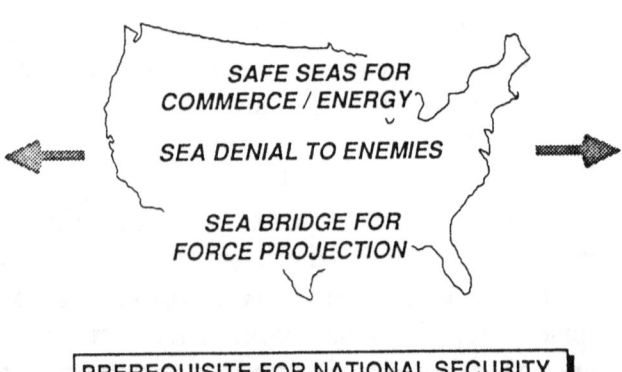

Each military service is structured to perform specific missions in implementing our overall national military strategy. That strategy is based on four principal elements: strategic deterrence, forward presence, crisis response and force reconstitution. Maritime superiority remains essential to successful implementation of each element of that strategy.

Bringing all services together for major force projection operations generates the greatest combat capability in the shortest period of time. Combining forces for joint operations represents the best, most economical use of our forces, and takes full advantage of the unique missions and functional capabilities of each service.

The Navy plays an essential role in the complex process of generating joint forces for a major power projection operation. The illustration on the next page shows a greatly simplified depiction of the process of sequencing joint forces for power projection. Initially, naval forces and regionally based Army and Air Force elements are forward deployed for deterrence, stability, and readiness for crisis response.

Naval forces are invariably among the first on scene in time of crisis or conflict. Often the presence of naval forces alone is enough to defuse a crisis. If the crisis erupts, naval forces can be rapidly augmented by airborne and Marine contingency forces airlifted into theater. At this point, naval forces play an "enabling" role, helping cover the introduction of follow-on ground and air forces. The joint force, once fully deployed, is capable of sustained heavy combat. At that point, the Navy complements and enhances the capabilities of land-based forces.

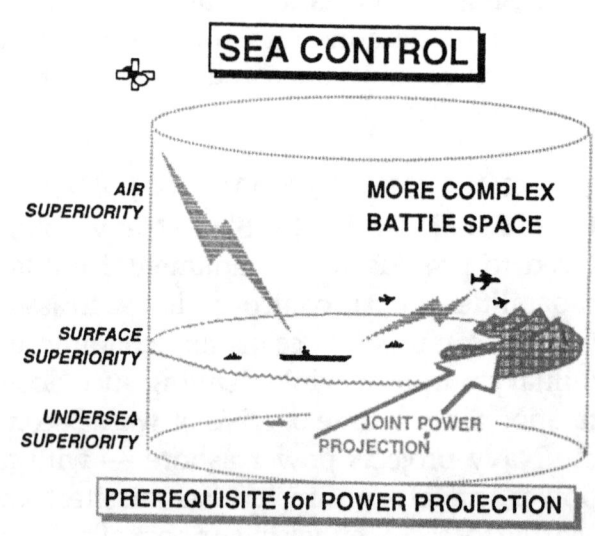

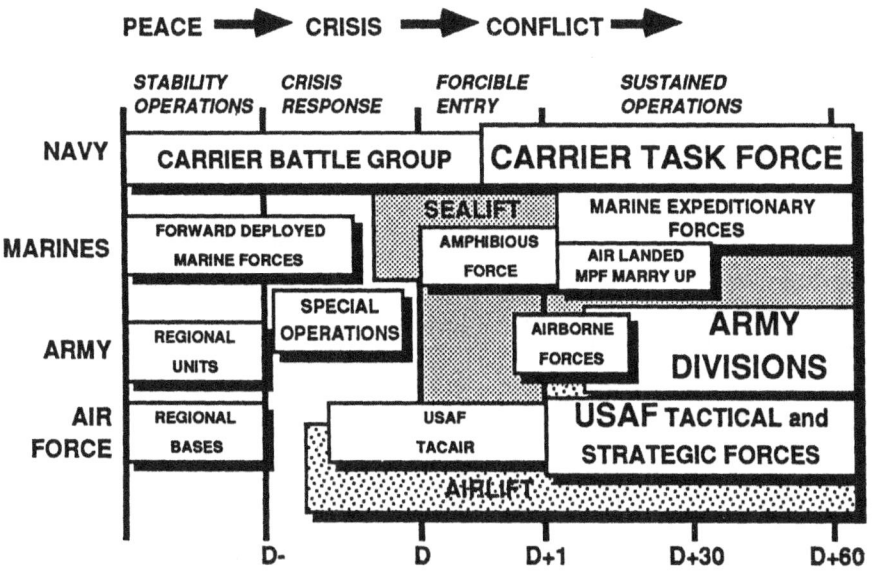

JOINT FORCE SEQUENCING

As mentioned previously, gaining control of the battle space in three dimensions — in the air, on the sea, and under the sea -- is a prerequisite for joint power projection. The Navy is responsible for achieving and maintaining the sea control and air superiority required for introduction of additional joint forces, and is structured to carry out that mission. Power projection cannot be sustained without control of the sea.

While DESERT SHIELD/STORM are not models for all future military operations, they do provide a regional prototype for certain joint power projection operations which might be anticipated in the decade to come. DESERT SHIELD/STORM unfolded in near text book fashion. We observed in the massive troop deployments an outstanding example of joint force sequencing in action. Forward deployed naval forces were first on scene — sustainable and combat ready on arrival. Their immediate combat capability provided cover for the introduction of ground and air forces. Sea control was assured from the outset, protecting the vital seaborne logistics train and enforcing U.N. sanctions. The forward presence of naval forces was a critical element in the rapid deployment of the joint force.

FLEXIBLE RESPONSE: THE NAVY-MARINE TEAM IN ACTION. The Navy-Marine Corps team lived up to its tradition of mobility and flexibility while deploying forces for DESERT SHIELD/STORM. While attention focused on Kuwait, Navy and Marine Corps

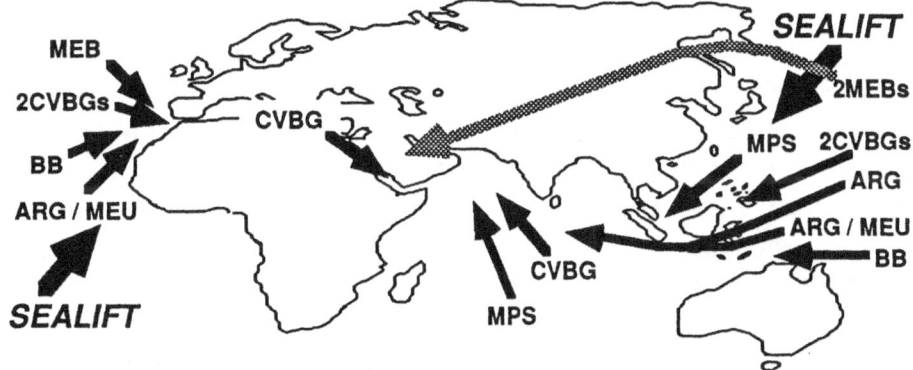

- JOINT POWER PROJECTION IN ACTION
- *"FORWARD PRESENCE"* - A KEY TO SUCCESS
- *"SEA CONTROL"* - AN ESSENTIAL ELEMENT
- MARITIME FORCES PLAYED AN *"ENABLING"* ROLE

units were evacuating civilians from two other hotspots on opposite coasts of Africa.

On 5 August, Marines from a U.S. Task Force off the coast of Liberia began an evacuation operation which eventually rescued 2,690 people, including 330 U.S. citizens, from the war-torn capital city of Monrovia. Operation SHARP EDGE began with a pre-dawn meeting in the wardroom of USS SAIPAN (LHA 2) to finalize a plan that had been in the works for nearly two months. During that time, SAIPAN and her Amphibious Ready Group, consisting of USS PONCE (LPD 15), USS SUMTER (LST 1181), Fleet Surgical Team TWO and the destroyer USS PETERSON (DD 969), waited off the coast for orders to begin evacuation.

Since December 1989, civil war had raged between rival Liberian factions, and the safety of American citizens could no longer be guaranteed. Tension grew as rebel leader Prince Johnson said he would begin rounding up foreigners to force foreign intervention in his fight against Liberian President Samuel Doe. Johnson threatened to attack U.S. Marines at the embassy if the United States did not intervene on the rebel side.

As dawn broke, more than 200 Marines from HOTEL Company, 2nd Battalion, 4th Marines climbed into CH-46 Sea Knight and CH-53 Sea Stallion helicopters for the 20-mile ride to the U.S. embassy compound in Monrovia and commenced the non-combatant evacuation operation. They evacuated not only Americans, but also Liberian, Italian, Canadian and French nationals during an operation which lasted until 30 November, when opposing forces agreed to a cease-fire. Sailors and Marines from the task force also provided humanitarian assistance, airlifting food, water, fuel and medical supplies to the ravaged city.

Navy support for the operation, the longest-running non-combatant evacuation operation in recent naval history, ended 9 January, when the amphibious transport dock USS NASHVILLE (LPD 13), Helicopter Combat Support Squadron FOUR (HCS 4) and elements of the 26th Marine Expeditionary Unit departed the Liberian coastal area known during the operation as "Mamba Station."

Just a few days before SHARP EDGE ended, another civil war threatened American lives. USS GUAM (LPH 9) and USS TRENTON (LPD 14) with Marines from the 4th Marine Expeditionary Brigade embarked, raced from their DESERT SHIELD stations in the North Arabian Sea to rescue Americans and foreign nationals threatened by war in Somalia.

The rescue, Operation EASTERN EXIT, was implemented within hours of an urgent plea from the U.S. Embassy in Mogadishu, the capital of Somalia. Indeed, from the time the U.S. Ambassador in Somalia sent his first message, "I really view this with concern, we've got to get out of here...," to the time the execute order was given, less than 48 hours had elapsed.

Marine Corps helicopters took off while the ships were still 460 miles from the Somali coast. They twice refueled in-flight courtesy of Marine Corps KC-130 tankers which took off from Bahrain in the Persian Gulf. The helicopters reached the Embassy, dropped off the Marines and brought back 62 evacuees. The first wave of Marines ashore set up defensive positions around the Embassy, while other waves conducted the evacuations. In all, 260 citizens from 30 nations, including 51 Americans, and the diplomatic contingent from the Soviet Union, were shuttled aboard the two waiting ships. A group of U.S. officials and the Kenyan ambassador were trapped by gunfire in an office two blocks from the U.S. Embassy. The Marines had to escort them through fierce firefights between the rival factions. Once all evacuees were safely aboard, the ships steamed back to the North Arabian Sea to rejoin DESERT SHIELD.

Marines and sailors have been perfecting non-combatant evacuation operations for many years. Since 1980, naval forces have responded to more than 50 international and regional crises. The capability to mount such operations — even while simultaneously responding to a major crisis elsewhere — is vital to protecting American interests and citizens around the globe.

THE UNITED STATES NAVY IN "DESERT SHIELD" / "DESERT STORM"

II: "THE GATHERING STORM"-- THE BUILD-UP OF U.S. FORCES

"If you look at the naval assets that have been deployed into the region, aircraft carrier battle-groups - four of them have been active at one time or another — as well as all other naval assets, I would agree there obviously isn't any other nation in the world that could do that today. We have in the first three weeks of the exercise deployed more capability than we had deployed in the first three months in 1950 when we were asked to go to Korea."

- **Defense Secretary Dick Cheney**
  6 September 1990

"We are doing this for the people of Kuwait, for our other friends in the region, for our own economic interest, for the safety of Americans who are in danger, and for the promise of a safer new world where disputes will not be solved by war."

- **General Colin Powell, USA**
  Chairman, Joint Chiefs of Staff
  11 November 1990

INTRODUCTION. We may never learn the extent to which on-scene naval forces influenced Saddam Hussein to stop short of invading Saudi Arabia. We do know that the sustainable combat capability and control of the sea provided by naval forces afforded protection for the introduction of ground and air forces arriving in theater in response to the deployment order. The joint teamwork of naval, air, and ground forces — together with our coalition partners — generated tremendous combat capability in a remarkably short period of time.

THE BUILDUP OF U.S. NAVY FORCES. The initial buildup of Navy forces for DESERT SHIELD/STORM drew upon the normal forward-deployed posture of the fleet. On 2 August, the ships of Joint Task Force Middle East were on station in the Persian Gulf, the EISENHOWER battle group was in the central Mediterranean in the last month of a scheduled six-month deployment, and the INDEPENDENCE battle group was in the Indian Ocean near Diego Garcia in the early stages of a scheduled Indian Ocean deployment. After the invasion, both battle groups moved toward the crisis area and by 8 August were on station and ready to conduct air strikes — EISENHOWER in the Red Sea and INDEPENDENCE in the Gulf of Oman. INDEPENDENCE could have launched long-range strikes as early as 5 August if required.

Thus, on C-day, 7 August — the day that President Bush committed U.S. forces to the protection of Saudi Arabia — naval presence in the crisis area consisted of two carrier battle groups with more than 100 fighter and attack aircraft plus a surface action group and command ship in the Persian Gulf. Those forces were later reinforced by four additional carrier battle groups and two battleships. The Navy also deployed the command ship USS BLUE RIDGE (LCC 19), a 31 ship amphibious task force, plus various support ships, combatants, mine warfare ships, and submarines.

The Navy forces requested by CINCCENT were geared toward defense of Saudi Arabia. Key elements of those forces came from both Atlantic and Pacific Fleets and from units stationed ashore in CONUS. This reinforcement was implemented quickly and effectively because:

- The Navy started from a forward deployed posture.

- The Navy is structured to deploy quickly and to be self-sustaining while deployed.

- The all-volunteer force was trained and ready to support the deployments.

"Forward presence meant Red Sea MIF operations could begin almost immediately [following enactment of U.N. sanctions]. We were also ready to conduct interception operations in the Med, with particular emphasis on the Northern approaches to the canal..."

-- Admiral J. T. Howe, USN, Commander-in-Chief U.S. Naval Forces Europe, Quick Look — First Impressions Report, 20 March 1991

THE BUILDUP OF AIRPOWER. The buildup of air power began immediately on 7 August. Fixed wing Navy and USAF combat aircraft were on scene the first day, and their number grew steadily, reaching a level of about 700 fighter and attack aircraft by the end of the first month. In addition to fixed wing aircraft, Marine and Army attack helicopters made a major contribution to U.S. airpower in theater, particularly with regard to close air support and anti-armor missions.

The first combat aircraft on scene were the air wings of INDEPENDENCE and EISENHOWER, followed closely by two Air Force F-15C squadrons flight-ferried from the U.S. directly to Saudi Arabia with the support of USAF tankers. The aircraft carriers provided more than 100 fighter and attack aircraft plus airborne early-warning, electronic warfare, and surveillance aircraft. The carrier aircraft were ready for sustained combat operations on arrival. Each battle group carried a full combat loadout of fuel and ordnance for its aircraft, plus a complete aircraft intermediate maintenance facility with its associated spare parts, test equipment, and maintenance personnel. The SARATOGA battle group arrived on 22 August to relieve EISENHOWER. The KENNEDY battle group reported on station 7 September.

Additional land-based fixed wing aircraft began arriving by 9 August. In theory, virtually all fixed-wing aircraft deployed to the Gulf within the first month were capable of deploying within the first few days. Actual deployment times were driven by the availability of aerial refueling (and airlift) and the practical realities of establishing a support infrastructure for sustained combat operations — including ground support equipment and personnel, maintenance equipment and personnel, spare parts, ordnance, ordnance storage and handling equipment, and general base operating support.

The Army, Air Force and Marine Corps have standing preparations to provide such support, but moving the equipment, supplies, and personnel takes time. For example, the large stocks of ordnance required for an air strike campaign must generally come by sea. In DESERT SHIELD/STORM, the transportation time was minimized because of the foresight in prepositioning ordnance aboard ships in Diego Garcia. The first maritime prepositioning ships with USMC air ordnance arrived on 14 August — 7 days after the deployment order. Two Afloat Prepositioned Force ships carrying USAF ordnance arrived in theater between 17 August and 19 August.

The experience in DESERT SHIELD/STORM has validated the Services' aviation deployment concepts. The Navy and Marine Corps fulfilled their assigned role in the sequencing of joint airpower — the early arrival of combat-ready, sustainable airpower. In DESERT SHIELD/STORM, as in any major air-land campaign, the Air Force provided the majority of fixed-wing aircraft.

Even after the initial buildup was complete, however, Navy and Marine airpower remained important elements of total U.S. airpower. One reason was limitation on facilities. Even the numerous airfields of Saudi Arabia and other Gulf states could only operate so many aircraft. The three aircraft carriers on scene in early September provided 20% of the total combat airpower. The three additional carrier battle groups deployed in response to the CINCs' request as part of the reinforcing buildup prior to the air war further increased the Navy's contribution. Marine aircraft not only added to overall numbers, but were integral to Marine air-ground task forces (MAGTFs).

THE BUILDUP OF GROUND FORCES. DESERT SHIELD/STORM illustrated that sizable U.S. ground forces and major deployments will still be required in the post cold war world. In Saudi Arabia, unlike Europe or Korea, the U.S. did not have significant ground forces or equipment on scene. The U.S. was faced with a major expeditionary operation in which speed of deployment was potentially crucial.

The U.S. was generally well-prepared for a major expeditionary operation. Creation of the Rapid Deployment Force (RDF), along with major improvements in expeditionary capabilities in the 1980s — particularly strategic sealift — provided a solid force structure on which to base DESERT SHIELD/STORM. Specific mobility enhancement programs included:

- **AFLOAT PREPOSITIONED SHIPS (APS).** Eleven ships, carrying ordnance, supplies, and fuel for the Army and Air Force, plus one ship carrying a naval field hospital. These ships are continuously manned by civilian crews under contract to the Military Sealift Command (MSC). Since initial deployment, most of the ships have been stationed at Diego Garcia in the Indian Ocean, but they can be quickly repositioned in response to a crisis elsewhere in the world.

- **MARITIME PREPOSITIONING SHIPS (MPS).** Thirteen ships, carrying unit equipment and 30 days of supplies for three Marine Expeditionary Brigades (MEBs). The ships form three MPS squadrons, which are normally based in Guam, Diego Garcia, and the Atlantic. They are manned continuously with civilian crews under contract to the MSC.

- **C-5B GALAXY.** The Air Force developed a new version of the C-5 airlifter and doubled the size of the C-5 fleet, greatly increasing the capacity to move outsized cargo via air.

- **FAST SEALIFT SHIPS (FSS).** The Navy purchased and modified eight SL-7 fast sealift ships capable of making over 30 knots for rapid deployment of Army equipment. The SL-7s are maintained in 96 hour readiness status in peacetime. Two large hospital ships (one on each coast) are maintained in a similar status.

- **READY RESERVE FORCE (RRF).** In the late 1970s, the Navy began purchasing militarily useful ships to bolster the aging mothballed fleet of World War II era cargo ships. Over the next ten years, the RRF grew to 96 ships — mostly roll-on/roll-off ships, barge carriers, breakbulk ships, and small tankers. These ships are maintained at various U.S. ports by the Maritime Administration in an inactive status, without crews. The RRF program was designed to allow activation of ships in 5, 10, or 20 days depending on readiness status. Upon receipt of an activation order, RRF ships are towed to a shipyard for mechanical preparation to sail. Crews are drawn from available U.S. civilian merchant mariners.

Those strategic lift assets were designed to support a rapid buildup in combat power based on the concept of joint force sequencing. The first ground-combat forces on scene for DESERT SHIELD/STORM were two brigades of the 82nd Airborne Division, which arrived via airlift to provide both initial presence and security for airbases and ports. These forces initially relied on support and provisions from Marine Corps supplies. They were quickly followed by two MPS MEBs, which provided additional firepower and greater sustainability. The heavy Army forces essential for modern mechanized warfare followed in turn — first the 24th Mechanized Division, primarily via fast sealift, and subsequently the 101st Air Assault Division, the 3rd Armored Cavalry Regiment, the 1st Armored Cavalry Division, and associated corps command element, also via sealift.

Strategic sealift was crucial to deploying Army forces. Although the soldiers were flown to the Gulf, the bulk of the equipment and supplies was too large to transport by air. The main exception is the 82nd Airborne Division, which is lighter than other Army divisions, has less organic sustainability, and is the lead Army division for rapid deployment. Otherwise, most Army unit equipment and resupply moved by sea.

Prior to the late 1970s, sealift was heavily dependent on the U.S. flag fleet and the National Defense Reserve Fleet (NDRF) of mothballed World War II-era ships. The procurement of APS, FSS, and RRF ships in the 1980s offset the decline in availability of militarily useful commercial shipping and the deteriorating condition of the NDRF. Sealift forces were sized for a global war growing out of a conflict in the Persian Gulf in which the initial Army deployment in the Gulf would be supported entirely by U.S. shipping. The eight SL-7 fast sealift ships were designed for rapid deployment of a heavy division. Deployment of succeeding divisions would depend on activation of the RRF, use of U.S. flag ships in the Sealift Readiness Program, charter of commercial vessels, and, if necessary, requisition of additional U.S. flag ships.

About three-fourths of DESERT SHIELD/STORM deliveries were made by ships resulting from the $7 billion investment in strategic sealift programs during the last ten years. Without these programs, there would have been no afloat prepositioning ships, no fast sealift, and no RRF. The APS/MPS ships prepositioned in Diego Garcia delivered ordnance and supplies two or three weeks sooner than sealift from the U.S. could have delivered it. Fast sealift ships delivered cargo at roughly twice the speed of most commercial shipping. The RRF provided militarily useful vessels — roll-on/roll-off ships, breakbulk cargo ships, LASH and SEABEE barge carriers — that are no longer readily available in sufficient numbers from the active U.S. flag fleet. The deployment in DESERT SHIELD/STORM was impressive and sealift performed close to its realistic potential in its first real test. More to the point, this experience has provided a sound basis for judging the nation's strategic lift requirements for the future.

NAVY MEDICAL BUILDUP AND FOLLOW-THROUGH. Shortly after Iraqi troops rolled into Kuwait, Navy medical personnel deployed to Saudi Arabia. From the corpsmen accompanying the Marines in the field to the hospitals stateside, Navy medicine proved itself ready. For example, three days after forces were committed to DESERT SHIELD, deployment orders went out to the hospital ships COMFORT and MERCY. Both ships were activated, manned, and supplied from a standing start. They were on station and ready in the Persian Gulf by 23 September.

More than 6,100 active-duty Navy men and women were deployed to provide medical care to coalition forces in DESERT SHIELD/ STORM. Additionally, 10,452 naval medical reservists were recalled to active duty. Many filled large staffing gaps at military medical facilities where manpower was cut to the bone to support DESERT SHIELD. Other reservists served on the hospital ships and fleet hospitals in theater.

In addition to personnel of the Navy medical corps, medical service corps, and nurse corps, more than 5,800 Navy hospital corpsmen served with Marines during DESERT SHIELD/STORM. Eleven corpsmen were attached to each company of Marines. Corpsmen are assigned to a specific Marine unit for the length of their Fleet Marine Force tour of duty.

After being treated by corpsman in the field, sick and injured personnel could be quickly moved up the medical treatment ladder as required. Battalion aid stations provide patients with a physician's skills and clinical judgement in a safer environment with sufficient time to accomplish a more complete examination. The next step up the ladder was a medical battalion surgical support company or a casualty receiving and treatment ship where patients were treated by teams of physicians and nurses supported by a staff of medical technicians with more complete medical facilities including a basic laboratory, holding wards, a pharmacy and greater surgical capacity. Casualties requiring more extensive treatment were transported to either a combat zone fleet hospital or a hospital ship. The scope of treatment available at these facilities mirrored fully-staffed hospitals in the United States.

Fleet Hospital (FH) 5 was the first such facility deployed to Saudi Arabia. Built in just 16 days, with the help of Navy Construction Battalion Units 411 and 415, FH5 saw its first patient five days after construction began. The entire facility had arrived in Saudi Arabia in more than 400 containers aboard the afloat prepositioning ship MV Noble Star on 15 August. In less than two weeks, the Seabees, and Navy medical and support personnel from Naval Hospital Portsmouth, Virginia, had transformed the shipping containers into a 500-bed, forward-deployed medical facility, complete with operating rooms, intensive care units and radiological facilities. FH5, along with FH6 and FH15 which were set up in late January, cared for more than 32,000 patients during DESERT SHIELD/STORM. Members of all coalition forces, expatriates, enemy prisoners of war (EPWs) and Kuwaiti refugees received care from the fleet hospitals.

FH6 and FH15 exemplified the Navy's Total Force concept, demonstrating how Naval Reserve units could be recalled to active duty and hit the ground running. While the fleet hospitals worked ashore, Navy hospital ships operated in the waters of the Persian Gulf, Red Sea and Gulf of Oman. Among the first ships deployed in support of DESERT SHIELD, USNS COMFORT (T-AH 20) and USNS MERCY (T-AH 19), are the only hospital ships of their size in the world. These 1,000-bed floating hospitals stood at the ready throughout DESERT SHIELD/STORM. Each hospital ship is equipped with 50 trauma stations that form the casualty receiving area, 12 operating rooms, a 20-bed recovery room, 80 intensive care beds and 16 light- and intermediate-care wards.

Navy medicine was ready stateside too. All Navy medical treatment facilities geared up to receive casualties from DESERT STORM if the need arose. In cooperation with the other armed services, the Navy designated certain hospitals to be casualty receiving centers (CRCs). The CRCs were set up to receive patients from all services as they were medevaced stateside. Patients were then transferred to facilities near their duty stations or hometowns, if available and as soon as possible, to ensure appropriate medical care.

NAVAL RESERVE SUPPORT. The call-up of reservists in support of DESERT SHIELD/STORM marked the largest activation of reservists since President Johnson mobilized reserve forces during the Vietnam Tet Offensive in 1968. On 22 August, President Bush issued the first executive order authorizing the call up of 48,800 members of the Selected Reserve to active duty.

Subsequent executive orders increased the authorization to 365,000 for all the services. Of those, the Navy was authorized a ceiling of 44,000. The full authorization was not used. Eventually, over 21,000 naval reservists were called to join active-duty units in and around the Arabian Peninsula, and fill critical gaps in military support positions in the United States and overseas. The Naval Reserve provided the Navy's only capability in many areas, including dedicated combat search and rescue, mobile inshore undersea warfare and logistic air transport.

The majority of reservists augmented their regular counterparts. They came from all parts of the country, representing many specialties: medical, naval construction, cargo handling, mine warfare, naval control of shipping, intelligence, public affairs, and the chaplain corps. Reservists made significant contributions, and provided meaningful training to their active-duty shipmates, enhancing the skills of both groups by the time the crisis was over.

Medical personnel composed the largest number of any specialty recalled — approximately 50 percent of the naval reservists were involved in health care. The reserves provided 90% of the Cargo Handling Battalion capability in DESERT SHIELD/STORM.

DESERT SHIELD/STORM validated the Navy's Total Force concept and underscored the importance and reliance our nation places on our reserve components. Navy Reservists proved a ready and an effective force for national security.

"The most important lesson learned from Operation DESERT STORM was that the system worked," said RADM James E. Taylor, USN, Director of Naval Reserve. "Our reservists were ready, they were well-trained, they did their job and they were highly motivated. We have proven that the investment we made in the past decade paid off — our taxpayer's dollars have been well spent. The reservists hit the ground running and I think the American public appreciates what they did for the country."

THE UNITED STATES NAVY IN "DESERT SHIELD" / "DESERT STORM"

III: "A COMMON GOAL" -- JOINT AND MULTINATIONAL OPERATIONS

"Joint service cooperation between the Navy-Marine Corps team, the U.S. Army and the U.S. Air Force has been superb — on the ground, in the air, and at sea. We are all here working toward a common goal."

-- **Lieutenant General W. E. Boomer, USMC, CG 1MEF
Commander U.S. Marine Forces Central Command
10 January 1991**

"The portrait of an American soldier in the desert has become the hallmark of Operation DESERT SHIELD in the minds of many American people. But it is the maritime forces of the Navy, Marines and Coast Guard who have been enforcing the U.N. sanctions against Iraq on a daily basis, and I will tell you they have been doing the job flawlessly."

-- **General H. Norman Schwarzkopf, USA
Commander-in-Chief U.S. Central Command,
COMUSNAVCENT Change of Command, 1 December 1990**

"One cannot think about this activity without mentioning the Navy — the very quiet, very professional way they put the embargo on, which continues to this day -- out of sight — but very, very effective — maybe one of the most important things we did."

-- **General Merrill McPeak, USAF
Chief of Staff of the Air Force
15 April 1991**

INTRODUCTION. The decade of the 1980s witnessed a tremendous increase in emphasis on joint operations. Since the Goldwater-Nichols Act codified that emphasis in 1986, the Navy has focused on better defining and understanding its roles and missions within the context of joint operations, particularly major joint power projection operations like DESERT SHIELD/STORM.

Earlier joint operations, including the Iran hostage rescue attempt and the contingencies in Grenada and Panama, demonstrated that there was considerable room for improvement. DESERT SHIELD/STORM reflected significant progress — progress based in large measure on the lessons learned in those earlier operations.

The unique missions and functional capabilities of each service are complementary, enabling and enhancing. Working together generates the greatest combat capability in the shortest period of time. It represents the best, most economical use of our military resources. A single unified chain of command with clear and direct lines of communication up and down is clearly the best way to ensure U.S. interests are translated into effective action.

JOINT OPERATIONS DURING DESERT SHIELD/STORM. The Navy was able to quickly and effectively integrate into virtually all aspects of DESERT SHIELD/STORM because of the significant experience gained during extensive involvement in joint operations in recent years. As an integral part of Joint Task Force Middle East in the Persian Gulf during the Iran-Iraq War, Navy ships routinely conducted complex data link and surveillance operations with USAF and Saudi AWACS aircraft — a valuable prelude to DESERT SHIELD/STORM. In other theaters, joint exercises have grown dramatically in scope and complexity, as the interoperable capabilities of all the services have matured.

That is not to say there were no problems during DESERT SHIELD/STORM. The communications systems of all the services are still not as interoperable and compatible as they should be. The U.S. Air Force computer assisted flight management system (CAFMS), for example, was not interoperable with Navy communications systems. When the Joint Force Air Component Commander (JFACC) used that system to develop the daily air tasking order (ATO), the lack of complete interoperability precluded timely delivery of the ATO to naval forces afloat.

In virtually every case where such problems arose, workable solutions were developed during the build-up of forces prior to DESERT STORM. The joint requirements process now in effect under the guidance of the Joint Requirements Oversight Council (JROC) will minimize such problems in the future.

The Navy quickly recognized that pre-deployment command arrangements were inadequate for a Navy force of the magnitude assigned to Central Command during DESERT SHIELD. A new Navy component command was identified and deployed. Nevertheless, the advantages of a peacetime planning organization which parallels wartime requirements are clear. A revised organization is being developed to meet those requirements.

DESERT SHIELD/STORM clearly demonstrated the tremendous importance and benefits of joint and combined operations. The significant progress made in the conduct of such operations over the past several years was dramatically reflected in success on the battlefield. That success further strengthened the Navy's commitment to the concept of joint operations.

THE MARITIME INTERCEPTION CAMPAIGN. Mounting a successful interception campaign in response to U.N. economic sanctions against Iraq required the ability to control nearly 250,000 square miles of sea lanes. Only the United States Navy has the forces and expertise to undertake such a monumental challenge.

Navy ships on station in the Persian Gulf following the Iraqi invasion of Kuwait were on guard against possible attack by air or sea — particularly against the U.S.-flagged tankers in the area. Ultimately, those warships became the "tip of the spear" for Operation DESERT SHIELD.

After around-the-clock diplomatic efforts failed, the U.N. Security Council passed Resolution 665, authorizing multinational naval vessels to begin enforcement of U.N. sanctions against Iraq and Kuwait. As diplomatic efforts continued, Navy ships patrolling the Persian Gulf, Gulf of Oman and Red Sea closely monitored merchant vessels transiting vast and busy shipping lanes. The mission of those ships was to stop the flow of oil out of Iraq and preclude the import of war materials into the country.

Oil produced 95% of Iraq's pre-war revenue. The landward flow of oil was quickly stopped with the closing of Iraqi pipelines through both Turkey and Saudi Arabia. Tankers loaded with crude were paralyzed in port as coalition naval forces controlled the Persian Gulf. Highly-dependent on imports of food and spare parts, Iraq soon felt the effects of the embargo. Before it was over, the effects of the embargo were felt by Iraqi soldiers in the trenches.

Overall coordination of the maritime interception forces fell Commander, Middle East Force. Under the guidelines in U.N. Security Council Resolutions 661, 665 and 670, he and his staff laid plans to intercept ships bound to and from Iraq and Kuwait, precluding all supplies except those intended strictly for medical purposes and, for humanitarian reasons, foodstuffs. An early alternative to war, the maritime interception forces soon captured the world's attention as they professionally demonstrated the international rejection of Iraq's aggression against Kuwait.

Battle group and destroyer squadron commanders in the Red Sea and North Arabian Sea coordinated the intercept operation as thousands of merchant vessels were tracked, challenged, identified, warned and then boarded and diverted if found in violation of sanction guidelines. The complexities of the interception mission required constant vigilance and attention to detail.

Challenges were issued over radios from warships, from P-3s flying maritime patrols, from embarked helicopters or tactical aircraft flying combat patrols to identify the vessel, its point of origin, destination and cargo. Information from satellite imagery, radar, intelligence, shipboard computer data bases and public shipping records was used to corroborate ship ownership and other facts while masters were queried via radio. After determining the vessel was not a threat, not bound for a belligerent's border and not carrying war goods, the merchant ships were sent on their way.

From the first days of the maritime intercept mission, warships like USS JOHN L. HALL (FFG 32), the first ship to challenge a merchant vessel, averaged 10 challenges daily — a process that became more determined following U.N. approval of the use of force to ensure compliance with the sanctions. Early in the interception effort, some Iraqi merchant masters appeared as obstinate as their leader.

On 18 August, two days after the interception mission began, the first shots of Operation DESERT SHIELD/STORM were fired across the bow of an Iraqi tanker that refused to alter its course in the Persian Gulf after being directed to do so by the guided-missile frigate

USS REID (FFG 30). A boarding team from USS ENGLAND (CG 22) became the first to climb over the side of a merchant vessel, the Chinese freighter Heng Chung Hai, for cargo and manifest inspection. After a short period at anchor in the Red Sea, Heng Chung Hai was found to be empty and proceeded to Iraq. Later, USS SCOTT (DDG 995) ordered the Cypriot merchant Dongola away from the Jordanian port of Aqaba after the vessel's master admitted carrying cargo bound for Iraq. The master complied with the order without the need for a boarding in DESERT SHIELD's first diversion.

Those actions demonstrated U.S. resolve to enforce the sanctions from the very first days of the interception mission. That signal became stronger 31 August when a team from the cruiser USS BIDDLE (CG 34) boarded the first Iraqi merchant vessel of the intercept operation as it headed for Aqaba, Jordan from the Red Sea. BIDDLE crewmen boarded the Al Karamah to inspect the manifest and holds for cargo that may have violated the U.N. sanction guidelines. A thorough search found the vessel empty, and BIDDLE allowed Al Karamah to proceed.

In the early morning hours of 4 September, the crew of USS GOLDSBOROUGH (DDG 20) boarded the Iraqi vessel Zanoobia. GOLDSBOROUGH's recently-embarked Coast Guard law enforcement detachment (LEDet) — one of 10 Coast Guard units embarked in Navy warships during DESERT SHIELD/STORM — accompanied the ship's boarding party.

The Coast Guard LEDets had the corporate knowledge needed to effectively implement the interception operation. Coast Guard experts, seasoned by their experience in drug interdiction boardings, provided essential training to Navy boarding teams. Zanoobia's holds carried only tea, but it was enough to supply the entire population of Iraq for a month. The Iraqi merchant was directed to divert his course to another port outside the Gulf. The Iraqi master was unwilling to divert, and the GOLDSBOROUGH was directed to take control of the ship. GOLDSBOROUGH crewmen were brought aboard to take Zanoobia to the port of Muscat, Oman, where Iraqi diplomats boarded and advised the master to return to his point of origin.

The LEDet team which boarded Zanoobia left GOLDSBOROUGH to go aboard the frigate USS BREWTON (FF 1086), where they participated in another historic encounter on 14 September — the first multinational boarding of an Iraqi vessel. After 24 hours of radio negotiations, the master of the Iraqi tanker Al Fao finally slowed when BREWTON and the Australian frigate HMAS DARWIN (F 04) fired warning shots across her bow.

Constant communication up the U.S. and Australian chains of command kept military leaders apprised of the situation throughout the operation. When it became apparent Al Fao would not agree to stop, the decision was made to proceed to the next step in the interception procedure. One hundred .50-caliber rounds later, DARWIN followed her American counterpart's lead with short bursts of fire ahead of the target. As Al Fao suddenly slowed, both warships launched their boarding teams. A 13-man team of four Coast Guardsmen, five BREWTON personnel and four Australians climbed to the tanker's main deck, the way lit by DARWIN's helicopter. Al Fao was found empty and sent on her way to the Iraqi port of Basra.

In early December, USS MISSISSIPPI (CGN 40) intercepted and boarded the M/V

Tilia outbound from Aqaba with a cargo of motor vehicles and household goods. Careful inspection revealed that most of the cars had been stolen from Kuwait. The cars, many of which had been vandalized, had been sold by Iraq for overseas shipment at bargin prices. The following day, USS SAMPSON (DDG 5) intercepted another ship with a similar load. Both vessels were sent back to Aqaba and required to offload the plundered material before being allowed to proceed.

From the early days of the interception mission, coalition warships effectively sealed off commercial shipping inside the Persian Gulf. Once-crowded Gulf ports emptied of oil shipping traffic within a few days following the Iraqi invasion, and incoming merchants changed course to avert confrontation with coalition maritime forces. Warships in the crowded Red Sea remained busy as vessels headed to Aqaba, Jordan, to try and offload contraband for overland shipment to Iraq. In fact, 45 of the 51 merchant diversions directed before the first week of March were performed by warships in the Red Sea.

While Coast Guard LEDet teams and Navy personnel performed the bulk of merchant boardings, Navy SEALs and Marines were deployed via helicopter to board some vessels considered potentially dangerous due to their origins, the crews' attitudes or other circumstances.

By Christmas, the number of maritime intercepts neared 6,000, with 713 vessels already boarded by U.S. and multinational boarding teams. Tensions rose in the Gulf of Oman when an Iraqi merchant, Ibn Khaldoon, carried not only sugar, milk, spaghetti and tea en route for Umm Qasar, but also hosted nearly 250 passengers later identified as "peace activists" protesting the allied embargo of Iraq by attempting to break through the "blockade" with prohibited cargo.

A boarding team of U.S. Marines and Navy SEALs arrived via helicopter from USS TRENTON (LPD 14) and USS SHREVEPORT (LPD 12) while a multinational boarding team of U.S. and Australian personnel from the destroyers USS OLDENDORF (DD 972), USS FIFE (DD 991) and HMAS SYDNEY (F 03) arrived via small boat to inspect the vessel's spaces.

The activists attempted to interfere with the boarding teams by forming a "human chain" to obstruct the team's passage. Team members fired warning shots into the air after several protesters grabbed for their weapons. Boarders also used non-lethal smoke and noise-maker grenades for crowd control. No injuries occurred, but it marked the only time boarding teams fired their weapons during a boarding. After inspectors located cargo which violated sanctions, the vessel which activists had dubbed the "peace ship," was escorted by U.S. and Australian ships to Muscat, Oman.

The early and continued success of the maritime intercept force was a reminder of the effectiveness of surface forces in maintaining control of the sea. U.S. and allied naval blockades during the Civil War and both World Wars were key to isolating the enemy by cutting off supply lines. The 1962 quarantine of Cuba during the missile crisis prevented deployment of Soviet ballistic missiles capable of striking key U.S. population centers and military sites.

The high degree of coordination exhibited by the multinational naval force in enforcing the U.N. sanctions reflected years of peacetime training and cooperation between the United States and her allies. Building on the experience of Operation EARNEST WILL escort missions during the Iran-Iraq war, the U.S. Navy and coalition partners paved the way for similar success in DESERT SHIELD/STORM. The maritime interception campaign was an example of multinational cooperation at its best. The smooth informal organization at sea provided a marked contrast to the problems faced by commanders ashore.

> *"Each naval force received maritime interception force tasking, reporting requirements, interception and VBSS [visit, boarding, search and seizure] guidance, patrol areas, restrictions and ROE from its own national command authority. Even without a formal international command and control structure, MIF demonstrated superb international cooperation, enhanced through monthly MIF conferences. Conferences facilitated cooperation, ensured mutual protection, and reduced redundancy."*
>
> -- **Vice Admiral S.A. Arthur, USN, Commander U.S. Naval Forces Central Command, Quick Look — First Impressions Report, 22 March 1991**

> *"Establishment and implementation of coalition command relationships were difficult. We relearned that national pride, politics and public perception play as large a role in determining relationships as military requirements. These factors resulted in formal command relationship structures which with all their attending bureaucratic problems, complicated rather than simplified the commands ability to execute the mission. In a perfect world, all military operations would have unity of command. However, in coalition warfare where several nations temporarily unite against a common enemy we may be obliged to seek an informal command relationship which will work in the execution of combat operations."*
>
> -- **General H. Norman Schwarzkopf, USA, Commander-in-Chief U.S. Central Command, Preliminary Report on Lessons Learned, 5 April 1991**

The coalition's naval effort to shut off Iraq's commerce assured there would be no resupply of war goods for the Iraqi army and no outflow of oil to supply Iraq with hard currency. Though not always an exciting mission that grabbed newspaper headlines, it proved highly effective in keeping pressure on Saddam Hussein while solidifying the international coalition. Each successful diversion proved the honorable intentions of the world to attempt resolution of the crisis and ejection of Iraqi forces from Kuwait through non-violent means.

Saddam Hussein's lack of concern for his people's suffering was the greatest obstacle in effecting a withdrawal from Kuwait through the flawlessly executed maritime embargo. The failure of a political solution through the first 177 days of Operation DESERT SHIELD caused coalition leaders to add offensive operations to the menu of options being played out against Iraq.

The multinational maritime interception force continued their demanding mission as DESERT STORM began. While the air war raged on, the maritime intercepts continued at a steady pace, especially in the northern Red Sea, where cargo holds were meticulously checked for Iraq-bound materials headed for Jordan, one of Iraq's strongest sympathizers throughout the crisis.

When hostilities ended on 28 February, the maritime interception force's demanding mission continued unabated to keep pressure on Iraq. As U.N. members debated the terms of a permanent cease-fire and Navy ships received their initial redeployment orders, the shipping lanes were flooded with merchants, still challenged by coalition warships.

The U.N. Sanctions Committee relaxed restrictions on food for civilian groups on 22 March, but food for the Iraqi military was still prohibited, complicating interception efforts. The committee also authorized other materials and supplies related to food and medical supplies, such as refrigeration units and generators. Medicine was exempt from sanctions from the outset.

As merchant shipping resumed its normal peacetime level, the now-smaller interception force adjusted its ongoing mission to allow the free flow of non-prohibited material to Iraqi, Jordanian and Kuwaiti ports, while barring the shipment of goods that could bolster Iraq's military machine.

Well in excess of one million tons of shipping carrying prohibited cargo was diverted during the maritime interception campaign. Intercepted cargo included surface-to-air missile systems, command and control equipment, early warning radar systems, weapons, ammunition, repair parts, food stuffs and general supplies required to maintain Iraq's industrial base.

Over an eight-month period, over 165 ships from 14 allied nations challenged more than 9,000 merchant vessels, boarded more than 1,100 to inspect manifests and cargo holds and diverted over 60 for violation of sanction guidelines. U.S. boarding teams conducted 582 of those boardings. Another 25 were combined U.S.-allied boardings.

- 26 -

THE UNITED STATES NAVY IN "DESERT SHIELD" / "DESERT STORM"

IV: "BEANS, BANDAGES AND BULLETS" -- LOGISTICS OPERATIONS

"You've got to consider coming from the sea because of the sustainability. Three or four ships carry as much beans, bandages and bullets as all the nation's airlift combined!"

-- **General A.M. Gray, USMC**
   Commandant of the Marine Corps
   Testimony before Congress, April 1990

"The overall logistics effort to mobilize and support DESERT SHIELD/STORM was herculean, especially in the weeks prior to initiating hostilities. The superb performance of the logistics community deserves high praise."

-- **General H. Norman Schwarzkopf, USA**
   Commander-in-Chief, U.S. Central Command
   Preliminary Report on Lessons Learned, 5 April 1991

SEALIFT INVESTMENTS OF THE 1980s. Following World War II the primary strategic sealift mission was to rapidly move men and equipment to Europe to defend against a Soviet/Warsaw Pact attack. The central front was 3,600 miles away and sealift would be provided by over 600 NATO merchant vessels and an active U.S. merchant fleet that still numbered 578 major ships as of 1978. Those 578 ships dwindled to 367 over the next 12 years.

The Iranian crisis and Soviet invasion of Afghanistan in the late 1970s focused emphasis on developing rapid deployment forces to respond to contingencies in distant regions, such as Southwest Asia, in addition to the continuing NATO mission in Europe. Planners recognized existing and emerging shortfalls in sealift capability. Alternative fast cargo ship and prepositioning programs were evaluated with respect to possible contingencies in the 1980s and 1990s.

Following a comprehensive examination of the alternatives, the Maritime Prepositioning Ship (MPS) and Afloat Prepositioning programs were approved in 1980. In 1984, the Secretary of the Navy formally recognized the increased importance of strategic sealift and accorded it equal status with the Navy's three other main missions: sea control, power projection and strategic deterrence.

In all, $7 billion was invested in improved sealift during the 1980s. That investment purchased, modified or long-term leased:

96 Ready Reserve Force (RRF) ships, 25 prepositioning force ships, eight Fast Sealift Ships (FSS), two hospital ships, and two aviation logistics support ships.

SEALIFT DURING DESERT SHIELD/ STORM. Within hours of the initial deployment orders, Navy and civilian merchant marine sailors aboard Military Sealift Command's (MSC) sealift force ships swung into action. Maritime Prepositioning Ships (MPS) loaded with Marine Corps supplies and equipment from Guam, Saipan and Diego Garcia headed for Saudi Arabia.

As in previous large logistic support operations during World War II, the Korean conflict and the Vietnam War, more than 90 percent of the heavy equipment, ammunition, fuel and other supplies for DESERT SHIELD/ STORM was carried by sealift. The strategic sealift mission includes both surge shipping during initial mobilization and resupply or sustainment shipping.

The first three ships of MPS Squadron TWO raced from their Diego Garcia homeport to reach Saudi Arabia 15 August, marking the first use of the MPS in an actual crisis. Within four days of their arrival in the port of Jubail, Navy cargo handlers averaging 100 lift-hours per day offloaded more equipment and supplies from the three 755-foot ships than could have been moved by 3,000 C-141 cargo flights. The 16,500 Marines of the 7th Marine Expeditionary Brigade (MEB), a component of the 1st Marine Expeditionary Force (MEF), arrived via the Military Airlift Command. They "married-up" with the MPS equipment and were ready for combat on 25 August — the first heavy ground combat capability in-theater.

The five ships of MPS Squadron TWO brought the essentials to support the 7th MEB Marines for 30 days of combat — food, water, fuel, millions of pounds of ammunition for aircraft, artillery and small arms, construction materials and medical supplies. The balance of the equipment for the 1st MEF arrived from Guam aboard the ships of MPS Squadron THREE. Delivering all the equipment delivered by MPS ships to the 45,000 men of the 1st Marine Division would have required 2100 lifts by C-5s, our largest military transport aircraft.

MSC's eight fast sealift ships (FSS), the fastest cargo ships in the world, sped eastward at 33 knots, carrying 24,000 tons of equipment for the Army's 24th Infantry (Mechanized) Division and the 1st Corps Support Command. Although normally on 96-hour standby, the first FSS, USNS CAPELLA (T-AKR 293), was ready to deploy in only 48 hours. The next two FSSs were only a day behind CAPELLA. A typical FSS load included more than 700 Army vehicles such as M-1 Abrams tanks, Bradley fighting vehicles and fuel trucks.

Ten afloat prepositioning ships (APS) carrying Army and Air Force equipment, fuel and supplies also headed for Middle East waters. Aboard the APS MV Noble Star the sprawling, 28-acre Fleet Hospital 5 was stored in over 400 international standardized containers. Those containers were soon offloaded in the first-ever deployment of a Navy fleet hospital.

MSC called on 40 Ready Reserve Force (RRF) ships to provide the surge sealift capability needed to sustain support for U.S. forces in Saudi Arabia. Civilian mariners answered the call and crews were quickly assembled. MSC also chartered commercial vessels to support the flow of cargo to Saudi Arabia.

Because Iraq was laying mines in the

northern Persian Gulf, MSC contracted the heavy-lift ship Super Servant III, to transport three Navy minesweepers plus the newly-commissioned mine countermeasures ship, USS AVENGER (MCM 1), to the Gulf.

USNS MERCY (T-AH 19) and USNS COMFORT (T-AH 20), 1000-bed floating hospitals, went from reduced operational status to fully-operational status within five days of the initial DESERT SHIELD deployment order. The two ships were quickly staffed by nearly 2,500 Navy doctors, nurses and corpsmen from Navy medical facilities on both coasts.

By September, more than 100 MSC controlled ships were supporting DESERT SHIELD. More than 100,000 U.S. military personnel and their equipment had been deployed to Saudi Arabia and the surrounding area in the first 30 days. Sea control — assured from the outset by the U.S. Navy — made possible the safe rapid deployment of MSC ships and assured the availability of required civilian charter vessels at reasonable rates.

When Sealift Phase I — supporting the initial deployment — ended in mid-December, more than 180 ships were assigned to or chartered by MSC. The entire sealift operation had already transported nearly 7 billion pounds of fuel and 2.2 billion pounds of cargo — moving more cargo farther and faster than any other time in history.

Sealift Phase II — which supported the additional reinforcement of DESERT SHIELD forces — saw 220 ships come under MSC control. Winter storms and nearly 40-foot seas did not slow the largest sealift effort since World War II. By March, an average of 84 million pounds of cargo was arriving in Saudi Arabia daily. That average is even more impressive when contrasted with the 57 million pound daily average during the 37-month-long Korean conflict and the 33 million pound daily average to the Pacific theater during World War II.

In the last week of December, dozens of ships loaded U.S. Army equipment in Northern European ports. MSC moved more than 2,000 tanks, 2,200 armored vehicles, 1,000 assorted helicopters, hundreds of self-propelled howitzers and other equipment for the Army alone. Hundreds of additional aircraft, trucks and other combat equipment were also transported for the Marines and Air Force. Ironically — but perhaps not surprisingly — only 4.4% of the dry cargo moved by sealift went to support naval forces. That total included tons of equipment for three Navy Fleet Hospitals, including ambulances, generators and other support gear. During DESERT SHIELD/STORM MSC also moved nearly 12 billion pounds of fuel and hundreds of millions of pounds of ammunition.

With the exception of the allied invasion of Normandy, during which — after two years of preparation — more than 20,000 vehicles and more than 176,000 troops assaulted five beaches in two days, sealift for DESERT SHIELD/STORM, with no prior buildup at all, represents the largest and fastest sealift to a single theater in the history of warfare. It was also the farthest, with the average voyage covering nearly 8,700 miles.

Sealift moved 2.4 million tons of cargo during the first six months of DESERT SHIELD. By comparison, that is more than four times the cargo carried across the English Channel to Normandy during the D-Day invasion and more than 6.5 times that of the peak force build-up during the Vietnam War during a similar period. On 2 January 1991, at the peak of the DESERT SHIELD deployment, MSC had 172 ships underway.

The sealift deployment was not without difficulties. One of the Fast Sealift Ships suffered an engineering casualty on its initial outbound voyage. There were additional engineering difficulties encountered on breakout of some of the RRF vessels, due in part to shortfalls in maintenance funding during the previous year. There were not enough roll-on/roll-off (RO/RO) configured ships to carry all the Army rolling stock. Despite these few problems, MSC got the job done.

MAINTAINING COMBAT READINESS. The material readiness of the ships deployed in support of DESERT SHIELD/STORM was sustained at an outstanding level. Measured in terms of overall readiness and significant equipment degradations reported on a day-to-day basis, approximately 90% of the ships were at the highest levels of combat readiness (C-1/C-2) at any given time. In fact, most of the ships were at a higher overall level of readiness at the end of the war than when initially deployed, demonstrating a high degree of self-sufficiency and staying power.

Navy aircraft exhibited similar readiness rates. Average mission capable (MC) rates were around 90% or better, with full mission capability (FMC) rates averaging near 85%. The typical aircraft carrier averaged only 15 to 20 off-ship requisitions per day. Such figures are outstanding considering the number of aircraft involved, consecutive high-tempo flying days, and length of supply lines.

Overall fuel support to Navy ships was outstanding. MSC and Navy tankers provided timely responsive support to meet all routine and emergent requirements.

NAVY COMBAT LOGISTICS. When DESERT SHIELD began in August, the top logistics priority was to ensure Navy ships in the Persian Gulf, North Arabian Sea and Eastern Mediterranean were ready for battle at a moment's notice. Additionally, ships making preparations for deployment from their U.S. homeports had to be stocked with all the goods and hardware they (and their embarked Marines and airwings in the case of amphibious ships and aircraft carriers) would need to carry the fight to Iraq, half a world away.

Naval Supply Center (NSC), Norfolk, for example, was flooded with requests from ships gearing up for deployment. Dozens of Norfolk-based ships were scheduled for short notice deployment. The USS JOHN F. KENNEDY (CV 67) battle group had to accomplish the normally 30-day process of locating and storing the supplies necessary for a six-month deployment in just four days.

KENNEDY alone requested some 700 pallets of food. By the time she departed, in company with her escorts, NSC Norfolk had provided the group with 2 million fresh eggs, 185,000 pounds of hot dogs, 250,000 pounds of chicken and 400,000 pounds of hamburger. During the first two weeks of August, NSC's fuels division delivered 525,000 barrels of fuel oil to departing ships and squadrons — more than twice the normal amount — forcing the center to dip into its reserve supply. NSC did one month of normal business ($1 million) in two days during its furious effort to supply deploying ships and aircraft.

DESERT SHIELD/STORM presented a major logistics challenge: coordinating the movement of a huge volume of supplies and equipment in the smoothest, most expeditious manner. The Naval Logistic Support Force (NAVLOGSUPFOR) was established specifically to meet the DESERT SHIELD logistic challenge and relieve operational commanders afloat and ashore from much of logistics management burden.

Keeping up to 115 combatant ships battle ready was a full-time job. Most resupply operations were carried out at sea by combat logistic force (CLF) ships, who were in turn supplied through expeditionary forward logistics sites. The CLF ships deployed during DESERT SHIELD/STORM, along with various Military Sealift Command and Ready Reserve Force ships, had the monumental task of supplying six carriers, two battleships, two command ships, two hospital ships, 31 amphibious ships and 40 other combatants including cruisers, destroyers, frigates, submarines and minesweepers.

Repair ships like the destroyer tenders USS YELLOWSTONE (AD 41), USS ACADIA (AD 42) and USS CAPE COD (AD 43) were deployed to fulfill another logistic requirement of sustained naval presence. Based in the Red Sea port of Jeddah, Saudi Arabia, YELLOWSTONE provided critical repair and rearming capability to the fleet. During seven months on station YELLOWSTONE alone completed more than 10,000 repair jobs on 30 U.S. and allied ships. The Navy men and women serving aboard tenders and other repair ships provided a wide variety of services simultaneously to as many as five ships moored alongside or nearby.

The Navy women serving in non-traditional roles aboard tenders joined nearly 2,500 other women serving aboard CLF ships, Military Sealift Command vessels, the two hospital ships, and at fleet hospitals and aviation and cargo handling detachments ashore to play a crucial role in the Navy's contribution to DESERT SHIELD/STORM.

Jeddah was also the site of the Combat Logistic Stores Facility (CLSF). CLSF Jeddah gave replenishment ships assigned to the Red Sea the ability to re-stock, repair and re-arm without depending on the Suez Canal as their logistics link. The replenishment and maintenance effort both ashore and underway, kept battle groups on-station and ready throughout DESERT SHIELD/STORM, a key factor in keeping Iraq locked in.

To support the logistics mission, airfields in Saudi Arabia and Bahrain were used as bases for a Navy "logistics air force" of 25 dedicated helos and fixed-wing aircraft. One of those helos, an H-53 from HC-1, was among the first coalition force aircraft to land in Kuwait City after the liberation. Within two days regularly scheduled logistic flights into Al Shuaiba, the main port for the country of Kuwait, had commenced in support of Navy explosive ordnance demolition (EOD) mine-clearing efforts.

Physical security against water-borne attack for three major ports in the Gulf region was a significant concern. LOGSUPFOR was responsible for coordinating the Port Security Harbor Defense (PSHD) force. Three PSHD groups — each consisting of a Mobile Inshore Undersea Warfare Unit that operates radar and sonar from the pier, a Coast Guard small boat security team and a Navy EOD diver unit — operated 24-hours a day from the beginning of the build-up. They protected the key ports of Bahrain, along with Jubail and Dammam in Saudi Arabia, as they received tanks, troops, ammunition and other supplies for U.S. and coalition forces.

Logistic support was also provided by sailors from Naval Mobile Construction Battalions, Cargo Handling Battalions, Navy Overseas Air Cargo Terminal units and Forward

Freight Terminal units. Seabees and cargo handlers were among the first to arrive in Saudi Arabia. Within 48 hours of President Bush's initial order, detachments of cargo handlers, the "combat stevedores," were airlifted to participate in off-loading supplies and equipment from the MPS. That massive logistic effort involved moving more than 2,400 people and nearly 40,000 tons of equipment and supplies.

Offloading was just the beginning for the Seabees. They proceeded to build mini-cities in the desert, undertaking airfield expansion projects, setting up berthing facilities and ammunition storage points, and building roads and military barriers. They also erected the first 500-bed fleet hospital, and a 400-bed Army field hospital — an example of joint-service cooperation at its best.

NAVY SEABEES—"CAN DO" IN ACTION. The Saudi landscape was quickly dotted with structures which looked hauntingly like the quonset huts built on the World War II battlefields of Guam, the Philippines or any of the other places where Seabees have supported U.S. troops. The roads, runways, buildings, bunkers and tank barriers carved into the desert sand stand as monuments to the "Can Do" spirit which is the trademark of the Naval Mobile Construction Battalion (NMCB). More than 5,000 Seabees — 4,000 active duty and 1,000 reservists — answered the call to duty during DESERT SHIELD/STORM.

NMCB ALFA Companies completed road construction and paving, while BRAVO Companies repaired air conditioning systems and sanitary facilities, and installed electrical distribution systems capable of servicing a small town. CHARLIE Companies erected huts, built new buildings and made additions to existing buildings, strung thousands of feet of fencing and erected 20-foot-tall security towers and building revetments to protect vital communications equipment.

Seabees used modern construction materials to build aircraft hangars, maintenance shops, berthing and headquarters facilities. Many were constructed by new processes such as the K-Span arches produced by automatic building machines, allowing a building to be erected 80% faster than by conventional means. Fabric membrane structures called "sprung instant" or "clamshells" consisting of fabric stretched over a steel arch superstructure were also quickly assembled on concrete slabs. The Seabees also built numerous mock artillery pieces and tank turrets and placed them at strategic points to deceive the Iraqi military.

The Seabees used more than 7.5 million board-feet of lumber, 92,000 sheets of plywood, 110,000 feet of PVC pipe, 1.4 million feet (262 miles) of electrical wire, 50,000 cubic yards of concrete and 250,000 cubic yards of select fill during DESERT SHIELD/STORM. In all, Seabees of the Naval Construction Force built 14 galleys capable of feeding 75,000 people; a 40,000-man EPW camp; 6 million square feet of aircraft parking apron after moving 9 million cubic yards of sand and dirt to prepare the sites; and four ammunition supply points that held $2 billion of ordnance. They also maintained and improved 200 miles of unpaved desert four-lane divided roads that were used as main supply routes and built 4,750 other buildings.

Just after the ground war began, an advance party from NMCBs 5, 24 and the 3rd Naval Construction Regiment entered the battleground of Kuwait to prepare positions for the 1st MEF command units to move into the following day. The plan, which was not fully executed due to the unexpectedly short duration of the ground war, called for Seabees to repair the Al Jaber airfield for use by Marine aircraft, maintain roads within Kuwait, construct enemy prisoner of war camps and finally, move up to Kuwait International Airport to support the Marine divisions there.

Perhaps the Seabee's most important contribution was the part they played in what General Schwarzkopf called the "end run". One of the attractions of a flank attack against the entrenched Iraqis was the trackless nature of the territory to the west — there were no roads big enough to support the large volume of troops and supplies required to successfully sustain an attack from that direction, so the Iraqis felt they could leave that flank unguarded. If an extensive road network could be quickly built from scratch, however, then such an attack would be feasible and make possible a crushing blow that would minimize allied casualties.

Building the road required to support the end run was made all the more challenging by the requirement to deceive the enemy because it necessitated last minute construction. Under the gun both figuratively and literally, the Seabees constructed more than 200 miles of road — a four-lane divided highway in the sand.

THE UNITED STATES NAVY IN "DESERT SHIELD" / "DESERT STORM"

V: "THUNDER AND LIGHTNING" -- THE WAR WITH IRAQ

"Soldiers, sailors, airmen and Marines of the United States Central Command, this morning at 0300, we launched Operation DESERT STORM, an offensive campaign that will enforce the United Nation's resolutions that Iraq must cease its rape and pillage of its weaker neighbor and withdraw its forces from Kuwait. My confidence in you is total. Our cause is just! Now you must be the thunder and lightning of Desert Storm. May God be with you, your loved ones at home, and our Country."

-- **General H. Norman Schwarzkopf, USA**
Commander-in-Chief U.S. Central Command,
in a message to the command, 16 January 1991

INTRODUCTION AND OVERVIEW. On 17 January, DESERT STORM began with a coordinated attack which included Tomahawk land attack missiles (TLAMs) launched from cruisers, destroyers and battleships in the Persian Gulf and Red Sea. The TLAM launches opened a carefully crafted joint strategic air campaign. The initial barrage of over 100 TLAMs took out heavily defended targets in the vicinity of Baghdad and made a critical contribution to eliminating Iraqi air defenses and command and control capabilities.

In all, 288 TLAMs were launched as part of the integrated air campaign. Launches were conducted from both the Red Sea and the Persian Gulf from nine cruisers, five destroyers, two battleships and two nuclear powered attack submarines. The top shooter was the destroyer USS FIFE (DD 991) which fired 58 missiles.

TLAM adds a dramatic new dimension to the offensive firepower of the United States Navy. Any future aggressor will have to contend with the demonstrated capability of U.S. forces to launch complex coordinated missile and air attacks from multiple axes. The TLAM and other precision-guided and high-tech munitions used by the Army, Navy, Marine Corps and Air Force clearly produced a revolution in the art of warfare.

The joint air campaign was successful beyond the most optimistic expectations. As full partners in that campaign, Navy and Marine Corps aviators flew from carriers and amphibious ships in the Red Sea and Persian Gulf, and from bases ashore, from the day hostilities began until the cease-fire was ordered. Navy aircraft struck targets up to 700 miles distant, with Red Sea sorties averaging 3.7 hours in length, and Persian Gulf sorties averaging 2.5 hours. As was also the case for their ground-based Air Force counterparts, many flights lasted as long as five hours, and virtually every flight required airborne refueling at both ends of the journey.

The four carrier battle groups operating in the Persian Gulf, together with the two additional battle groups in the Red Sea, complemented the striking power of land-based coalition air forces in Saudi Arabia and other coalition Gulf states, and the USAF units in eastern Turkey. This effectively surrounded Iraq with strike capability and demonstrated the mobility, flexibility and firepower which naval forces bring to the battlefield.

Critical to the success of all aviation missions was the role of electronic countermeasures, "jamming" or "defense suppression" aircraft. Navy EA-6B Prowlers determined threat location then jammed and destroyed enemy radars. Navy defense suppression aircraft supported all U.S. and coalition forces — in fact, availability of the EA-6Bs was a go/no-go criterion for many strike missions. If Navy defense suppression wasn't available, the missions didn't fly.

The presence of U.S. naval forces on both flanks of coalition land and air forces ashore complemented and enhanced the air-ground campaign. It helped ensure the continued flow of logistics throughout the war and provided the "insurance" which allowed the Gulf states to confidently participate in the coalition without fear of retaliation.

Naval forces destroyed the Iraqi Navy and contributed directly to the liberation of Kuwait. They continued the maritime interception campaign throughout the war. They supported the ground campaign with air power and naval gunfire.

To fully appreciate the contribution of the Navy and Marine Corps to the campaign ashore, one need only consider the large scale models of Iraqi defenses discovered in Kuwait City. Those defenses were pointed seaward. Iraqi forces were committed to defend Kuwait against amphibious attack. This diversion of forces was a critical element in the overall campaign plan. It set the stage for coalition armored forces on the western flank to rapidly envelop the Iraqi forces facing seaward and southward towards the central thrust spearheaded by the Marines.

THE AIR WAR. Navy and Marine Corps pilots, aircrews and support personnel joined in the most powerful and successful air assault in the history of modern warfare. From "H-hour" on 17 January when the air campaign began, until the end of offensive combat operations 43 days later, Navy and Marine aviators destroyed key targets and helped ensure the United States military and its coalition partners owned the skies over Iraq and Kuwait.

Operating from six aircraft carriers, two large amphibious assault ships (LHAs), various other amphibious ships, plus ground bases and makeshift airstrips ashore, Navy and Marine fixed- and rotary-wing aircraft were an integral part of the coalition air campaign. Of more than 94,000 sorties flown by U..S. aircraft during the war, Navy and Marine aircraft flew close to 30,000. Sea-service pilots flew around 35 percent of the sorties, which was in direct proportion to their numbers in the U.S. air inventory.

More than 1,000 Navy and Marine Corps aircraft joined the U.S. Air Force, Army and coalition partners to knock out the Iraqi military machine. The air campaign was conducted in four phases. Phase I was to gain air superiority by destroying Iraq's strategic capabilities. That phase was accomplished within the first seven days. Phase II required the suppression of air defenses in the Kuwaiti Theater of Operations. During Phase III, the coalition airmen continued to service Phase I and II targets as needed, but also shifted emphasis to the field army in Kuwait. Finally, Phase IV entailed air support of ground operations.

At around 0300 (Persian Gulf time) 17 January, along with a blitz by more than 100 TLAMs, wave after wave of coalition aircraft — including those flown by Navy and Marine pilots — began hammering strategic targets inside both Iraq and Kuwait, signaling the start of offensive combat operations. Throughout the war, air strikes were conducted from six aircraft carriers operating in the Red Sea and Persian Gulf. USS AMERICA (CV 66) and USS THEODORE ROOSEVELT (CVN 71) departed Norfolk 28 December 1990, and arrived just in time for the beginning of DESERT STORM. They joined USS MIDWAY (CV 41), USS SARATOGA (CV 60), USS JOHN F. KENNEDY (CV 67) and USS RANGER (CV 61) who were already on station.

After blinding the enemy's early warning systems with Navy EA-6B Prowlers and destroying critical radar sites with high-speed anti-radiation missiles (HARM) fired from Navy tactical aircraft and Air Force F-4 Wild Weasels, allied aircraft poured into Iraq and began bombing command and control centers, Scud missile launchers and nuclear, biological and chemical weapons facilities. The Navy/Marine Corps team launched more than 80% of the HARM missiles that paved the way for the coalition attack.

During those early hours of the war, Navy and Marine pilots contributed to the destruction of Iraq's air and naval forces, anti-air defenses, ballistic missile launchers, communications networks, electrical power and more. They joined their joint and allied partners in inflicting heavy military losses with precision bombing from high-tech aerial weaponry, while at the same time minimizing civilian casualties.

On "D-day," four Navy Hornets from VFA-81, embarked in SARATOGA, were on a bombing mission targeted against an Iraqi airfield when they detected two Iraqi MiG-21s seven miles away. They switched their F/A-18 strike-fighters from bombing profile to air-to-air, and downed both aircraft using Sidewinder missiles. They then continued their mission and scored direct hits on the enemy airfield. That encounter produced the Navy's only air-to-air kills, while taking the versatile Hornet through its dual-roled paces. All told, coalition aircraft scored 35 air-to-air fixed wing kills.

The Iraqi air force quickly went underground or flew to safe haven in neighboring Iran. Navy pilots from KENNEDY, flying a daytime mission over southwestern Iraq early in the offensive, said that a group of MiGs stayed 40 or 50 miles away, falling back and refusing to engage each time the U.S. planes advanced. It was a pattern repeated throughout the war. Each time Navy crews energized the powerful, long-range AWG-9 radar in the F-14, Iraqi pilots turned away. In the course of the war, more than 234 Iraqi aircraft were taken out of the fight: 90 were destroyed in combat operations, 122 flew to Iran, 16 were captured by ground forces and six were non-combat losses.

E-2C Hawkeyes operated around-the-clock in concert with coalition AWACs to keep track of Iraq's air force and provide air traffic control. Navy and Marine aircraft flew continuous combat air patrols to protect sealift ships and airfields, provide reconnaissance and on-call anti-surface strike capability.

U.S. Air Force, Marine Corps and Navy airborne tankers played a crucial role. Without airborne tankers, coalition warplanes wouldn't have been able to hit targets deep in Iraq. The large, land-based Air Force KC-10 and KC-131 tankers carried the bulk of the load. Coordination of the airborne tanking effort was superb.

While Navy strike-fighters and bombers were doing their job, shore-based P-3C Orions and carrier-based S-3 Vikings continued to patrol the shipping lanes. Specially equipped EP-3Es provided electronic reconnaissance. While performing routine surface reconnaissance in the northern Persian Gulf on 20 February, an S-3B from VS-32, based aboard the carrier AMERICA, became the first aircraft of that type to engage and destroy a hostile vessel using bombs. Guided by the Aegis cruiser USS VALLEY FORGE (CG 50), the S-3 searched the area with its forward-looking infrared system and inverse synthetic aperture radar (ISAR), pin-pointed the position of the high-speed, heavily-armed craft, and sank it.

The Navy also had a large helo contingent which employed a variety of rotary-wing aircraft for search and rescue, medical evacuation and logistics. DESERT STORM marked the first combat operations for the HH-60H Seahawk strike rescue helicopter. The Navy's newest helicopter can also perform medical evacuations, provide logistics support or deliver up to eight members of a special operations (SEAL) team.

Naval aviators made a major contribution to the destruction of the Iraqi navy. Within the first three weeks of the air campaign, Intruders and Hornets using Harpoon missiles, Skipper and Rockeye bombs, sank and disabled many of Iraq's missile gunboats, minesweepers, patrol craft and other small ships. Silkworm anti-ship missile sites and several armed hovercraft were also destroyed. During that same three week period, Navy and Marine Corps units contributed more than one-third of the total 42,000 sorties flown.

As the war progressed, the Navy-Marine team's mission changed from strategic and battlefield preparation to tactical targets and close-air support. Tanks, vehicles and artillery moved to the top of the target list, especially during the border incursions in and around the Saudi town of Khafji on 29 January, and following the start of the ground campaign on 24 February. Marine Harriers and Navy and Marine Intruders shifted from hitting pre-selected, stationary targets to striking roving quarry.

OV-10 Broncos and AH-1 Cobra attack helicopters provided close-air support during these operations and helped clear the way for the fast-moving 1st and 2nd Marine Divisions. Close-air support, with constant danger from small-arms fire, shoulder-fired missiles and possible "friendly fire," was not a new mission for the A-6 or the Cobra, both of which saw action in Vietnam.

The AV-8B, on the other hand, saw its first sea-based combat action. Flying from the amphibious assault ships USS TARAWA (LHA 1) and USS NASSAU (LHA 4) as well as from ground bases, the Harrier demonstrated the Navy/Marine team's versatility and effectiveness, as did the OV-10 ashore. Twelve Broncos transited the Atlantic aboard AMERICA and ROOSEVELT. As the carriers entered the Mediterranean, the Broncos flew off to finish their trip to Saudi Arabia.

DESERT STORM marked the first combat use of some of the Navy's newest aircraft including the F-14A+, the F/A-18C and the F/A-18D night-attack aircraft. The multi-mission F/A-18 Hornets of the Navy flew 4,435 sorties, while the Marines flew 5,047 sorties in the durable fighter-attack aircraft. Navy pilots flew 4,071 sorties in their battle-proven, all-weather A-6 Intruders, and Marine pilots flew 854 sorties in their Intruders.

Because a wide variety of ordnance was used to match specific weapons to specific targets, Navy/Marine tactical aviation units put the logistics system to the test. Not counting missiles, allied air forces dropped over 88,500 tons of ordnance on the battlefield. The heavy demand for repair parts was satisfied by the supply system as well. Navy squadrons maintained 85 to 95 percent of their aircraft at a fully mission-capable status throughout DESERT SHIELD/STORM.

On the last full day of war, Navy aviators of the six carrier battle groups flew 600 combat missions, reducing the remaining combat capability of Saddam Hussein's forces as the Iraqis fled from Kuwait. Over the course of the war, Navy pilots, crews and aviation support personnel helped give the United States and her coalition partners early and undisputed ownership of the airspace over Iraq and Kuwait. Launching up to 140 sorties a day from a single flight deck, the carriers and their battle groups contributed significantly to coalition air dominance and effectively eliminated Iraq's naval capability. The performance of the nearly 30,000 Navy men and nearly 500 aircraft aboard the carriers was unparalleled, and their mission statistics were impressive. At the end, Navy sorties, both fixed and rotary wing, totaled nearly 20,000.

THE WAR AT SEA. The war at sea was integral to the liberation of Kuwait. While continuing their high-tempo maritime interception mission, U.S. and coalition warships conducted a wide variety of contingency actions, from TLAM launches to naval gunfire support.

A multinational naval force of 115 U.S. and 50 allied warships had already severed Iraq's economic lifeline during the five-month-old maritime interception campaign when DESERT SHIELD turned into a STORM. The battleships USS WISCONSIN and (BB 64) and USS MISSOURI (BB 63) took up stations in the northern Persian Gulf ready to contribute the firepower of their 16-inch guns and Tomahawk cruise missiles to the ejection of Iraqi forces from Kuwait.

The Aegis cruiser USS SAN JACINTO (CG 56) fired the first Tomahawk missile toward Iraq from her position in the Red Sea. USS BUNKER HILL (CG 52) followed suit moments later from the Persian Gulf. It was an historic moment soon duplicated 100 times over aboard seven other Navy warships during the first day of DESERT STORM.

WISCONSIN served as the TLAM strike commander for the Persian Gulf, directing the sequence of launches that marked the opening of DESERT STORM and firing a total of 24 TLAMs during the first two days of the campaign. Within sight of WISCONSIN, missile after missile rose from other ships in the area, including her sister ship MISSOURI.

Navy surface forces made an impact early in DESERT STORM, when USS NICHOLAS (FFG 47) and the Kuwaiti fast attack craft ISTIQLAL (P 5702) conducted the first surface engagement of the war. Supporting combat search and rescue operations for the air campaign, NICHOLAS and her helicopters scouted the Dorrah oilfield, about 40 miles off the Kuwaiti coast. Nine of Dorrah's 11 oil platforms were occupied by Iraqi troops who were using them as observation posts to gather intelligence on U.S. and allied aircraft and ship movements.

In a daring night-time operation, well within range of Iraqi Silkworm missiles and near Iraqi combatant ships and aircraft armed with Exocet ship-killer missiles, NICHOLAS and ISTIQLAL attacked the enemy positions.

NICHOLAS crept to within a mile of the southernmost platforms under cover of darkness. Armed for air-to-surface combat, embarked Army AHIP helicopters, joined by NICHOLAS' own SH-60 Seahawk helicopter from HSL-44, headed north — toward the enemy's "back door." Once in range, the helicopters launched a volley of precision-guided missiles that destroyed enemy positions on the two northernmost platforms. Seconds later, as six Iraqi soldiers attempted to escape to a waiting small craft, ammunition stockpiled on the platforms exploded, illuminating the night sky.

NICHOLAS and her Kuwaiti counterpart came within range of their objectives. While Iraqis on the other platforms were staring at their neighbors' flaming fortifications, the two ships opened fire, quickly neutralizing the remaining platforms. No enemy troops had returned fire since the beginning of the lightning-fast operation.

An Arabic-speaking crewman called out over the ship's loudspeaker that anyone who wished to surrender should raise his hands. A monitor in NICHOLAS' combat information center displayed a flickering infrared image of an Iraqi waving weakly. Several hours later, the first 23 enemy prisoners of war (EPWs) were taken as teams boarded the platforms to destroy the remaining fortifications. Five Iraqis were killed during the engagement.

Searchers found caches of shoulder-launched surface-to-air missiles — an unpleasant surprise for the Seahawk pilots who had flown near the platforms during the past two days. Navy demolition teams destroyed the remaining weapons and long-range radio equipment.

NICHOLAS' relatively low-tech victory contrasted vividly the high-tech hailstorm of sea-launched TLAMs during the opening days of DESERT STORM. The Navy's distributed firepower concept — of which TLAM is one example — was further demonstrated on 19 January when a TLAM was fired by the attack submarine USS LOUISVILLE (SSN 724) submerged in the Red Sea. By the end of DESERT STORM's second day, Navy ships in the Middle East had launched 216 TLAMs while continuing to conduct maritime intercept and other sea control operations.

During DESERT SHIELD/STORM attack submarines not only fired TLAMs, but provided an array of multi-mission capabilities to battle group commanders. Prior to and during hostilities, eight SSNs were involved in surveillance and reconnaissance operations. They also provided indications and warning for the battle groups. After hostilities began, an additional five submarines bolstered Navy forces already on station.

As Navy A-6 Intruders pounded Iraqi minelayers on 22 January, NICHOLAS and her Seahawks were again busy in the northern Persian Gulf. As the northernmost allied ship, NICHOLAS launched her helicopters to attack Iraqi patrol boats operating less than a mile from the Kuwaiti coast. In the battle that followed, Seahawk gunners sank or heavily damaged all four enemy craft. The following day, A-6s hit the mark again, disabling an Iraqi tanker used to gather intelligence, an enemy hovercraft and another Iraqi patrol boat.

Navy air power struck again on 24 January, when A-6s destroyed an enemy minelayer, a minesweeper and another patrol boat. A second enemy minesweeper sunk after hitting one of its own mines while attempting to evade the A-6. Near Qurah Island, embarked Army helicopters from USS CURTS (FFG 38) pulled 22 EPWs from the sea. As the helicopters assisted the survivors, Iraqi forces on Qurah fired at the airborne rescuers.

As CURTS' helicopters returned the enemy fire, the ship maneuvered closer to the island and trained its guns ashore, commencing an intense six-hour struggle to retake the first parcel of Kuwaiti territory. When the enemy gunfire ceased, three Iraqis lay dead and 29 others knelt in surrender. Navy SEALs from Naval Special Warfare Group 1 landed on Qurah aboard helicopters from USS LEFTWICH (DDG 984). With NICHOLAS and CURTS keeping watch close by, the island was reclaimed, and 51 EPWs were taken into custody.

On 29 January, in the northern Persian Gulf, the five ships of Amphibious Ready Group (ARG) ALFA — USS OKINAWA (LPH 3), USS OGDEN (LPD 5), USS FORT MCHENRY (LSD 43), USS CAYUGA (LST 1186) and USS DURHAM (LKA 114) — with embarked Marines from the 13th Marine Expeditionary Unit (special operations capable) — steamed near the Kuwaiti island Umm al Maradim. The Marines assaulted the 300-meter by 400-meter island 12 miles off the Kuwaiti coast using embarked Marine helicopters, liberating the second Kuwaiti island. After destroying Iraqi anti-aircraft weapons and artillery stored on the island, which had been used as an early warning post by the enemy, the Marines raised the Kuwaiti flag over the second parcel of reclaimed territory.

Later that day, 20 Iraqi small craft fired upon Navy helos investigating reports of surrendering Iraqis on neighboring islands. The helos returned fire, sinking four boats and damaging twelve others. By 2 February all Iraqi craft capable of delivering missiles had been destroyed, and the Iraqi naval force was considered combat ineffective.

CURTS, using advanced mine-avoidance sonar, led MISSOURI northward. MISSOURI gun crews sent 2,700-pound shells crashing into an Iraqi command and control bunker near the Saudi border. It marked the first time her 16-inch guns had been fired in combat since March 1953 off Korea. MISSOURI's gun crews returned to action 5 February, silencing an Iraqi artillery battery with another 10 rounds. Over a three-day period, MISSOURI bombarded Iraqi strongholds with 112 16-inch shells.

WISCONSIN, escorted by NICHOLAS, relieved MISSOURI on the 6th, answering her first combat call for gunfire support since March 1952. The most recently recommissioned battleship sent 11 shells across 19 miles of space to destroy an Iraqi artillery battery in southern Kuwait. Using an Unmanned Aerial Vehicle (UAV) as a spotter in combat for the first time, WISCONSIN pounded Iraqi targets and Iraqi boats that had been used during raids along the Saudi coast. WISCONSIN's turrets boomed again on 8 February, blasting bunkers and artillery sites near Khafji after the Iraqis were ousted from the city by Saudi and Qatari armor. The two battleships alternated positions on the gun line, using their 16-inch guns to destroy enemy targets and soften defenses along the Kuwait coastline for a possible amphibious assault.

Soon after the Iraqi invasion, it became clear that Iraq was laying mines in international waters. U.S. ships discovered and destroyed six mines during December. The U.S. Mine Countermeasures Group (USMCMG) was established with the objective of clearing a path to the beach for a possible amphibious landing and battleship gunfire support.

The minesweepers USS ADROIT (MSO 509), USS IMPERVIOUS (MSO 449), and USS LEADER (MSO 490) along with the newly commissioned mine countermeasures ship USS AVENGER (MCM 1) arrived in the Gulf aboard the heavy-lift ship Super Servant III. More than 20 Navy Explosive Ordnance Disposal (EOD) teams were also deployed to support the mine countermeasures force. Allied minesweepers from Saudi Arabia, Great Britain and Kuwait, and the MH-53 Super Stallions of Mine Countermeasures Helicopter Squadron 14 joined the MCM effort.

After months of training off Dubai, United Arab Emirates, USMCMG staff embarked in USS TRIPOLI (LPH 10) on 20 January, and proceeded to the northern Gulf waters to perform their mission. As flagship for the combined operation, TRIPOLI's flight deck was the base for the mine-sweeping helicopters. Six British minesweepers joined their U.S. counterparts, with British and U.S. warships providing air defense.

USMCMG began its work 60 miles east of the Kuwaiti coastline, working initially to clear a 15-mile long, 1,000-yard wide path. The mine-clearing task force spent the first few weeks of DESERT STORM pushing 24 miles to "Point FOXTROT," a 10-mile by 3.5-mile box which became the battleship gunfire support area south of Faylaka Island.

While sweeping further toward shore, the task group was targeted by Iraqi fire control radars associated with Silkworm missile sites inside Kuwait. Task force ships moved out of Silkworm range and worked to locate the radar site. During those maneuvers on 18 February, Iraqi mines found their mark. Within three hours of each other, TRIPOLI and USS PRINCETON (CG 59) were rocked by exploding mines. As damage control teams successfully overcame fires and flooding aboard TRIPOLI and PRINCETON, IMPERVIOUS, LEADER and AVENGER searched for additional mines in the area. ADROIT led the salvage tug USS BEAUFORT (ATS 2) toward PRINCETON to tow her to safety.

TRIPOLI was able to continue her mission for several days before she was relieved by USS LASALLE (AGF 3) and USS NEW ORLEANS (LPH 11) and proceeded to Bahrain for repairs. NEW ORLEANS provided the helicopter deck while the mine group staff moved aboard LASALLE to coordinate the operation. PRINCETON restored her TLAM strike and AEGIS anti-air warfare defense capabilities within fifteen minutes of the mine strike, whereupon she reassumed duties as local anti-air warfare coordinator and remained on station, providing defense for the mine countermeasures group for an additional 30 hours, until relieved.

Charts and intelligence captured from Iraq showed the mine field where TRIPOLI and PRINCETON were hit was one of six laid in a 150-mile arc from Faylaka Island to the Saudi-Kuwaiti border. Within that arc, there were four additional mine-lines — a total of more than 1,000 mines — laid over a five month period.

Three days later, the massive 31-ship amphibious task force moved north to assist in battlefield preparation as the deadline for the ground offensive neared. As WISCONSIN and MISSOURI steamed in the vicinity of recently-cleared "Point FOXTROT," their gun crews continued to pound Iraqi targets. Marine AV-8B Harriers launched from the flight deck of NASSAU conducted strikes ashore.

The night before the 24 February ground offensive began, MISSOURI trained her guns on Faylaka Island in a pyrotechnic display intended to convince Iraqi troops along the Kuwaiti coast that the sea-borne invasion was at hand. WISCONSIN, accompanied by USS MCINERNEY (FFG 8) moved in close to drive that point home.

Twenty-four hours into the ground campaign, Iraqis manning the Kuwait Silkworm missile sites fired two anti-ship missiles at MISSOURI. The first landed harmlessly between MISSOURI and USS JARRETT (FFG 33). The second, headed straight for MISSOURI, but was intercepted by two Sea Dart missiles from the British warship HMS GLOUCESTER (D 96).

With the allied ground force plowing through Iraqi defenders, Iraqi forces on the Kuwaiti coastline prepared a counter-attack. To diffuse that possibility, Marine helicopters from USS GUAM (LPH 9) and other ships of the amphibious task force conducted operations designed to keep the enemy wary of an amphibious assault. GUAM's helicopters conducted early-morning strike missions on both Faylaka and Bubiyan Islands. OKINAWA conducted a simulated helicopter assault against Kuwaiti beaches, turning back after drawing small arms and anti-aircraft artillery fire from the enemy's coastal bunkers. The maneuvers held the attention of 80,000 Iraqi coastal defense personnel as the coalition's "end run" swarmed around their flank. By the time the enemy realized an amphibious assault was not headed their way, it was too late. Coalition victory was less than 24 hours away.

WISCONSIN and MISSOURI's guns continued to fire. Both battleships passed the million-pound mark of ordnance delivered on Iraqi targets by the time President Bush ended hostilities on 28 February. With one last salvo from her big guns, WISCONSIN fired the last naval gunfire support mission of the war.

Though the cease-fire ended ground hostilities, the Navy's mission didn't slow. Navy warships continued working with allied counterparts to enforce U.N. sanctions. Both battleships' UAVs combed the coastline and outlying islands in reconnaissance support for occupying allied forces. Over Faylaka Island, MISSOURI's UAV observed hundreds of Iraqi soldiers waving white flags following the battleship's pounding of their trenchlines — the first-ever surrender of enemy troops to an unmanned aircraft.

The mine-clearing effort continued unabated. By the time the cease-fire was called, the job of reaching the Kuwaiti port of al-Shuaibah was nearly complete. Minesweepers and EOD teams from the U.S., Britain, Holland and Belgium continued to clear the path to Kuwait's main port.

LASALLE arrived at Al Shuaibah on 12 March, after she assisted the British minesweeper HMS CATTISTOCK (M 31) in escorting two tankers filled with fresh water and supplies through a channel to the newly-liberated Kuwait. USMCMG assets were busy sweeping channels into other ports north and south of Shuaibah and around Kuwait City.

"The Iraqis might have agreed to a cease-fire, but their mines have not yet surrendered," said RADM Raynor A. K. Taylor, USN, Middle East Force commander aboard LASALLE. "There are lots of them out there." Further complicating the minesweeping operation was the huge oil slick Iraqi forces spilled into the Gulf, hampering mine-sighting efforts and complicating the work of EOD divers. By mid-March, more than 220 mines had been destroyed by the coalition force.

On 27 February, AVENGER, the Navy's newest mine countermeasures ship, detected, classified and marked a bottom-influence mine similar to the two that rocked PRINCETON nine days earlier. Divers from EOD Mobile Unit 6 placed neutralizing charges and detonated the mine — the first bottom influence mine ever found intact during combat. During the week of 18 April, using her mine-hunting sonar and remote-controlled mine neutralization vehicle, AVENGER located and destroyed five additional bottom-influence mines.

As of 14 March, the day Sheikh Jaber Ahmad al-Sabah, Kuwait's Emir, returned to his home after a seven-month exile, more than 70 U.S. ships remained on station. Mine clearing and maritime intercepts continued, with USS BIDDLE (CG 34) completing the coalition's 1,000th boarding of a merchant vessel since the operation began in early August.

Battle damage repair crews from USS JASON (AR 8) completed six month's work in 30 days to enable TRIPOLI to return to the northern Gulf in the first week of April to relieve NEW ORLEANS as flagship for ongoing allied mine-clearing operations. Twenty-one minesweeping ships from six coalition countries continued to scour the Kuwait coastline and northern Persian Gulf for mines. By April 11, the day the U.N. Security Council declared the end of the Persian Gulf war following Iraq's acceptance of cease-fire terms, coalition divers and minesweeping forces had located and destroyed 553 of Iraq's 1,000-plus mines.

AMPHIBIOUS OPERATIONS. During the early days of DESERT SHIELD, a powerful 18,000-man amphibious task force steamed into the North Arabian Sea to add an important element to the allied arsenal. Within less than a month after the Iraqi invasion of Kuwait, more than 20 amphibious ships from Norfolk, Little Creek, and San Diego had completed the 10,000-mile trip to the Gulf of Oman, where nearly 8,000 Marines and 10,000 sailors commenced full-scale preparations to "hit the beach" to eject Iraq's army from Kuwait.

The task force, with Marines from the 4th Marine Expeditionary Brigade (MEB) and 13th Marine Expeditionary Unit (MEU) embarked, included air, land and sea assets tailor-made for coastal assault — Harrier attack jets and assault helicopters to provide air cover for infantry, and armor that would hit the beach aboard high-speed air-cushion landing craft (LCAC). The Task Force, quickly forged from several amphibious ready groups (ARGs), represented the largest amphibious assault force assembled in more than 30 years. It was also represented fastest deployment of an amphibious force of this magnitude. Load-out and departure were completed within 11 days.

During the transit and following arrival, "gator" Navy sailors and fleet Marines underwent constant chemical weapons defense, cultural and intelligence training, just like their counterparts ashore. They also completed demanding shipboard drills and amphibious assault training on coalition beaches. That training grew more intense as the amphibious forces performed high-visibility exercises off the coast of Saudi Arabia to heighten the enemy wariness of an invasion from the sea.

Along with massive amphibious exercises, embarked Marines responded to calls for assistance from maritime interception force warships. Marines aboard the five ships of ARG ALFA were among the first combat troops placed aboard uncooperative Iraqi tankers during maritime intercepts in the early days of DESERT SHIELD. Along with Navy SEALs, fleet Marines backed up boarding and search teams composed of surface sailors and Coast Guard law enforcement detachment personnel during hostile boardings.

Amphibious forces also played a major role in mine countermeasures operations. Helicopters performing airborne mine countermeasures used versatile amphibious flight decks inside the mine-infested waters off the Kuwaiti coast. USS TRIPOLI, LASALLE, NEW ORLEANS and other amphibious ships acted as home base for the MH-53E mine sweeping helicopters. Marine AH-1W Cobras acted as armed escorts. The largest mine-clearing effort since World War II enabled the battleships to pummel Kuwait's shoreline with naval gunfire.

The amphibious presence grew larger following President Bush's 8 November decision to nearly double U.S. forces in theater. The 13 ships of PHIBGRU THREE arrived from three West Coast ports with nearly 15,000 Marines of the 5th MEB embarked to join the amphibious task force.

As the ground war commenced, nearly 17,000 Marines stood ready aboard the largest combined amphibious assault force since since the Inchon landing in Korea. Only then did the Sailors and Marines of the amphibious force learn that their warfighting skills would not be immediately required as they had expected. But their preparation had not been in vain. It was at the core of the deceptive tactics which played a major role in the quick allied victory.

SUPPORT FOR THE TROOPS: THE GROUND WAR. During the weeks prior to "G-day," Marine units, including artillery, reconnaissance and combined arms task forces, were busy disrupting Iraqi defensive positions. Marine artillery and Army multiple-launch rocket systems, using Air Force airborne spotters as well as Marine forward and aerial observers and clandestine recon teams inside enemy territory, had enormous success with artillery raids and roving gun tactics. Coalition air forces pounded the enemy day and night. Naval gunfire from the battleships MISSOURI and WISCONSIN provided the "Sunday punch" that helped soften up the future battlefield.

On the night of 23 February, Marine units all along the Kuwait border moved into final attack positions and waited for the order to commence the ground offensive. Real-time and near-real-time tactical reconnaissance were provided by Navy and Marine Corps UAVs and Navy F-14s equipped with the tactical air reconnaissance pod system (TARPS). The deadline set by President Bush for Iraq to get out of Kuwait had expired.

Iraq had no "eyes" over the battlefield with which to observe the allied strategy. While the United States and its coalition partners unleashed General Schwarzkopf's "Hail Mary" play, the Iraqis were convinced that the battle would be joined at the center of their defensive lines along the Saudi-Kuwait border, and by amphibious assault.

What the Iraqis could not realize was that the allies had secretly moved two entire corps of American forces (the Army's 7th and 18th), supported by British and French divisions, far to the west in one of the largest and swiftest battlefield troop movements in history. This giant "end run" by more than 250,000 soldiers spread over several hundred miles, moved deep into Iraqi territory from the Saudi border behind the Iraqi forces to deliver a fatal "left hook." The flanking maneuver not only cut off all avenues of retreat north and west of Kuwait, it fulfilled Chairman of the Joint Chiefs of Staff, General Colin Powell's prediction that the coalition — specifically the American military — were going to "cut off the head ... and kill" the Iraqi army.

The Marine Corps, with the support of Navy air power, was tasked with going for the jugular. After performing their own deception by shifting both Marine divisions some 40 to 50 miles northeast from their original staging area, the Marines stepped off into battle. The 1st and 2nd Marine Divisions, each more than 18,000 strong, and the U.S. Army 1st Brigade ("Tiger Brigade"), 2nd Armored Division, plunged into the attack. They were supported by the 3rd Marine Aircraft Wing and thousands of combat service support staff from the 1st and 2nd Force Service Support Groups, and by Navy air forces.

On their way, the Marines had to cross two belts of minefields, 12-foot high sand berms, barbed-wire defenses, booby traps and fire trenches, all the while under sporadic attack by Iraqi artillery. These "impenetrable barriers" were quickly breached by the Marine teams. As the two Marine divisions advanced, two Saudi and Qatari task forces moved up Kuwait's east coast in a similar drive. The initial Marine advance was described by Schwarzkopf in his 27 February briefing as follows:

"It was a classic, absolutely classic military breaching of a very, very tough minefield, barbed wire, fire trench-type barrier. They went through the first barrier like it was water. Then they brought both divisions steaming through that breach. Absolutely superb operation -a textbook, and I think it will be studied for many, many years to come as the way to do it."

Overhead, Cobras, Harriers and Intruders provided close-air support as the Marines pushed forward meeting occasional resistance. Navy A-6 Intruders laid down heavy barrages. Marine aircraft attacked in waves as engineers continued to shoot line charges and drop bundles of plastic pipes near trenches so the blade tanks could form makeshift bridges. Even though the 1st Division Marines encountered artillery fire and a mechanized counter-attack, their attack proved unstoppable. Most Iraqis fought for only a few minutes before surrendering. Massive artillery and air support from Navy and Marine aircraft sparked a frenzy of surrender that, at times, slowed the progress of advancing Marine units.

The 2nd Marine Division enjoyed equal success. With the Army's Tiger Brigade on the west flank, the 8th Marine Regiment to the east, and the 6th Marine Regiment in the center, the division kicked off its attack. Within hours they too had breached both defensive belts. Facing enemy mortar and small arms fire, the 2nd Division drove into Kuwait and took more than 5,000 EPWs by the end of the first day.

As Marines continued their attack the sea-based arm of the Navy-Marine Corps team continued to provide support. The battleships continued rapid, responsive gunfire on targets designated by Navy and Marine spotters on the ground and in the air. The amphibious task force in the Persian Gulf continued to demand difficult decisions from the Iraqi generals. Because of the threat of an amphibious landing and the uncertainty of where and when it to ten divisions, totaling 80,000 men, to the defense of the Kuwait coastline. In addition they garrisoned troops and equipment on Bubiyan and Faylaka Islands which command sea approaches to vital areas.

About 7,500 Marines from the 5th MEB were off-loaded from amphibious ships at Saudi Arabian ports at the beginning of the ground attack to serve as the 1st MEF reserve force. Marine AV-8B Harriers, AH-1 Cobra helicopters and special operations units from the 4th MEB aided the Arab forces in the east coast drive. On the second day of the ground war, both Marine Divisions faced sporadic resistance as they pushed further into Kuwait. They fought some intense battles along the way, and by the time Kuwait's International Airport was secured on the fourth day of the ground war, the two Marine divisions had defeated an Iraqi force of 11 divisions.

At 0800, Persian Gulf time, 28 February, American forces ceased offensive combat operations by order of the President. In 100 hours of offensive combat, the Marines and one Army Brigade, supported by Navy, Marine and coalition aircraft, destroyed or damaged 1,060 tanks, 608 artillery pieces, five Frog launchers and two Scud launchers, and captured more than 20,000 Iraqi soldiers.

THE WEAPONS OF WAR. The coalition attack on Iraq began early on 17 January when U.S. naval forces launched a barrage of Tomahawk land attack cruise missiles (TLAMs) from the Persian Gulf and the Red Sea against strategic targets in Iraq and Kuwait. As Americans watched the evening news, we heard the the correspondents in Baghdad say, "I hear bombs but I don't see any planes." The reason they saw no planes was because the only systems sent to destroy the critical, but heavily defended targets in Baghdad were TLAMs and Air Force F-117 "stealth" fighter-bombers.

The initial TLAM attack was followed by nearly 600 coalition aircraft striking from desert bases and carrier flight decks. TLAM's outstanding performance and accuracy — about 85% of the 288 missiles fired during the war hit their targets — helped neutralize Iraqi defenses and paved the war for coalition strike aircraft. While avoiding the necessity of risking the life of a pilot in attacking a heavily defended target, TLAM further minimized the loss of life on both sides by reducing unintended collateral damage to civilian targets and reducing or eliminating the threat to allied aircraft.

The success of TLAM validated the results of years of operational testing. "Tomahawk doesn't know the difference between war and peace," said one officer describing its baptism in combat. "It just does its job."

The TLAM uses an array of advanced technology to reach its target. Launched with a solid-rocket booster and propelled by turbofan engine, the missile follows complex guidance directions from its on-board computer. Skimming the ground at 100 to 300 feet, it literally reads the terrain to avoid enemy radar. Although the TLAM warhead is fairly small in comparison with some bomb payloads, it is highly accurate. It also has the advantage of being fast, hard to detect or shoot down and immune to human traits such as nervousness. More importantly, it can fly day or night, in all weather, to safely attack targets deemed too dangerous for human pilots.

The overland routes flown by Tomahawks are developed by theater mission planning centers at Atlantic and Pacific Fleet Headquarters with the help of the Defense Mapping Agency. Programming the missile's flight from ship to shore is done aboard ship.

Two types of Tomahawk were used during DESERT STORM; the conventional land-attack missile, TLAM-C, and a version equipped with submunitions, the TLAM-D. The TLAM-C accurately delivers a single 1,000 pound warhead. TLAM-D can dispense up to 166 bomblets in 24 packages. The submunitions can be armor-piercing, fragmentation or incendiary. TLAMs were used against chemical and nuclear weapons facilities, surface-to-air missile sites, command and control centers and Saddam's presidential palace.

Tomahawks were used in DESERT STORM to both destroy important targets and save allied aircraft by attacking defensive positions in advance of the air assault. "It costs a lot of money," said Senator Sam Nunn, chairman of the Senate Armed Services Committee, "but when you look at the precious savings of lives, I think the dollars are well invested."

Anti-ship attacks were carried out using the smaller Harpoon cruise missile system, previously used against Iranian warships in 1988 after the mine attack on USS SAMUEL B. ROBERTS (FFG 58). The Navy also recorded the first combat use of the stand-off land-attack missile (SLAM). SLAM, a variant of the Harpoon, allows pilots to attack high-value targets from more than 50 miles away.

Deployed from carrier-based aircraft, SLAMs use targeting data loaded into the missile before take-off, Global Positioning System mid-course guidance assistance and video aim-point control to provide a precision strike capability that minimizes collateral damage. SLAM's data link system allows the missile to be launched by one aircraft and be guided to the target by another aircraft, normally positioned out of danger more than 60 miles away from the target.

The high-speed anti-radiation missile (HARM) proved especially effective in the destruction and suppression of Iraqi electronic emitters, particularly those associated with radar sites used to direct anti-aircraft guns and surface-to-air missiles.

Another system dedicated to insuring the survival of sailors and their ships is the AEGIS combat system. The system can defeat an extremely wide range of targets. One AEGIS cruiser even detected and tracked four Iraqi SCUD missiles fired at great ranges. AEGIS cruisers coordinate anti-air defense of the battle group in a multi-threat environment. This high-tech command and control system allows the battle group to concentrate on its offensive tasks by reducing the resources needed for its defense. The AEGIS ships themselves made a formidable contribution to offensive firepower: more than 25% of the TLAMs fired during DESERT STORM were fired by seven of the nine AEGIS cruisers on station.

Among the other ways the Navy used "high-tech" weaponry to minimize the need to place American pilots in danger is the Unmanned Aerial Vehicle (UAV), or Remotely Piloted Vehicle (RPV) as they are sometimes called. The UAV was another Gulf War success story. Several times larger than the remote control airplane a hobbyist might own, the UAV is equipped with a television camera that relays live battlefield pictures to the control site. Launched from ships, or from the ground, it can operate for several hours at a distance of more than 100 miles from the launch point. Information gained from the UAV is used to direct gunfire and gather other real-time information from behind enemy lines without risking the lives of airborne or ground-based forward spotters.

The "smart" weapons and laser-guided

bombs used in the war with Iraq introduced a new age of weaponry to nearly everyone in America. Millions of people had a birds-eye view of enemy command and control centers enveloped in clouds of smoke and debris as television broadcast vivid images of the bombs hitting their mark. There were many success stories in DESERT STORM, including new weapons, previously fired only in testing, evaluation or training exercises. For the most part, they performed exactly as they were intended. The "old reliables" also proved to be just that. The ships, planes, bombs, and missiles all worked well. However, the ingredient which made it all work was the one cited by Defense Secretary Dick Cheney when he said, "Everybody talks about the wonder weapons, but the most impressive capability we have is our people."

THE POST WAR PERIOD. Regardless of when the majority of DESERT SHIELD/STORM forces return home, the Navy will still be representing the U.S. in the Persian Gulf. Naval forces have transited the region since 1801, and the reasons behind our stationing a permanent naval presence in the Gulf since 1948 have been revalidated by this most recent conflict.

The President has announced that naval presence in the region will be beefed up, and we are busy working on how to best carry out that tasking. Naval forces will once again provide the primary United States presence in the region, perhaps supplemented by additional prepositioned equipment and a strengthened program of military exercises with our allies.

THE UNITED STATES NAVY IN "DESERT SHIELD" / "DESERT STORM"

VI: LESSONS LEARNED AND SUMMARY

"The United States Armed Forces, with the forces of allied coalition countries, achieved a great victory in the liberation of Kuwait from Iraqi aggression. We must ensure that the lessons of Operations DESERT SHIELD and DESERT STORM inform our decisions for the future."

— **Memorandum from Defense Secretary Dick Cheney, 8 March 1991**

"I believe the magnificent performance of our forces and the totality of their victory have clearly established the tenor of after action discussions — success. We planned, mobilized, deployed, and executed this operation farther from the shores of the continental United States than ever before. We applied military power beyond what our coalition partners — and indeed many Americans — could have imagined. Our accomplishments and successes greatly overshadow any identified shortfalls or deficiencies."

— **General H. Norman Schwarzkopf, USA
Commander-in-Chief U.S. Central Command,
Preliminary Report on Lessons Learned, 5 April 1991**

"It is absolutely essential that we review the performance of our people, platforms, weapons, and tactics while memories are fresh. We want to find out what worked well and what didn't work so well."

— **Statement by Admiral F. B. Kelso, II, USN
before the House Armed Services Committee, 24 April 1991**

INTRODUCTION: From almost any vantage point Operations DESERT SHIELD and DESERT STORM were tremendously successful. There has not been sufficient time to collect, sort and analyze all the data required for detailed tradeoff analyses between specific systems and programs. Nevertheless, some useful broad trends and conclusions are already apparent. This initial recapitulation of lessons learned underscores keys to victory which must be nurtured and reinforced. It also highlights areas for improvement.

The lessons of DESERT SHIELD/ STORM can be usefully separated into three broad categories: (1) areas not tested, (2) old lessons revalidated, and (3) new lessons learned. Areas not tested encompass systems and capabilities which, because of the special circumstances of those operations, were not realistically stressed, tested or evaluated.

> *"...Lessons should be interpreted in light of [the] DESERT SHIELD/STORM scenario, and in some cases may be less applicable generally. For example, we did not test our open ocean concepts. Equipment, tactics, and CWC organizations designed to fight in blue water were modified, often significantly, in this geographically limited joint arena. Some areas such as ASW were not played at all due to lack of a threat. As the budget process focuses on the very positive results of DESERT SHIELD/STORM, these facts must not be forgotten."*
>
> -- Vice Admiral S.R. Arthur, USN, Commander U.S. Naval Forces Central Command, Quick Look — First Impressions Report, 22 March 1991

AREAS NOT TESTED. Nearly every early attempt to extract the lessons of DESERT SHIELD/STORM has begun with a cautionary note concerning the "unique aspects" of those operations and the "lessons not learned". This assessment reviews those "areas not tested" in context with the old and new lessons to foster critical examination of the entire range of naval warfare capabilities. Reviewing the areas not tested also helps avoid learning the wrong lessons.

DESERT SHIELD/STORM was not a model for all future operations. The conditions which existed in Saudi Arabia and the other Gulf states are unique, and not likely to be fully duplicated in other remote areas where U.S. interests require protection. We cannot plan on the advantages of a cohesive coalition, outstanding infrastructure, or six months of preparation time. For 20 years, Saudi Arabia has been over-building industrial, commercial, and transportation facilities, including more than 30 air bases and eight modern port facilities. Nor can we plan on the availability of unlimited free fuel and ample supplies of water in a desert environment.

Those assets — and the close cooperation of Bahrain, Qatar, Oman and the United Arab Emirates — were key to our ability to quickly base over 500,000 troops and over 2,000 aircraft ashore in Saudi Arabia and the other Gulf States. Even six months would not have provided time to build such infrastructure from scratch. In many places we would have to operate without it.

Given our present understanding of Iraq's military capabilities, our nearly six months preparation and an uninterrupted logistics train, we enjoyed, in the words of defense analyst Jeffrey Record "...a set of circumstances so fortuitous that it is highly unlikely it will ever be duplicated again." For this discussion, those "fortuitous circumstances" have been catalogued under three general headings: (1) the galvanizing threat posed by Saddam Hussein, (2) opposition strategy, and (3) infrastructure and environment.

A GALVANIZING THREAT: Although there were clearly additional forces at work, Saddam Hussein's repugnant behavior aroused unprecedented international opposition, secured U.N. legitimacy, helped minimize the potential for a significant split with the Soviets or China, and ensured overwhelming domestic and international support for military action. Despite his best efforts, Saddam was unable to broaden the conflict. Israel remained on one of the sidelines while international terrorists and Iraq's potential allies stood by on the other. Additionally, other international actors did not seek to exploit the possible opportunities presented by our major commitment of forces to Southwest Asia.

AREAS NOT TESTED:

- Limited access to critical enroute support bases, aircraft refueling facilities and overflight rights.

- An opponent who receives support from allies with significant capabilities such as the USSR or China.

- Non-availability of overseas bases from which to conduct offensive or support operations.

- U.S. action without strong regional or international support.

- Force and mobility requirements of a second major simultaneous crisis in another region.

OPPOSITION STRATEGY: Because Iraq did not press their attack into Saudi Arabia in the days following annexation of Kuwait, or attack coalition ground and air forces in Saudi Arabia early in the build-up, we were able to fine tune our forces and plans. Once conflict began, Iraq's burrowing, defensive, survival-oriented strategy, precluded a realistic test of our tactics and systems against a modern, well-led, well-trained, highly motivated adversary. Also, Iraq's strategy was shaped in part by the fact that it was not a maritime power, possessed no submarines, and had only limited ability to threaten forces enroute to the theater.

AREAS NOT TESTED:

- Rapid transition to hostilities.

- Requirement for forcible entry, significant naval opposition, and antisubmarine warfare.

- Confrontation by an integrated defense and strong resistance from a capable adversary with modern high-tech weapons. Neither close air support nor anti-air warfare were fully tested by this conflict.

INFRASTRUCTURE AND ENVIRONMENT: Our regional allies provided a well-developed infrastructure in what could have been a difficult operating environment. The modern ports and airfields of Saudi Arabia accommodated the rapid build-up of coalition forces with relative ease. There was an ample supply of fuel close at hand. The flat, featureless terrain of the region, and the demanding environmental conditions proved both a help and a handicap during operations. The terrain is well-suited for air warfare, but navigation and concealment were more challenging for ground forces. Sand, heat and unusual radio wave propagation conditions hindered operations. The normally clear air-mass of the region is well-suited for flight operations although unusually poor weather encountered during the air campaign hampered battle damage assessment, forced modification of plans and precluded delivery of some precision ordnance. The lack of a significant coastline and the "bottleneck" effect of the Northern Persian Gulf made the option of amphibious assault more challenging than would be the case in other regions.

AREAS NOT TESTED:

- Limited host-nation support and infrastructure.

- While the extreme and unique topographical and climatological conditions of Southwest Asia posed special challenges, DESERT SHIELD/STORM only tested our capabilities to operate in one of many extreme environments.

- Amphibious assault was not fully tested.

OLD LESSONS REVALIDATED. DESERT SHIELD/STORM reaffirmed the importance of clear-cut military objectives, political cohesion and civic support. Established principles of war such as concentration of force, unity of command, effective leadership, the will to fight, and detailed planning were also reaffirmed.

DESERT SHIELD/STORM demonstrated in unmistakable fashion the value and effectiveness of joint and combined military operations. The unique capabilities of each of the U.S. military services — and those of each of our allies — were exploited during various phases of both operations. The combined force provided a synergistic combat capability which brought the greatest possible military power of the coalition force to bear against the opponent. Likewise, our experience also reaffirmed the importance of joint and combined training, the value of forward presence and the validity of joint force sequencing for power-projection.

DESERT SHIELD/STORM underscored the principle that control of the sea is essential for successful power-projection. Maritime superiority afforded the United States a position of leadership in implementing and enforcing the U.N. sanctions. The traditional role of sealift in moving heavy equipment and supplies into the theater was clearly highlighted.

The strategic advantage of high technology was re-confirmed. We must continue to emphasize research and development to retain that edge. At the same time, we were also forcefully reminded that possession of high-tech weapons alone is not a sure defense against simple, low-tech weapons like mines. Finding and neutralizing mines is always challenging. We cannot always afford to provide the minelayer unimpeded opportunity to lay mines. No known or projected technology could have quickly neutralized over 1000 enemy mines once they were in place. Nevertheless, we must clearly focus our high-tech resources on developing the best mine countermeasures capability available.

THE LESSONS OF DESERT SHIELD/STORM. The following summary highlights the preliminary U.S. Navy lessons learned.

QUALITY PEOPLE AND REALISTIC TRAINING. The excellent quality of our people and their high state of training were fundamental to success. The all-volunteer force worked and worked well. Our men and women knew their jobs, knew their equipment, and knew how to fight. Naval forces arrived in theater trained, ready and sustainable. The Navy-Marine Corps team quickly assembled a composite force from literally all corners of the globe, then executed a complex series of maritime intercept, strike, naval gunfire support and amphibious operations, under the most demanding circumstances. Teamwork was evident at all levels.

- <u>We will continue to emphasize joint operations in our training</u>. Some minor training shortfalls were observed with respect to new systems and joint procedures not widely practiced prior to DESERT SHIELD. We made good use of the nearly six month build-up prior to commencement of combat operations to overcome such problems.

"Routine training must include joint terminology and procedures. Joint flight training detachments (Red Flag, Solid Shield, Fallon) should actively seek to combine operations on available ranges. The Navy should work to incorporate KC and AWACS assets routinely. When deployed, joint and multinational operations/exercises should focus on

interoperability issues — comms, tactics, limitations."

— Vice Admiral S.R. Arthur, USN, Commander U.S. Naval Forces Central Command, Quick Look — First Impressions Report, 22 March 1991

- We must continue emphasis on people programs which are the foundation of the all-volunteer force. High retention and the experience level of our forces contributed to victory.

"The quality of our personnel deployed in theater set new standards of excellence. I cannot say enough about the performance of our people. The speed of their advance on the battlefield, their expert employment of weapons systems, exceptionally low UCMJ violation rate, and their strong positive showing on media events all support the services quality force programs... The credit for this goes to the troops and their commanders. The all volunteer force is a winner."

— General H. Norman Schwarzkopf, USA, Commander-in-Chief U.S. Central Command, Preliminary Report on Lessons Learned, 5 April 1991

- High quality, realistic training is difficult, time consuming and expensive, but it is fundamental to success in combat. As our force gets smaller, we will focus continued attention and resources on training. Just one of many examples of the superb level of training readiness enjoyed by our forces from the outset was provided by the amphibious force:

"There was no pre-deployment work-up, yet four of the five largest amphibious operations since INCHON (number one was STEEL PIKE in 1964) were executed flawlessly and without injury or damage. The training was realistic — and at times dangerous (but never unsafe): in full EMCON, darkened, at night the ATF executed simultaneous launch of 50 AAVs, simultaneous landing of 12 LCAC, and air assault from seven LHA/LPHs in a very narrow sea echelon area."

— Rear Admiral J. B. LaPlante, USN, CTF 156, "Quick Look" Report, 11 March 1991

TOTAL FORCE CONCEPT. Over 99% of the Naval Reservists called to duty in support of DESERT SHIELD responded to that call. They augmented the active force with the mix of skills required to get the job done. Reserves had major roles in cargo handling, medical support, combat construction and control of shipping. Like their active duty counterparts, they proved to be well-trained and highly professional. While some specific functional areas and administrative matters requiring additional emphasis were noted, DESERT SHIELD/STORM clearly validated significant aspects of the Navy's total force concept.

- Over the past decade, the United States has invested heavily in Naval Reserve manpower, training, and equipment. This investment really paid off in DESERT SHIELD/STORM:

  - Seabees: about 2/3 of all Seabees were reservists.

  - Mine countermeasures: the Naval Reserve provided more than half of the total dedicated MCM personnel.

  - Combat Search and Rescue: all of the Navy's dedicated Combat Search and Rescue personnel are reservists.

  - Cargo Handling Battalions: all of the so-called "combat stevedores" who loaded and offloaded the largest military sealift in history are reserve personnel.

- Intelligence: 400 Naval Reserve intelligence personnel were activated and stood watches, conducted analyses, and interrogated prisoners.

- Harbor Defense: all of the Navy's Mobile Inshore Undersea Warfare personnel are part of the Naval Reserve.

- Other reserve key personnel provided vital medical, logistics, public affairs, and religious support.

"Reservists activated to support USNAVEUR forces during DESERT SHIELD/STORM validated the Total Force Concept. Most reservists arrived well trained from previous annual training periods in theater and were fully and easily integrated into day-to-day operations in minimum time. This was particularly true of the USCOMEASTLANT reserves who were all well exercised under TF 137 and its concept of operations. We are currently looking at the feasibility of creating a new MED logistics task force augmented with reserves, patterned after TF 137, for use in contingencies."

-- **Admiral J. T. Howe, USN, Commander-in-Chief U.S. Naval Forces Europe, Quick Look First Impressions Report, 20 March 1991**

JOINT OPERATIONS. DESERT SHIELD/STORM illustrated the importance and benefits of joint and combined operations. The significant progress made in the past several years was reflected in success on the battlefield. That <u>success firmly cemented the commitment of the Navy to joint operations</u>.

• Working as a team with the other services and our coalition partners generated tremendous combat capability in a short period of time. That teamwork extended into fully integrated combat operations of unprecedented scope, complexity and speed. Clearly, joint operations require continued emphasis.

• Years of close cooperation and coordination with the navies of our NATO allies and other coalition partners, not only in regular multi- and bi-lateral exercises but particularly as part of a multi-national cooperative naval effort during the Iran-Iraq war, laid a strong foundation of interoperability and common procedures. During DESERT SHIELD/STORM, that prior experience facilitated strong informal multi-national naval cooperation even before formal agreements/procedures were developed and implemented.

• Some problems were encountered, particularly in command and control, communications, interoperability, and matters of joint doctrine. For example, regardless of who serves as the Joint Force Air Component Commander (JFACC), all services must have significant representation on his staff to ensure strike planning is fully integrated. Although the nearly six month build-up enabled us to overcome most obstacles and build the teamwork required to resolve problems which arose during combat, the JFACC doctrine must be further refined to ensure it is flexible and enables us to optimize use of our resources.

FORWARD PRESENCE. <u>DESERT SHIELD reaffirmed the importance of forward presence as a pillar of our national military strategy</u> and underscored the role of the Navy

- 56 -

in sustaining that presence. Our maritime forces clearly benefited from years of experience in the harsh operating environment of Southwest Asia. Over 40 years of continuous naval presence in the Persian Gulf — largely independent of political access — demonstrated U.S. interest and resolve. Over those years, our coalition partners in the region came to recognize and respect the depth of our commitment and gradually afforded additional access, paving the way for the massive deployments required by DESERT SHIELD.

- Forward presence made possible the rapid positioning of naval forces in response to the invasion of Kuwait.

- Deploying forces augmented ships already on station in the Persian Gulf. Naval forces were prepared to launch strikes had Iraqi forces continued southward into Saudi Arabia. Their sustainable combat capability and control of the sea provided protection for the introduction of ground and air forces into the theater and enabled immediate enforcement of U.N. sanctions.

SEA CONTROL. DESERT SHIELD underscored that sea control is a fundamental prerequisite for power projection operations. As demonstrated during the "tanker war" with Iran, Iraq's mines, missile-firing patrol boats and aircraft were capable of damaging and disrupting seaborne commerce. Sealift carried 90% of the cargo required for DESERT SHIELD/STORM. Without control of the sea, that cargo would have been at risk, slowing the deployment, threatening our ability to charter foreign merchant ships and significantly increasing costs. Because our naval forces were on station and ready, we were never seriously challenged, and sea control was assured from the outset.

MARITIME INTERCEPTION. The role of our naval forces, working with our coalition partners to implement the U.N. sanctions through a comprehensive maritime interception campaign, is a major DESERT SHIELD/STORM success story. Through April 1991, over 9200 merchant ships were challenged, over 1200 were boarded for inspection, and at least 67 were diverted for carrying prohibited cargo. Iraq's GNP was reduced by approximately one-half. The impact of the embargo was clearly felt by Iraqi soldiers in the trenches — with corresponding impact on morale and will to fight.

- Sanctions against seaborne commerce are enforceable. How effective they will be in achieving their ultimate objectives depends on other factors such as agricultural development, support by neighbors and other allies, and geography.

- Aircraft, especially those with inverse synthetic aperture radar (ISAR), made a vital contribution to our ability to conduct round-the clock maritime surveillance.

- The training and advice of U.S. Coast Guard Law Enforcement Detachments (LEDets) proved invaluable.

"The success of MIF ops was due in no small measure to experience and training provided by LEDets. Drug interdiction operations in the Caribbean have allowed LEDets to become familiar with many Navy procedures, capabilities, and support assets for conducting boardings from Navy platforms. LEDets provided Navy personnel with training in boarding procedures and authority, and indoctrinated personnel in policy for use of force, as well as team duties."

-- **Vice Admiral S.R. Arthur, USN, Commander U.S. Naval Forces Central Command, Quick Look — First Impressions Report, 22 March 1991**

WARFIGHTING. Conducting complex joint operations in a geographically constrained near-land/overland environment poses special challenges for naval forces. Those challenges were met through innovation and teamwork. In general, combat systems, tactics, and organization worked as well or better than expected. While not every naval warfare area was stressed or even tested, naval forces participated in virtually every aspect of the campaign. For example, about one-quarter of all air sorties were flown by Navy and Marine Corps aircraft. Marine forces spearheaded the drive into Kuwait. Platforms capable of multi-mission operations proved especially valuable, making major contributions in cross-warfare areas where demand was greatest.

- **COMMAND RELATIONSHIPS.** After commencement of Desert Shield, Commander, U.S. Seventh Fleet was designated naval component commander. While that new organization worked well, it also highlighted the importance of peacetime planning relationships and staffs which parallel wartime responsibilities and requirements. The Navy is working with CENTCOM to establish permanent command relationships that will support both peacetime planning and wartime requirements.

- **ANTISUBMARINE WARFARE.** ASW was not tested as there was no threat. While Iraq did not have any submarines, many third world and regional powers do, and regional submarine threats are expected to increase in the future. Primary ASW systems such as P-3s, S-3s and LAMPS helicopters used multi-mission capabilities to good advantage in both the maritime interception campaign and in the destruction of the Iraqi navy. S-3s also provided critical tanker and EW support.

- **ANTI-AIR WARFARE.** DESERT SHIELD/STORM presented an unprecedented AAW deconfliction challenge. All operations were conducted safely and successfully from pre-hostilities through re-deployment. There were no "blue-on-blue" air engagements. Restricted geography, unusual RF propagation conditions, proximity of the threat from Iraq and potential threat from Iran, the large number of commercial airfields and air routes in the vicinity, the joint/combined nature of the operation and the limited time available to establish positive identification of potential hostiles prior to their entry into engagement envelopes combined to form a most complex, demanding AAW environment. Coalition air and surface units were controlled through a complex sea-air-land data link architecture. Some problems were noted — primarily in the areas of communications interoperability — but the overall success of joint/combined AAW during DESERT SHIELD/STORM will provide a solid foundation for future operations.

"The Arabian Gulf link network was the most complex ever attempted, and combined U.S. and MNF link-11 ships, USN, USAF, RSAF, AE W aircraft, USAF TACC, and USMC TACCs and TAOCs in a combined TADIL A/B/ JTIDS architecture."

-- **Vice Admiral S.R. Arthur, USN, Commander U.S. Naval Forces Central Command, Quick Look — First Impressions Report, 22 March 1991**

- **STRIKE WARFARE.** The Joint Force Air Component Commander (JFACC) used the air tasking order (ATO) as a centralized planning and execution tool. It was effective in managing the high volume of sorties generated to concentrate coalition air power against Iraq, especially during the preplanned, structured stages of the campaign. There were some problems with production of the ATO and its delivery to naval forces. The flexibility of the ATO must be improved to account for changes, shifting priorities and real time target requirements as the campaign progresses.

    "The ATO... was effective in managing the volume of sorties generated to concentrate coalition air power against Iraq, especially during the preplanned structured stages of the campaign... After the first two days, late completion of the ATO impacted operations. As hostilities progressed and key targets had been struck (with delayed BDA) the ATO proved increasingly unresponsive to rapidly moving events... The "kill box" concept was an improvement, as it allowed decentralized target selection and coordination with airborne assets for real time target priorities..."

    -- Vice Admiral S.R. Arthur, USN, Commander U.S. Naval Forces Central Command, Quick Look — First Impressions Report, 22 March 1991

    - **STRIKE AIRCRAFT.** The A-6 aircraft was a workhorse for long range strike. It performed extremely well in an environment of established air superiority, but its survivability would be reduced against future high-tech air defenses. It was clear the A-6 requires upgrade and eventual replacement. The performance of the F-117 demonstrated the value of stealth and <u>validated the requirement for a follow-on, long range, all weather, stealthy strike aircraft (AX)</u> as a replacement for the A-6. In addition, the excellent performance of the F/A-18 <u>confirmed the validity of the multi-mission strike/fighter concept</u>.

    - **TOMAHAWK CRUISE MISSILE.** <u>Tomahawk was a tremendous success, and its first use in combat fully confirmed the results of previous extensive operational testing.</u> The value of distributed firepower was demonstrated by TOMAHAWK launches from surface combatants and submarines. DESERT STORM highlighted the importance of rigorous training on this complex weapon system, not only for shooters, but for all levels of command, including joint staffs involved in strike planning. Knowledge grew rapidly throughout the build-up period. Planned improvements in the Tomahawk missile and mission planning systems will further enhance the capabilities and potential contributions of this formidable weapon.

    "...The objective is not always to reduce a target to rubble, but to significantly disrupt operations. TLAM [the Tomahawk land attack missile] proved to be an excellent weapon to accomplish this, especially TLAM-D."

    -- Vice Admiral S.R. Arthur, USN, Commander U.S. Naval Forces Central Command, Quick Look — First Impressions Report, 22 March 1991

    "The use of TLAM has validated the effectiveness of these weapons for a number of contingencies..."

    -- Admiral J. T. Howe, USN, Commander-in-Chief U.S. Naval Forces Europe, Quick Look First Impressions Report, 20 March 1991

- **DEFENSE SUPPRESSION.** The outstanding performance of the EA-6B, other Navy defense suppression aircraft and weapon systems was <u>a noteworthy strength</u> in high demand for strike support of all services and coalition forces during the campaign. Their performance was instrumental in the early achievement of air superiority.

"Suppression of enemy air defenses (SEAD) was one of the Navy's noteworthy strengths. The EA-6B performed very well and was the clear choice. USN HARM (high-speed anti-radiation missile) and jam doctrine was successful..."

-- Vice Admiral S.R. Arthur, USN, Commander U.S. Naval Forces Central Command, Quick Look — First Impressions Report, 22 March 1991

- **SMART WEAPONS.** Although not all weapons were used in sufficient numbers to draw definitive conclusions (the standoff land attack missile (SLAM) for example), "smart" or precision weapons clearly demonstrated their capabilities against point targets and we will be procuring more of them. We also reaffirmed a requirement for highly accurate penetrating weapons for use against heavily bunkered or hardened structures.

"Laser Guided Bombs (LGBs) were consumed at a much greater rate than anticipated in pre-hostilities planning. LGBs quickly became the weapon of choice for a variety of missions against relatively low-value, non-hardened targets. MK-83 LGBs were particularly useful..."

-- Vice Admiral S.R. Arthur, USN, Commander U.S. Naval Forces Central Command, Quick Look — First Impressions Report, 22 March 1991

"DESERT STORM demonstrated the necessity for precision guided munitions. Laser guided bombs (and their advanced successors such as inertially aided munitions), SLAM, and TLAM have all proven their worth, both militarily and politically. We need to maintain the technological edge these weapons give, both through continued research and development, preplanned product improvement (P3I), and in maintenance of sufficient munitions in our arsenal to cope with likely future contingencies."

-- Admiral J. T. Howe, USN, Commander-in-Chief U.S. Naval Forces Europe, Quick Look First Impressions Report, 20 March 1991

"The 2000 pound penetrator is the weapon you need to kill the really hard, important, war-winning targets."

-- Rear Admiral R.D. Mixson, USN, Commander Battle Force YANKEE (Red Sea), during OPNAV debrief, 18 April 1991

- **TACTICAL RECONNAISSANCE.** The importance of real-time and near-real-time tactical reconnaissance in support of strike planning, naval gunfire support (NGFS), and battle damage assessment (BDA) was clearly demonstrated during DESERT STORM. Navy platforms such as the tactical air reconnaissance pod system (TARPS) equipped F-14 and unmanned aerial vehicles (UAVs) performed as designed, but could not meet the demand.

- **AIRBORNE TANKING.** Geography dictated extensive land-based tanking support for both USAF and naval air strikes into Iraq. Tanker coordination went extremely well. But tankers were stretched thin, and their apportionment necessarily limited the Navy's long-range strike contribution.

- **SURFACE WARFARE.** DESERT STORM demonstrated the enduring value of long range naval gunfire support. Unmanned aerial vehicles (UAVs) were effective in target selection, spotting the fall of shot and damage assessment. We are actively looking for alternative long range naval fire support systems to replace the battleships in future conflicts. The firepower of surface action groups was augmented with attack helicopters (U.S. Army AHIPs and Royal Navy Lynx). The combination of the attack helos working in conjunction with SH-60B (LAMPS Mk III) and surface combatants provided a highly effective enhancement to surface warfare offensive/reconnaissance capability. Naval forces used the offensive firepower of strike aircraft (A-6s and F/A-18s) and surface combatants to destroy the Iraqi navy. At last count, 105 Iraqi vessels had been destroyed.

"...Ship/aircraft [helicopter] surface action groups (SAGS) proved to be indispensable in achieving ASUW offensive/RECCE coverage.

"Maritime patrol aircraft (MPA) played a major role in the ASUW success. P-3/NIMROD availability and reliability were outstanding, as was the quality of the surveillance and targeting provided from the beginning of maritime interception force operations to the present, including DESERT STORM. P3C with and without ISAR... were fully integrated with battle force operations."

> -- Vice Admiral S.R. Arthur, USN, Commander U.S. Naval Forces Central Command, Quick Look — First Impressions Report, 22 March 1991

- **AMPHIBIOUS WARFARE.** The entire spectrum of amphibious capability and force structure was used during DESERT SHIELD/STORM. Amphibious operations focused enemy attention on the threat from seaward and tied down at least seven Iraqi divisions, even after the coalition ground campaign was well underway. The responsiveness and flexibility of amphibious forces was highlighted by successful raids, rehearsals and feints. The large deck amphibious assault ship (LHA) proved its versatility, operating significantly more AV-8s than planned (20 vice 6) while serving as flagship and conducting the full spectrum of other amphibious operations.

- **MINE WARFARE.** DESERT STORM again illustrated the challenge of mine countermeasures (MCM) and how quickly mines can become a concern. Because of the difficulty of locating and neutralizing mines, we cannot afford to give the minelayer free rein. Future rules of engagement and doctrine should provide for offensive operations to prevent the laying of mines in international waters. Our Cold War focus on the Soviet threat fostered reliance on our overseas allies for mine countermeasures in forward areas. The MCM assets of our allies — on whom we have relied for MCM support in NATO contingencies for years — proved their mettle in the Gulf, both in Operation EARNEST WILL (during the Iran-Iraq war) and DESERT STORM. Both operations highlighted the need for a robust, deployable U.S. Navy MCM capability. We are undertaking a comprehensive review of both our mine countermeasures strategy and the readiness of our forces to ensure our ability to conduct independent mine countermeasures operations when required.

INTELLIGENCE. Intelligence support for Desert Shield/Desert Storm reflected application of proven principles coupled with outstanding innovation. A joint intelligence doctrine and architecture are needed to support both joint and component commanders. More interoperable intelligence systems are also required.

COMMUNICATIONS. Almost every aspect of naval command and control communications capability was stressed to the limit during Desert Shield/Desert Storm. Problems were solved through aggressive management, work-arounds, innovation, close cooperation and coordination, equipment upgrades and new installations. The volume of communications traffic, the scope of the USN/joint/combined connectivity requirements, and the high precedence of a large percentage of the message traffic, presented a communications challenge of previously unimagined proportions. The STU-III, INMARSAT, SHF installations, portable communications vans, and high speed modems stood out among many systems which contributed to success. We are focusing increased attention on improving our ability to communicate with other services and nations, strengthening jam-resistant communications, and using high speed computer networks to increase capacity.

LOGISTICS. Naval forces arrived in theater with full, self-sustained logistic support capability. Aircraft readiness averaged nearly 90% with a full mission capability rating near 85%. The readiness of our ships was equally impressive. Those high readiness levels were virtually constant throughout the operation and reflect a high degree of unit self-sufficiency. There were ample supplies of fuel and ammunition, although inventories of laser guided bomb kits (a high demand item) were limited, and the aviation fuels provided by USAF airborne tankers posed safety problems aboard ship. Naval forces required minimal airlift and sealift for deployment and support. In fact, only 4.4% of strategic sealift was used for support of naval forces. Logistics messages were delayed by other operational traffic in the overworked communications system. The combat logistics force (CLF) performed superbly — meeting all requirements. Doing so, however, required nearly every CLF ship in the fleet. Versatile RRF sealift vessels augmented the CLF as ad hoc ammunition ships. DESERT SHIELD/STORM showed we must move carefully as we plan future CLF reductions.

"PHIBGRU TWO deployed in a week-and-a-half from a standing start (the first ship left after three days). At this writing we are approaching the seven month point, and the average ship has had less than three weeks in port (only ten days of which was maintenance time). ...The list of out of commission equipment is shorter than at INCHOP. Aside from parts and the occasional large motor rewind, the ships have become fully self-sufficient and could apparently stay out here indefinitely."

-- **Rear Admiral J.B. LaPlante, USN, CTF 156, "Quick Look" Report, 11 March 1991**

STRATEGIC SEALIFT. The contribution of strategic sealift was one of the major success stories of Desert Shield/Desert Storm. Major investments in sealift in the '80s paid great dividends. Throughout the deployment, Military Sealift Command (MSC) controlled ships delivered 3.4 million tons of cargo halfway around the world. Cargoes were loaded in over 40 ports in CONUS and Europe and were downloaded at two primary ports in Saudi Arabia. Additionally, 6.8 million tons of fuels were delivered. This cargo represents four times the cargo moved across the English Channel to Normandy in support of the D-Day invasion, and over six times the peak force build-up during a similar six month period of the Vietnam conflict. Sealift continues to do the heavy lifting: over 90% of all cargo was moved into theater by sea, and more than 95% will return the same way.

- Early, accurate identification of lift requirements was difficult and changed often. Close coordination between MSC and the Military Traffic Management Command (MTMC) kept the cargo flowing.

- We need more roll-on/roll-off (RO/RO) ships to meet unit equipment surge requirements. Problems encountered during the breakout of some RRF ships reflected shortfalls in maintenance funding in previous years.

- World-wide sea control afforded by our naval forces contributed to a responsive charter market, which reduced the need for activation of the Sealift Readiness Program (SRP) or ship requisitioning.

"The successful patchwork of MSC/RRF/charter and foreign charter vessels used to support DESERT SHIELD/STORM demonstrated the need for MSC to be given higher national priority and to integrate their operations more closely with the Navy."

-- Admiral J. T. Howe, USN, Commander-in-Chief U.S. Naval Forces Europe, Quick Look First Impressions Report, 20 March 1991

MARITIME PREPOSITIONING. The afloat prepositioning concept was validated in Desert Shield. No other alternative could achieve such early force closure dates. Two squadrons of Maritime Prepositioning Ships (MPS) deployed from Diego Garcia and Guam to deliver unit equipment and 30 days supplies for two Marine Expeditionary Brigades (MEBs). The first heavy ground combat capability in theater (105,000 tons) arrived by 15 August (C+8). The MEBs were "married-up" and combat ready by 25 August. Eleven additional prepositioned ships from Diego Garcia, the United Kingdom and the Mediterranean delivered 102,000 tons of Army, Air Force and Navy equipment and supplies that same week.

MEDICAL SUPPORT. Navy medical ships and fleet hospitals provided well over two-thirds of in-theater medical capability during the first four months of the operation. In accordance with plans, the hospital ships MERCY and COMFORT were activated and deployed on five days notice. Together with the Fleet Hospitals, they provided the most comprehensive medical care facilities in theater and the capability to deal with a major influx of combat casualties.

SUMMARY. The naval forces and capabilities put to the test in DESERT SHIELD/STORM were not achieved by decisions made in the last few years. The high quality people, aircraft, ships and weapons systems involved in this crisis were products of decisions made in the throughout the 1980s. So a final lesson might well be that the decisions we make today do have important ramifications for the future.

Affordability has always been a factor in such decisions, but current economic realities give it greater weight than at any time in the recent past. We will have a smaller force — that much is certain — and a smaller force, no matter how capable, will not be present in as many places, or respond as quickly, as the force which executed DESERT SHIELD/STORM.

In an evolving world which contains unknown numbers of Saddam Husseins, and a clear dependence on regional stability for economic, social and political progress, it is imperative that the United States retain the capability to protect its interests wherever and whenever they may be challenged. To defend America's interests around the world, future force structure must enable us to continue to employ the winning strategy of concentrating superior force anywhere rapidly enough to deter aggression or achieve quick success in combat.

> *"Force reductions now under review should preserve sufficient flexibility to cope with a wide range of realistic contingencies, because levels that cause potential adversaries to question U.S. capabilities could degrade deterrence and involve the United States in otherwise preventable wars."*
>
> -- John M. Collins, Congressional Research Service Senior Specialist in National Defense, in "Desert Shield and Desert Storm Implications for Future U.S. Force Requirements", 19 April 1991

> *"Deterrence, both nuclear and conventional, costs less than any level of conflict, and will remain the cornerstone of U.S. defense policy."*
>
> -- from "THE WAY AHEAD" by H. Lawrence Garrett III, Secretary of the Navy, Admiral F. B. Kelso II, USN, Chief of Naval Operations, and General A.M. Gray, USMC, Commandant of the Marine Corps, Proceedings, April 1991

While there were problems encountered, the outstanding first impression generated by the performance of our forces in DESERT SHIELD/STORM is being reinforced by the "post game analysis". Now we face the challenge of translating the lessons of DESERT SHIELD/STORM into decisions, programs and actions which will shape our forces, guide our training and ensure our continued readiness to forcefully defend America's interests whenever and wherever required.

THE UNITED STATES NAVY IN "DESERT SHIELD" / "DESERT STORM"

EPILOGUE

"From the moment OPERATION DESERT STORM commenced on January 16th, until the time the guns fell silent at midnight one week ago, this nation has watched its sons and daughters with pride; watched over them with prayer. As Commander in Chief, I can report to you: Our armed forces fought with honor and valor. As President, I can report to the nation: Aggression is defeated. The war is over."

-- **President George Bush before Congress, 6 March 1991**

"Already we sense that there is a growing disinclination in some places to give George Bush and his government and the military who were involved the credit due them for the prosecution and outcome of the war. Increasingly one reads of how mere "technology" defeated Saddam Hussein or how the administration must have stupidly and grossly (or knowingly and cynically) overestimated the size and strength of the Iraqi military forces or how the result was clearly foreordained since we didn't pick on someone our own size, etc.

But there was nothing foreordained about what happened, and many of those now implying that there was should go back and quietly reconsider their own warnings throughout this episode as to how dangerous and unpredictable, if not downright disastrous, a military encounter would be, some even recommending that Saddam Hussein be given those Kuwaiti islands and oil fields he so coveted. No, it was not foreordained, and it was not a mere function of automatic pilot and vastly superior firepower either. The people who did it did it."

-- **Editorial, <u>The Washington Post</u>, 1 March 1991**

APPENDICES

APPENDICES

APPENDIX A

CHRONOLOGY

DESERT SHIELD CHRONOLOGY

1990

2 Aug   **Iraq invades Kuwait**-Six U.S. Navy Middle East Force ships in Persian Gulf (continuous Middle East Force presence since 1949).
USS INDEPENDENCE Carrier Battle Group is in Indian Ocean and USS DWIGHT D. EISENHOWER Carrier Battle Group is in the Mediterranean.

4 Aug   USS INDEPENDENCE Carrier Battle Group en route North Arabian Sea.

5 Aug   **Operation SHARP EDGE, noncombatant evacuation operation, authorized by State Department to remove U.S. citizens caught in civil war in Liberia.**
USS SAIPAN (LHA-2), USS PONCE (LPD-15), USS SUMTER (LST-1188), USS PETERSON (DD-969), off Liberia inserts USMC reinforced rifle company into U.S. Embassy compound in Monrovia for increased security.

6 Aug   SECDEF travels to Saudi Arabia to discuss request for assistance and deployment of U.S. forces in country. SECDEF then travels to Egypt and gets permission to send U.S. warships through Suez Canal.

7 Aug   USS INDEPENDENCE Carrier Battle Group arrives in the Gulf of Oman.
USS DWIGHT D. EISENHOWER Carrier Battle Group transits Suez Canal en-route Red Sea.
USS SARATOGA Carrier Battle Group and battleship USS WISCONSIN depart East coast ports on scheduled deployment.

8 Aug   **The President of the United States orders U.S. Armed Forces to Saudi Arabia.**
The first elements of the 82nd Airborne Division arrive in Saudi Arabia.

10 Aug F-16's from Shaw AFB and C-130's from Pope AFB begin arriving in Saudi Arabia.
Hospital ships USNS MERCY and USNS COMFORT activated and prepare to deploy.

12 Aug F-15E's deploy to area.
Army's 11th Air Defense Artillery Brigade arrives in Middle East.
Department of Defense deploys the DoD National media pool and regional pools of reporters currently in the Persian Gulf to cover deployment of U.S. forces.

13 Aug USS WISCONSIN transits Strait of Gibraltar en route Persian Gulf.
4th Marine Expeditionary Brigade (MEB), embarked on 13 amphibious ships, departs East Coast ports.
USS BLUE RIDGE, command ship for Commander, SEVENTH Fleet, en route Persian Gulf.

14 Aug Advanced elements of the 1st Marine Expeditionary Force (MEF) and the 7th Marine Expeditionary Brigade (MEB) arrive Saudi Arabia.
Elements of 1st MEF, which includes units from the 1st Marine Division, the 3rd Marine Aircraft Wing (MAW) and the 7th Marine Expeditionary Brigade, depart for region.
Hospital Ship USNS COMFORT deploys for Middle East.

15 Aug <u>USS SARATOGA Carrier Battle Group transits Strait of Gibraltar enroute to Mediterranean Sea.</u>
<u>USS JOHN F. KENNEDY Carrier Battle Group departs East coast ports enroute to Mediterranean Sea.</u>
1st MEB departs Hawaii.
Ships from Maritime Prepositioned Squadron 2 (Diego Garcia) begin unloading in Saudi Arabia.
Hospital Ship USNS MERCY deploys for Middle East.

16 Aug **Multi-national maritime intercept operation began intercepting ships going to or from Iraq and Kuwait, consistent with U.N. Security Council Resolution 661.**
Thirteen amphibious ships announced to be deploying with the 4th MEB embarked.

17 Aug <u>USS WISCONSIN transits Suez Canal en route Persian Gulf.</u>
MSC Fast Sealift Cargo Ships (T-AKRs) ALTAIR and CAPELLA depart Savannah, GA carrying the 24th (Mechanized) Infantry Division.
Stage one of the Civil Air Reserve Fleet plan is activated to meet mounting airlift requirements.

18 Aug In separate incidents, USS REID and USS BRADLEY fire warning shots across the bows of two Iraqi oil tankers leaving the Persian Gulf. Also, USS ENGLAND and USS SCOTT divert freighters in the Arabian Gulf and N. Red Sea, **the first diversions by Navy ships.**

19 Aug **Secretary of Defense Cheney announced that VADM Henry H. Mauz, Jr., USN, Commander U.S. SEVENTH Fleet assumed new duties as Commander, U.S. Naval Forces Central Command (COMUSNAVCENT).** He will control all U.S. naval forces assigned to the U.S. Central Command, to include the maritime intercept force.

21 Aug Command of Operation SHARP EDGE shifted from COMSIXTHFLT to CO USS WHIDBEY ISLAND (LSD-41), joined by USS BARNSTABLE COUNTY (LST-1197), off Liberia.

22 Aug **The President of the United States authorized the "call up" of members of the Selected Reserve to active duty in support of Operation DESERT SHIELD, or by filling critical military support vacancies in the United States or elsewhere.**
<u>USS SARATOGA Carrier Battle Group transits Suez Canal en route Red Sea.</u>

24 Aug	<u>USS WISCONSIN transits Strait of Hormuz into Persian Gulf.</u>
25 Aug	F-111 aircraft announced to be deploying to Saudi Arabia.
26 Aug	**United Nations Security Council votes, without dissension, to allow use of military force to uphold trade embargo on Iraq.** Commander-in-Chief, United States Central Command, General H. Norman Schwarzkopf, establishes his command headquarters in Saudi Arabia. Department of Defense national media pool is officially disbanded due to decision by the government of Saudi Arabia to allow reporters from the U.S. and other countries to cover the military operation in the gulf region.
27 Aug	**The first two Fast Sealift Cargo Ships, ALTAR and CAPELLA, arrive in Saudi Arabia carrying components of the 24th (Mechanized) Infantry Division.**
28 Aug	Department of Defense announces that there have been about 170 intercepts since maritime intercept operations began. USS SAMPSON (DDG 10) diverts freighter in the N. Arabian Sea.
29 Aug	Three minesweepers and Mine Counter Measures Ship USS AVENGER, loaded on board Super Servant III, depart Norfolk en route the Persian Gulf area. Two of the ships are Naval Reserve ships - USS ADROIT and USS IMPERVIOUS. Operation SHARP EDGE, the noncombat evacuation operation being conducted off the coast of Liberia by the USS WHIDBEY ISLAND and the USS BARNSTABLE COUNTY, continues as 76 more people, including 6 Americans, are evacuated from Liberia.
30 Aug	Department of Defense announces that there have been about 250 intercepts and about 4 boardings since maritime intercept operations began. Hospital Ship USNS COMFORT transits Suez Canal. <u>USS JOHN F. KENNEDY Carrier Battle Group transits Strait of Gibraltar en-route Mediterranean Sea.</u> Operation SHARP EDGE continues as 15 more people are evacuated from Liberia.
31 Aug	USS BIDDLE (CG -34) intercepted and boarded the Iraqi merchant vessel Al Karamah. The tanker was the first Iraqi ship to be boarded since the intercept operations began on 16 August. The tanker was empty and allowed to continue to Aqaba, Jordan. MARG 3-90, consisting of USS INCHON, USS NASHVILLE, USS FAIRFAX COUNTY and USS NEWPORT, with the 26th MEU embarked, arrive Rota en route Mediterranean Sea. Navy's Fleet Hospital Five announced to be deploying to the Middle East.

1 Sept	USS BLUE RIDGE, command ship for Commander, SEVENTH Fleet, arrives in the Persian Gulf.
3 Sept	Operation SHARP EDGE continues as 63 more people are evacuated. This brings the total number of people evacuated from Liberia to 1,858, including 147 Americans. USS DWIGHT D. EISENHOWER and USS TICONDEROGA transit Strait of Gibraltar en route East coast homeports.
4 Sept	Department of Defense announces that there have been about 550 intercepts and about 20 boardings since maritime intercept operations began. USS GOLDSBOROUGH (DDG 20) intercepted and an embarked U.S. Coast Guard Detachment boarded the Iraqi bound and Iraqi registered motor vessel ZANOOBIA. The motor vessel, loaded with tea, had refused orders to either return to its port of origin or proceed to a non prohibited port. Amphibious ships USS SHREVEPORT, USS TRENTON, USS GUNSTON HALL, USS PORTLAND, and USS SPARTANBURG COUNTY, with components of the 4th MEB embarked, transit Suez Canal. The Fast Sealift Cargo Ship ALGOL, with elements of the 24th (Mechanized) Infantry Division embarked, arrives in Saudi Arabia.
5 Sept	The Navy lifts the firing suspension for USS WISCONSIN's 16 inch guns. **USS ACADIA (AD-42) departs San Diego with crew of 1,260, including 360 women. This is the first war-time test of the combined male-female fighting force.**
6 Sept	Department of Defense announces that there have been about 580 intercepts and about 25 boardings since maritime intercept operations began. Amphibious ships USS NASSAU, USS RALEIGH, USS PENSACOLA and USS SAGINAW, with components of the 4th MEB embarked, transit the Suez Canal. The Fast Sealift Cargo Ship DENEBOLA, with elements of the 24th (Mechanized) Infantry Division embarked, arrives in Saudi Arabia. Effective today, Liberia and Kuwait are designated as countries at which Imminent Danger Pay is authorized. Operation SHARP EDGE continues as 76 more people are evacuated. This brings the total number of people evacuated from Liberia to 1,936, including 151 Americans.
7 Sept	ARG ALFA units USS OKINAWA, USS OGDEN, USS FORT MCHENRY, USS DURHAM and USS CUYUGA, with the 13th MEU embarked arrive in the Gulf of Oman. **Hospital Ship USNS COMFORT arrives in Gulf of Oman.**
8 Sept	Amphibious ships USS IWO JIMA, USS GUAM, USS LA MOURE COUNTY and USS MANITOWOC, with elements of the 4th MEB embarked, transit Suez Canal. Hospital Ship USNS COMFORT arrives in the Persian Gulf.

9 Sept	Operation SHARP EDGE continues as 94 more people are evacuated, including 10 Americans. This brings the total number of people evacuated from Liberia to 2030, including 161 Americans.
11 Sept	ARG BRAVO units USS DUBUQUE, USS SCHENECTADY and USS SAN BERNADINO, with the 1/6 Battalion embarked, arrive in the Gulf of Oman. Amphibious ships USS SHREVEPORT, USS TRENTON, USS GUNSTON HALL, USS PORTLAND, and USS SPARTANBURG COUNTY, with components of the 4th MEB embarked, arrive in the Gulf of Oman.
12 Sept	Operation SHARP EDGE continues as 12 more people are evacuated, including 6 Americans. This brings the total number of people evacuated from Liberia to 2042, including 167 Americans. USS BIDDLE (CG-34) diverts freighter in N. Red Sea.
13 Sept	ARG BRAVO units USS DUBUQUE, USS SCHENECTADY and USS SAN BERNADINO, with the 1/6 Battalion embarked, arrive in Saudi Arabia.
14 Sept	<u>USS JOHN F. KENNEDY Carrier Battle Group transits Suez Canal into Red Sea.</u> Hospital ship USNS MERCY arrives in the Gulf of Oman. Amphibious ships USS NASSAU, USS PENSACOLA and USS SAGINAW, with components of the 4th MEB embarked, arrive in the Gulf of Oman.
16 Sept	**USS O'BRIEN (DD-975) intercepted the Bahamian-flagged merchant tanker DAIMON, logging the 1,000th intercept since the multinational operations began** (averaging 40 intercepts and 4 boardings per day). Amphibious ships USS IWO JIMA, USS GUAM, USS RALEIGH and USS LA MOURE COUNTY, with the remainder of the 4th MEB embarked, arrive in the Gulf of Oman.
20 Sept	SECDEF announces that effective 17 Sept 1990, personnel on duty in the Middle East will receive Imminent Danger Pay (IDP). USS MONTGOMERY (FF-1082) diverts freighter in N. Red Sea.
21 Sept	Off the coast of Liberia, Operation SHARP EDGE units embark 25 additional evacuees, including one American. This brings the total number of evacuees to 2,116, including 162 Americans.
23 Sept	**USNS MERCY (T-AH-19) and USNS COMFORT (T-AH-20) steam together for the first time in the Arabian Gulf, making Naval medical history.**
27 Sept	With Operation SHARP EDGE, U.S. Marine helicopters carried more than a ton of emergency medical supplies from the U.S. Embassy in Freetown, Sierra Leone, to the U.S. Embassy in Monrovia. The USS BARNSTABLE COUNTY and the USS WHIDBEY ISLAND, the two amphibious ships remain off-shore.

27 Sept (continuing)	To-date, the number of evacuations is 2100, and that included more than 200 U.S. citizens. **USS ELMER MONTGOMERY (FF-1082) fires the first warning shots by U. S. forces during a merchant interception**, and then boarded the Iraqi tanker TADMUR, as it was proceeding south out of the Gulf of Aqaba.
29 Sept	USS MONTGOMERY diverts a freighter in N. Red Sea.
1 Oct	<u>**USS INDEPENDENCE (CV-62) transited the Strait of Hormuz en route the Persian Gulf (first time a carrier in the Gulf since 1974)**</u>. The carrier will remain in the Gulf for a short period and conduct normal operations. SUPER SERVANT III arrived Bahrain with her cargo of Minesweepers, and is scheduled to offload 4-5 Oct. **ARG Alfa units and CTG 150.6 conduct the first major amphibious rehearsal operation, "CAMEL SAND" off Ras Madrakah, Oman.**
2 Oct	<u>USS MIDWAY (CV-41) Carrier Battle Group deploys from Yokosuka, Japan.</u>
4 Oct	**USS INDEPENDENCE (CV-62) leaves the gulf after successfully completing its mission (to demonstrate that it is possible to put a carrier in the Gulf and carry out operations).**
15 Oct	**USS ELMER MONTGOMERY (FF-1082) completed the 2500th intercept action by the multi-national intercept force since the operation began on 12 Aug 90.** The USS ELMER MONTGOMERY hailed the Indian-registered cargo vessel "JAY GAYATRI" in the Northern Red Sea.
21 Oct	USS O'BRIEN (DD-975) fired warning shots across the bow of the Iraqi merchant vessel AL BAHAR AL ARABI in the Persian Gulf after it failed to alter its course to a non-prohibited port.
22 Oct	The Iraqi merchant vessel AL BAHAR AL ARABI was cleared to proceed by a multi-national boarding team including Navy and Coast Guard personnel from the USS REASONER (FF-1063) in the North Arabian Sea. The merchant had apparently disposed of its prohibited cargo.
30 Oct	A major steam leak in the fire room of the USS IWO JIMA (LPH-2) resulted in the deaths of 10 crewmembers. Off Ras al Madrakah Oman, ARG Alfa units, along with the remaining CTG 150.6 units - 4th MEB (Amphibious) embarked - began amphibious rehearsal exercise SEA SOLDIER II. Operation SHARP EDGE continues, with a total of 2393 evacuations, including 213 U.S. citizens.
1 Nov	USS MIDWAY Carrier Battle Group relieves USS INDEPENDENCE in Gulf.
3 Nov	In Operation SHARP EDGE, USS NEWPORT (LST-1179) relieves BARNSTABLE COUNTY off Liberia.

8 Nov	<u>Secretary of Defense Dick Cheney announced that in addition to the 230,000 forces in the Persian Gulf region, more heavy divisions, Marines and ships will be headed for the Persian Gulf. Navy elements to be sent include:</u> three aircraft carriers with appropriate escorts; one battleship, USS Missouri (BB-63); Amphibious Group Three, San Diego California; and Maritime Prepositioning Ship Squadron 1, Norfolk, Virginia.
13 Nov	<u>USS MISSOURI (BB-63)</u> deploys for Persian Gulf region from Long Beach.
14 Nov	Secretary of Defense Dick Cheney authorized activation of 72,500 more military reservists, taking the first step toward fulfilling President Bush's decision to deploy up to 200,000 additional troops in the Middle East. The Navy's authorization ceiling was raised from 6300 to 10,000.
15-21 Nov	Joint Combined exercise <u>IMMINENT THUNDER</u> conducted inside Saudi Arabia, including amphibious exercises in the eastern province, air to air and close air support exercises and ground force training. The exercise included 16 ships, 1000 marines and 1100 aircraft. Authorization approved to extend Reserve call-up from 90 to 180 days. SECNAV announces call-up of 30 Naval Reserve units from 13 states and the District of Columbia.
22 Nov	USS BIDDLE (CG-34) diverts a freighter in the N. Red Sea.
26 Nov	Operation SHARP EDGE continues, with a total of 2430 evacuations, including 225 U.S. citizens. Department of Defense announces 3800 merchant ships have been challenged, 450 ships boarded, 16 ships diverted since maritime intercept operations began. USS PHILIPPINE SEA (CG-58), USS THOMAS C. HART (FF-1092), and two multinational craft intercept KHAWLA BINT AL ZAWRA in northern Red Sea. The Iraqi-flagged cargo ship refused repeated requests to stop, permitted boarding and search after the PHILIPPINE SEA fired warning shots across the bow.
27 Nov	DOD announces post-Christmas deployment of <u>USS THEODORE ROOSEVELT (CVN-71)</u> and <u>USS AMERICA (CV-66)</u> Carrier Battle Groups with appropriate escorts and embarked airwings. KHAWLA BINT AL ZAWRA was cleared to proceed on after boarding team of Navy personnel determined vessel was not carrying prohibited cargo. DOD updates numbers of intercepts - 4162; boardings - 500; diversions - 19; 85,635 Reserves recalled: 5421 Navy, 12,865 USMC.
28 Nov	**With OPERATION SHARP EDGE, <u>ceasefire is accepted by opposing factions in Liberia.</u>**
29 Nov	<u>United Nations Security Council approves resolution authorizing use of military force unless Iraq vacates Kuwait by 15 January 1991.</u> DOD announces 1 December deployment of 13-ship Amphibious Group Three,

29 Nov (continued)	homeported in San Diego and Long Beach, with 5th Marine Expeditionary Brigade (MEB) embarked. DOD also announces new U.S. troop strength at over 240,000 in region; updates numbers of intercepts - 4217; boardings - 517; diversions - 19; 86,128 Reserves recalled: 5421 Navy, 12,865 USMC.
30 Nov	In Operation SHARP EDGE, limited evacuation of noncombatants from Monrovia terminated. 2609 evacuated, including 330 U.S. citizens.
1 Dec	**VADM Stanley R. Arthur relieves VADM Henry H. Mauz, Jr., as Commander, Navy Central Command/Commander, 7th Fleet.** 18-ship Amphibious Group Three, with V Marine Expeditionary Brigade (MEB) embarked, departs 3 West coast ports. SECDEF increases activation authority of 63,000 more military reservists. The Navy's authorization ceiling was raised from 10,000 to 30,000.
2 Dec	Iraqi Armed Forces conducted activity that included the firing of surface-to-surface missiles within Iraq; missiles landed in Iraq. The flight path was away from U.S. and coalition forces. In Operation SHARP EDGE, USS NASHVILLE (LPD-13) relieves USS WHIDBEY ISLAND and USS NEWPORT off Monrovia, Liberia.
4 Dec	Navy implements DOD-authorized limited stop loss action to retain personnel previously scheduled for retirement, release from active duty and completion of reserve recall orders considered essential to national security and serving in positions and skills critical to Operation Desert Shield. **The Navy's first use of this authority,** effective 1 January 1991, affects Navy personnel (medical, religious support, other specialities) assigned to Marine Corps units and complements 8 November Marine Corps stop-loss implementation. SECNAV announces activation of additional Naval Reserve units.
6 Dec	DOD announces new U.S. troop strength at over 250,000 in region; updates numbers of intercepts - 4605; boardings - 569; diversions - 22; 117,313 Reserves/National Guard recalled: 6691 Navy, 15,893 USMC. Navy ship strength: 19 (Arabian Gulf), 21 (North Arabian Sea/Gulf of Oman), 9 (Red Sea), 15 (Mediterranean). In Operation SHARP EDGE, USS WHIDBEY ISLAND and USS NEWPORT deploy to Mediterranean. Situation quiet.
7 Dec	DOD announces 8 December deployment of USS RANGER (CV-61) Carrier Battle Group with appropriate escorts and embarked airwings. USS HORNE (CG-30), San Diego, and USS JARRETT (FFG-33), Long Beach, deploy to Persian Gulf.
8-18 Dec	Amphibious exercise conducted by elements of IV Marine Expeditionary Brigade (MEB) and Amphibious Task Group Two off the coast of Oman.

10 Dec	II Marine Expeditionary Force (MEF), 24,000 Marines, deploys from Camp Lejeune, NC.
11 Dec	DOD announces new U.S. troop strength at over 260,000 in region; updates numbers of intercepts - 4833; boardings - 583; diversions - 22; 121,940 Reserves/National Guard recalled: 6877 Navy, 16,495 USMC. Coalition forces strength in excess of 220,000.
13 Dec	USS SAMPSON (DDG-10) diverts a freighter in N. Red Sea. SECNAV activates 2,388 Naval Reserve personnel to staff Navy Fleet Hospitals 20 and 22.
14 Dec	<u>Navy implements DOD-authorized limited stop loss action</u> to retain personnel with skills which are critical and in short supply due to extended medical requirements of Operation Desert Shield. The Navy's second use of this authority affects all Navy doctors, nurses, hospital corpsmen and medical service corps personnel whose dates of retirement or separation fall on or after 2 January 1991. SECNAV activates 769 additional Naval Reservists from 44 units.
15 Dec	USS MISSISSIPPI (CGN-40) diverts a freighter in the N. Red Sea.
16 Dec	USS MISSISSIPPI diverts a freighter in the N. Red Sea.
18 Dec	DOD announces new U.S. troop strength at over 270,000 in region; updates numbers of intercepts - 5393; boardings - 668; diversions - 26; 124,943 Reserves/National Guard recalled: 7249 Navy, 17,066 USMC. USS MONTGOMERY diverts a freighter in the N. Red Sea. <u>Sealift update</u>: 253 ships in support, 200 under MSC operational control; 188 offloads completed (approximately 10.2 billion pounds of unit equipment and petroleum products).
20 Dec	DOD announces new U.S. troop strength at about 280,000 in region; updates numbers of intercepts - 5509; boardings - 679; diversions - 27; 127,293 Reserves/National Guard recalled: 7314 Navy, 17,375 USMC. <u>USS INDEPENDENCE (CV-62)</u> returns to San Diego homeport from Persian Gulf deployment. Members of Reserve Squadrons HCS-4 and HCS-5, the Navy's only combat Search and Rescue squadrons, are deployed in the Middle East. SECNAV activates 289 additional Naval Reservists from 28 units.
21 Dec	An Israeli-chartered liberty ferry shuttling crewmembers of the USS SARATOGA (CV-60) capsized and sank off Haifa, Israel, resulting in 20 deaths. Additional crewmember is missing/presumed drowned.
23 Dec	A truck on a liberty excursion in Abu Dhabi, United Arab Emirates, carrying crewmembers of the USS MIDWAY (CV-41) overturned, killing 2 sailors, injuring 5 others.

23 Dec (continuing) USS MISSISSIPPI diverts a freighter in the N. Red Sea.

26 Dec USS FIFE (DD-991), USS OLDENDORF (DD-972), USS TRENTON (LPD-14), USS SHREVEPORT (LPD-12), USS CURTS (FFG-38), and two multinational craft intercepted IBN KHALDOON ("Peace Ship") in the Arabian Sea after the Iraqi-flagged freighter refused repeated requests to stop. Crewmembers attempted to restrain boarding team of Navy personnel and grab their weapons, resulting in warning shots being fired in the air and a smoke grenade and noise grenade set off for crowd control. IBN KHALDOON was diverted to port after search revealed prohibited cargo.
SECNAV activates 480 additional Naval Reservists from 3 units.

28 Dec <u>USS THEODORE ROOSEVELT (CVN-71) and USS AMERICA (CV-66)</u> Carrier Battle Groups with appropriate escorts and embarked airwings deploy from Norfolk. Total of 17 ships depart from 5 East coast ports.
Iraqi Armed Forces fires 5th surface-to-surface missile within Iraq; missile landed in Iraq. The flight path was away from U.S. and coalition forces.
DOD announces chemical/biological vaccination program for U.S. forces.
SECNAV activates 172 additional Naval Reservists from 40 units.

31 Dec USS MISSISSIPPI diverts a freighter in the N. Red Sea.

1991

1 Jan <u>USS MISSOURI (BB-63)</u> arrives in the Gulf of Oman.
USNS MERCY (T-AH 19) records 1,000th helicopter landing.

2 Jan CINCCENTCOM announces new U.S. troop strength at over 325,000 in region (35,000 USN, 55,000 USMC); updates numbers of intercepts - 6221; boardings - 749; diversions - 32.
Navy ship strength: 25 (Arabian Gulf), 20 (North Arabian Sea/Gulf of Oman), 10 (Red Sea).
6 anti-ship mines discovered floating in Gulf during December, all destroyed. Investigation of origin/date of deployment continues.
USNS ANDREW J. HIGGINS (T-AO 190) runs aground on an unchartered reef off Oman, hull rupture leaks undetermined amount of mixed fuels. No injuries.

4 Jan <u>USS GUAM (LPH-9) and USS TRENTON (LPD-14) conduct Operation EASTERN EXIT.</u> Embarked elements of 4th Marine Expeditionary Brigade evacuated 65 U.S. citizens and other foreign nationals caught in civil war in Somalia. Evacuees helicoptered from U.S. Embassy in Mogadishu to ships offshore. No injuries or incidents.
USS MISSOURI responded to distress call from Saudi-flagged tanker TABUK (2 small fires, inoperative fire pump) near Dubai. MISSOURI fire party and repair officer transferred onboard, and extinguished fire.

4 Jan (continued)	<u>Spanish frigate intercepts and diverts Soviet-flagged cargo ship DIMITRIY FERMANOV</u> in Northern Red Sea after multinational boarding team, including Navy personnel from USS MISSISSIPPI (CGN-40), discovered improperly-manifested military equipment on board. DIMITRIY FERMANOV, enroute from Odessa, USSR to Aqaba, Jordan, anchors while manifest awaits reconciliation and is found to be in accordance with U.N. Security Council resolutions. SECNAV activates 438 additional Naval Reservists from 55 units.
5 Jan	<u>With Operation EASTERN EXIT</u>, the U.S. Ambassador, the Soviet ambassador, and 193 additional foreign nationals evacuated in four helicopter roundtrips from U.S. Embassy in Mogadishu, Somalia to USS GUAM and USS TRENTON. <u>The rescue operation was initiated from a range of 460 miles, and involved the first in-flight night refueling of helicopters by USMC KC-130s.</u> 60 U.S. Marines provided rear security until 48-hour evacuation completed. Evacuees taken to undisclosed location for processing and return to respective countries.
6 Jan	<u>USS SARATOGA (CV-60) transits Suez Canal en route Red Sea</u> for the fifth time, a record canal transit by any Navy ship during a single deployment. USS MISSISSIPPI diverts a freighter in the N. Red Sea.
7 Jan	In Operation SHARP EDGE, USMC Fleet Antiterrorist Security Team (FAST) relieves Marine Amphibious Readiness Group at U.S. Embassy in Monrovia, Liberia providing security.
8 Jan	DOD announces new U.S. troop strength at over 360,000 in region (540,000+ Iraqi troops); updates numbers of intercepts - 6566; boardings - 785; diversions - 34; 147,300 Reserves/National Guard recalled: 9939 Navy, 18,155 USMC. <u>Navy ship strength in region - 63:</u> 18 (Arabian Gulf), 21 (North Arabian Sea/ Gulf of Oman), 12 (Red Sea), 12 (Mediterranean). <u>Sealift update:</u> 245 ships in support, 218 under MSC operational control; 253 offloads completed (12 billion pounds of equipment/fuel). Soviet-flagged DIMITRY FERMANOV remains in the Red Sea. Cargo ship will be allowed to proceed to its destination of Aqaba when the intercept force has determined the cargo is properly manifested.
9 Jan	Anti-ship contact mine discovered in Arabian Gulf, the 9th in last week. USS MISSOURI (BB-63) explosive ordnance disposal team retrieved/destroyed. <u>USS NASHVILLE (LPD-13) departs Liberian coast, ending Operation SHARP EDGE.</u> USS ELMER MONTGOMERY boards 100th ship, designated MIF Centurion as first ship in theater to reach this milestone. SECNAV activates 1868 additional Naval Reservists from 333 units.
10 Jan	USS MISSISSIPPI diverts a freighter in the N. Red Sea.

10 Jan (continued)   8-ship Amphibious Task Force enters Arabian Gulf to conduct routine operations. Led by USS NASSAU (LHA-2), task force carries complement of nearly 10,000 sailors and Marines.

12 Jan   <u>U.S. Congress approves joint resolutions authorizing the use of force against Iraq.</u>
<u>USS RANGER (CV-61) Carrier Battle Group arrives on station in the North Arabian Sea.</u>
<u>Amphibious Group Three (with 5th MEB embarked) arrives on station in the Arabian Sea.</u> The 18-ships, USS OKINAWA (LPH-3), USS TARAWA (LHA-1), USS TRIPOLI (LPH-10), USS NEW ORLEANS (LPH-11), USS OGDEN (LPD-5), USS VANCOUVER (LPD-2), USS DENVER (LPD-9), USS JUNEAU (LPH-10), USS FORT MCHENRY (LSD-43), USS GERMANTOWN (LSD-42), USS ANCHORAGE (LSD-36), USS MOUNT VERNON (LSD-39), USS DURHAM (LKA 114), USS MOBILE (LKA 115), USS CAYUGA (LST-1184), USS BARBOUR COUNTY (LST-1195), USS PEORIA (LST-1183), and USS FREDERICK (LST-1184) will join amphibious group presently deployed creating the largest amphibious task force since the Korean War.
<u>USS MIDWAY Carrier Battle Group reenters the Arabian Gulf.</u>
USS MISSOURI explosive ordnance disposal team retrieves/detonates another anti-ship contact mine in the Arabian Gulf.
USS OLDENDORF (DD-972) and USS TRENTON (LPD-14) team boarded/inspected IBN KHALDOON, and after determining Iraqi-flagged cargo ship was no longer carrying prohibited cargo, vessel was cleared to proceed to stated destination Basrah, Iraq. No incidents.

14 Jan   <u>USS THEODORE ROOSEVELT (CVN-71) Carrier Battle Group transits Suez Canal, arrives on station in the Red Sea.</u>
<u>Navy ship strength in Central Command Area of Responsibility - 91:</u> 35 (Arabian Gulf), 35 (North Arabian Sea/Gulf of Oman), 21 (Red Sea).
SECNAV activates 423 additional Naval Reservists from 36 units.
In second call-up, SECNAV activates 357 additional Naval Reservists from 19 units.

15 Jan   <u>USS AMERICA (CV-66) Carrier Battle Group transits Suez Canal, arrives on station in the Red Sea.</u>
<u>USS RANGER (CV-61) Carrier Battle Group transits to station in Arabian Gulf.</u>
DOD announces new U.S. troop strength at about 415,000 in region (545,000 Iraqi troops); updates numbers of intercepts - 6913; boardings - 823; diversions - 36; 157,716 Reserves/National Guard recalled: 10,952 Navy, 21,628 USMC.
<u>Navy ship strength in region - 108:</u> 34 (Arabian Gulf), 35 (North Arabian Sea/Gulf of Oman), 26 (Red Sea), 13 (Mediterranean).
17 anti-ship mines discovered in Arabian Gulf since 21 December 1990. 16 are believed to be of Iraqi origin.

15 Jan (continued) Soviet-flagged DIMITRY FERMANOV is diverted, not allowed to proceed to its destination of Aqaba. Vessel departs Northern Red Sea for transit back through the Suez Canal to a non-prohibited port as determined by her master.

16 Jan At weekly briefing, CINCCENTCOM announces new U.S. troop strength at about 425,000 (60,000 USN, 75,000 USMC); 19 countries have deployed ground forces; 14 nations are participating in naval efforts (U.S., 100 ships [80 combatants]/50 multinational ships); updates numbers of intercepts - 6960; boardings - 832; diversions - 36.

Completion of two naval exercises announced; Operation CANDID HAMMER: communication techniques/mine warfare drills in central Arabian Gulf (Participants: USN, Royal Saudi, French, British, Canadian, and Australian naval forces); Operation CAMELOT: personnel and equipment trained in various areas, to include anti-air warfare/vertical replenishment in central Red Sea (Participants: USN, Royal Saudi naval forces).

At 1900 (EST), White House announced commencement of OPERATION DESERT STORM, offensive action against Iraq under provisions of U.N. Security Council/U.S. Congressional resolutions.

DESERT STORM CHRONOLOGY

1991

16 Jan At 1900 (EST), White House announced that "the liberation of Kuwait has begun!" The offensive action against Iraq, codenamed OPERATION DESERT STORM, is being carried out under provisions of twelve U.N. Security Council resolutions and resolutions of both houses of the U.S. Congress.
Following President Bush's address to the nation, SECDEF Dick Cheney and CJCS General Colin Powell announce at Pentagon briefing hundreds of U.S./coalition airstrikes on missile and anti-aircraft targets in Iraq and Kuwait to "destroy Saddam Hussein's offensive military capabilities"; Cheney reports "initial attack appears to have gone very, very well"; no casualty reports provided.

17 Jan DOD announces that over 100 TOMAHAWK cruise missiles were launched at pre-programmed targets by 9 U.S. Navy ships in the Arabian Gulf and Red Sea. USS SAN JACINTO (CG 56) fired the first TOMAHAWK missile from the Red Sea between 0100-0200 Gulf Time; moments later, USS BUNKER HILL (CG-52) fired the first TOMAHAWK missile from the Arabian Gulf. Then, over 1,000 aircraft sorties (E2-Cs/AWACs-controlled) were flown by A-6s, A-7s, AV-8s, A-10s, B-52s, EA-6Bs, EF-111s, F-4s, F-14s, F-15s, F-16s, F/A-18s, F-111s, F-117As, AH-64s, Saudi/British Tornados, French Jaguars, Kuwaiti A-4s.
The Navy launched 228 combat sorties on the first day of OPERATION DESERT STORM from six aircraft carriers in the Red Sea and Arabian Gulf.
CJCS GENERAL Colin Powell reports TOMAHAWK cruise missiles "were extremely effective" (against precision targets where Iraqi air defenses threatened manned aircraft); of all sorties, 80% were effective, 20% ineffective due to mechanical/weather problems; Iraqi SCUD missile fixed-sites destroyed, targeting SCUD launchers; Iraqi planes destroyed, but "Iraqi Air Force is still intact"; U.S. engaged in air-to-air battles with Iraqi aircraft; Iraq fired multiple SAMs and anti-aircraft artillery, little or no effect; Iraqi elite Republican Guard units attacked in Iraq and Kuwait; did not target President Hussein, focused on disrupting/destroying command/control network.
An F/A-18 is shot down, the first Navy aircraft loss in combat. The F/A-18 crewman, LCDR Michael Speicher of USS SARATOGA's Strike Fighter Squadron 81, is listed as missing.

17 Jan (continuing) 3 USMC/1 USN injured in bunkers in Saudi Arabia by Iraqi artillery fire near Kuwaiti border.

Eight Iraqi SCUD missiles impact in Tel Aviv and Haifa, Israel. Seven civilian injuries. U.S. Patriot missile intercepts one SCUD over Dhahran, S.A.

SECNAV activates 421 additional Naval Reservists from 36 units.

18 Jan DOD announces 196 TOMAHAWK cruise missiles have been launched. Additionally, 2,107 attack sorties have been flown by USN, USMC, USAF, USA and coalition forces; assessed as 80% effective.

In air-to-air engagements, eight Iraqi MIG-29s and Mirage F-1s are destroyed; two by 2 USN F/A-18s of USS SARATOGA-based Strike Fighter Squadron-81 (directed by E-2Cs from Carrier Air Wing-17). **First Navy combat "kills".** F/A-18s then transitioned, and bombed targets.

Navy has lost two additional aircraft, both A-6s. The crewmen, LT Jeffrey Zaun and LT Robert Wetzel of the USS SARATOGA's Attack Squadron 35, and LT Charles Turner and LT William Costen of USS RANGER's Attack Squadron 155 are missing.

A USMC OV-10 is downed, **the first Marine combat aircraft loss.** The two aircrewmen, LtCol Clifford Acree and CWO Guy Hunter are missing.

USS NICHOLAS (FFG-47), operating with embarked Helicopter Anti-Submarine Squadron (Light) 44, Det. 8/USA helos and a Kuwaiti patrol boat, engaged and neutralized Iraqi forces firing on coalition aircraft with anti-aircraft artillery and shoulder-fired SAMs from eleven Kuwaiti oil platforms in northern Arabian Gulf. **In the first combined helicopter missile and surface ship gun engagement,** five Iraqis are killed, 3 wounded and 23 Iraqis, **the first enemy prisoners of war,** were taken board USS NICHOLAS for transfer to USMC holding facility and Saudi Arabian EPW camp.

USS MOOSBRUGGER (DD-980) SEALs board Sudanese vessel EL OBEID, **the first boarding by a Navy ship since commencement of hostilities.**

Iraqi SCUD missiles impact in Israel, 10-12 civilian injuries.

<u>SECDEF declares an airlift emergency</u>, activates Stage II of Civil Reserve Air Fleet (CRAF) plan, authorizing government to contract with civil air carriers to use up to 181 aircraft to move supplies and equipment in support of OPERATION DESERT STORM.

SECNAV activates 498 additional Naval Reservists from 37 units

19 Jan DOD announces that U.S. troop strength is 460,000 (75,000 USN, 85,000 USMC) and over 100 ships in AOR. 216 TOMAHAWK cruise missiles have been launched and over 4,000 sorties (bombing, combat, attack suppression, refueling) have been flown. Air campaign is satisfactory, causing Iraq to move aircraft north.

USN A-6s and A-7s from USS JOHN F. KENNEDY and USS SARATOGA **successfully launch a Standoff Land Attack Missile (SLAM) against an Iraqi target for the first time.**

USS LOUISVILLE (SSN-724) fires the first submarine-launched TOMAHAWK cruise missile in combat history while submerged in the Red Sea.

19 Jan (continuing) **Missile was directed against an unidentified Iraqi target.**

USS SYLVANIA (AFS-2) achieves historic quadruple underway replenishment in the Red Sea. 4 ships were resupplied at once.

DOD announces the deployment of European-based U.S. Patriot surface-to-air defensive missiles, with American crews, to Israel to assist defenses against SCUD missiles.

DOD also announces loss of USAF F-4G with the crew later rescued in Saudi Arabian desert. U.S. has lost 6 aircraft and has 7 personnel listed as missing.

State Department announces transfer of diplomatic notes with Iraq reaffirming U.S intention to abide by its legal obligations under the 1940 Geneva Convention relative to the protection of POWs, and expects Iraq (a signatory) to reciprocate; second note affirms legal protection from attack on U.S. military hospital ships in regional waters.

Ten Iraqi aircraft (6 MIG-29s, 3 Mirage F-1s, 1 MIG-23) have been destroyed in air-to-air engagements.

<u>President Bush signs authorization to extend call-up of up to one million National Guard/Reserves for up to two years</u>; DOD will implement incrementally raising ceiling on 161,887 National Guard/Reserves currently called up to 360,000. The Navy's authorization ceiling was raised from 30,000 to 44,000, USMC from 23,000 to 44,000.

20 Jan DOD announces that over 7,000 sorties have been flown.

Iraq launches nine SCUD missiles against Saudi Arabia. Two SCUDs aimed at Dharhan and six aimed at Riyadh are intercepted by U.S. Patriot missiles. One SCUD lands in Gulf waters off Dhahran.

Five additional Iraqi aircraft have been destroyed in air-to-air engagements for a total of fifteen (10 MIG-29s, 4 Mirage F-1s, 1 MIG-23).

DOD reports the loss of a USAF F-15 and two USAF F-16s. DOD reports 4 additional personnel listed as missing. U.S. has lost 8 aircraft and has 11 personnel listed as missing.

DOD announces that, to-date, 19 anti-ship mines have been discovered and destroyed in the northern Arabian Gulf. DOD also announces that there have been 6,968 intercepts and 830 boardings.

DOD announces that Iraqi artillery battery was destroyed by USN A-6 and USAF A-10 aircraft. USMC and USA troops continue in defensive mode in forward positions and there has been no direct ground confrontations.

SECNAV activates 498 additional Naval reservists from 26 units.

21 Jan DOD announces over 8,000 sorties have been flown; air operations focus continues on neutralizing fixed/mobile SCUD launch sites and troop concentrations.

A USN F-14 is downed by surface-to-air missile over Iraq. Pilot, LT Devon Jones and Radar Intercept Officer, LT Lawrence Slade of USS SARATOGA's Fighter Squadron 103 are missing.

U.S. has lost 10 aircraft and has 13 personnel listed as missing.

21 Jan (continuing) U.S. ships have conducted nearly 7,000 maritime interceptions operations in regional waters. No direct ground confrontation.

U.S. warns Iraq will be held accountable for mistreatment of U.S. prisoners of war after Iraq announces captured Americans will be placed at strategic target sites as "human shields."

6 Iraqi SCUD missiles fired into Saudi Arabia in three attacks over 12 hours. U.S. Patriot missiles intercept two SCUDs, one landed in the sea northwest of Al Jubayl, two others fell into the desert. No injuries.

<u>USS THEODORE ROOSEVELT (CVN-71) Carrier Battle Group arrives on station in the Persian Gulf region.</u>

22 Jan DOD announces that over 10,000 sorties have been flown, no U.S. aircraft lost in air-to-air engagements. Oil storage tank fires started by Iraqis in Wafra, Shuaiba and Mina Abdullah, Kuwait having little effect on air operations.

USAF special operations forces recovered one crewmember of F-14 downed on 21 January, LT Devon Jones. Second aircrewmember is missing.

4 USN A-6s attacked and disabled an Iraqi T-43 class ship--capable of laying 20 mines--in the northern Arabian Gulf. Vessel was seen sinking.

U.S. ships attacked 3 Iraqi patrol boats, disabling one, and chasing off two others. 3 additional mines were found and destroyed.

Iraqi launches SCUD missile against Israel. U.S. Patriot missile crew had a generator problem, Israeli Defense Forces fired a Patriot missile. SCUD impacted in Tel Aviv killing 3 and wounding nearly 100.

U.S. troop strength has increased to 474,000 (Iraqi - 545,000) and there are 165,797 Reserves/National Guard recalled (13,303 Navy, 22,048 USMC).

23 Jan <u>At D+7 days</u>, 12,000 sorties have been flown (6,000 attack, 6,000 support). USAF F-16 downed by artillery fire over Kuwait; pilot ejected over Persian Gulf, rescued by Helicopter Anti-Submarine Squadron (Light)-44, Detachment Eight, embarked on USS NICHOLAS, **first over-water combat search and rescue.** DOD reports 2 noncombat-related aircraft losses: USMC AV-8 in training accident, pilot killed, and USA AH-64 in ground mishap, no injuries. 14 total U.S. aircraft lost: 11 fixed wing (9 from hostile ground-fire), 3 helos (non-combat).

USN A-6s disable an Al Qaddisiyah-class Iraqi tanker that had been collecting and reporting intelligence data, setting off three explosions, and killing three. A-6s also attacked and sank a Winchester-class hovercraft being re-fueled by the tanker, and a Zhuk patrol boat.

SECDEF Dick Cheney and CJCS General Colin Powell assess first week of Operation DESERT STORM: Objectives are being achieved and campaign has achieved air superiority over Kuwait and Iraq; have destroyed Iraq's two operating nuclear reactors and is neutralizing Iraqi ground radar/air defenses. Air-to-air engagements are no match. Warns Iraq still has significant military capability, may be "hunkering down", expecting range of responses including air strikes, more SCUDs, ground attacks or terrorism. Will continue air campaign as part of overall land,

23 Jan (continuing) air and sea campaign, with goal to "cut off the Iraqi army and kill it."
5 Iraqi SCUD missiles fired at Saudi Arabia (2 Riyadh, 2 Dhahran, 1 at King Khalid Military Center). U.S. Patriot missiles successfully intercepted four, one fell into gulf waters. No injuries. In second attack, 1 SCUD is intercepted over Israel by U.S./Israeli Patriot missiles. No injuries.

24 Jan DOD announces 15,000 sorties (8,000 combat, 7,000 support) have been flown and more than 220 TOMAHAWK cruise missiles have been launched at Iraqi targets. Air strikes are directed at SCUD missile launchers, lines of transportation and communication, control sites and airfields. At Al Quara West airfield, 3 Soviet-built TU-16 Badger heavy bombers were caught on the ground, ready to take off, and destroyed. Coalition has been joined by forces from Qatar and Bahrain. The UK has lost a Tornado. Two crewmembers are missing.

USN A-6s attacked and destroyed an Iraqi Spasilac minelayer. An A-6 sank an Iraqi Zhuk-class patrolboat and another Iraqi minesweeper hit an Iraqi mine while attempting to evade the A-6 fire. Twenty-two survivors were taken from the sea by a helo from USS CURTS (FFG-38), near the island of Jazirat Qurah. During rescue, helo comes under attack, returned fire from Iraqi forces on the island, killing 3. 29 additional Iraqis subsequently surrendered. 51 enemy prisoners of war were taken into custody by SEAL Platoon from Naval Special Warfare Group One on Helicopter Anti-Submarine Squadron 12 and Helicopter Anti-Submarine Squadron 9 helos from USS LEFTWICH (DD-984) and USS NICHOLAS, and the island is reclaimed, **the first liberated Kuwaiti territory.** Also, A-6s and F/A-18s attacked the Umm Qasr Naval Base, hitting four Iraqi ships.

In first air-to-air engagement between Saudi Arabian and Iraqi aircraft, a Royal Saudi F-15 downed 2 Iraqi F-1s (armed with Exocet anti-ship missiles and bombs). USS WORDEN (CG-18) vectored aircraft for shootdown. To-date, 19 Iraqi aircraft have been destroyed in air-to-air engagements, with no U.S. or coalition losses.

U.S. ships continue multiple operations including locating and destroying 25 mines to-date in the northern Arabian Gulf.

Using Harpoon anti-ship missile, Royal Saudi vessel sinks an Iraqi minelayer in northern Persian Gulf. No survivors reported.

U.S. ground forces continue to be attacked by sporadic Iraqi artillery fire, but no injuries or damage. No direct ground confrontations. Troops continue maneuvering for any possible engagement at Saudi-Kuwaiti border.

DOD announces U.S. troop strength has increased to 475,000 (75,000 Navy, 90,000 USMC).

Elements of IV and V Marine Expeditionary Brigades, and 13th Marine Expeditionary Unit, embarked on ships from Amphibious Task Groups Two and Three, are conducting amphibious exercise Operation Sea-Soldier IV, the largest amphibious force assembed since the 1950 landing at Inchon, Republic of South Korea.

25 Jan   DOD announces 17,500 sorties have been flown (a record 2,700 today) and 236 TOMAHAWK cruise missiles have been launched. Iraq has lost 43 aircraft, 19 in air-to-air engagements, 24 on the ground. <u>The U.S. has lost 10 aircraft to ground fire and the coalition has lost 7 aircraft,</u> including 5 UK Tornados hit by anti-aircraft fire flying low-level missions to crater airfields. <u>The total of 17 aircraft losses represents two-tenths of 1 percent of all combat missions flown to-date.</u>

U.S. ships engage an Iraqi vessel laying mines near Sea Island Terminal, setting part of terminal and surrounding water afire.

<u>Iraq has dumped several million barrels of oil into the Arabian Gulf</u> from the Sea Island crude oil tanker loading terminal, off the coast of Kuwait. 5 pre-positioned Iraqi tankers in the occupied Kuwaiti port of Mina al Ahmadi have been drained of oil, and oil is being pumped from storage tanks ashore through an underwater pipeline into the gulf. Described by DOD as "an act of environmental terrorism", the spill is approximately 20 miles long, 3 miles wide, and three feet deep, and threatens to foul the intakes of Saudi Arabia's desalinization plants as well as the gulf.

U.S. troop strength in the region has increased to 482,000. To-date, 192,965 National Guard and Reservists have been recalled to active duty (14,702 Navy, 22,142 USMC). Fifteen percent of U.S. servicemembers in the DESERT STORM field of operation are Guard and Reserve.

Iraq fires 3 SCUD missiles at Riyadh, Saudi Arabia. U.S. Patriot missiles successfully intercept, but warhead debris kills at least one person, 23 injured. In a second attack, 7 SCUDs impact in Tel Aviv and Haifa, Israel, killing one person, injuring dozens.

SECNAV activates 298 additional Naval Reservists from 41 units.

26 Jan   DOD announces 20,000 sorties have been flown as the air campaign's focus shifts from strategic interdiction to battlefield preparation, with targeting on military storage facilities, military production facilities, Republican Guard troop fortifications and SCUD launchers. Bomb damage assessments confirm significant destruction of Iraqi biological/chemical production capability.

The Navy has lost an F/A-18 in non-combat operations. The aircrewman ejected over the Persian Gulf and was recovered safely.

Total of Iraqi aircraft destroyed in air-to-air engagements climbs to 22 as USAF F-15s down 3 Iraqi MIG-23s.

USN aircraft attack an Iraqi patrol boat in Kuwait harbor. Boat last seen burning. A-6s have engaged and left a TNC-45 patrol boat burning.

DOD announces that at least a dozen Iraqi MIG-29s/F-1s and a dozen transport aircraft have landed in an undisclosed location in Iran, a declared neutral country. DOD ascertaining whether Iraqi planes are seeking a safe haven from bombing attacks, whether this is a mass defection or a husbanding of resources for future combat operations.

<u>An estimated 120 million gallons of oil continues to spew into the Persian Gulf</u> from the Sea Island Terminal, and the oil slick -- partly afire from January 25 engagement between USN and Iraqi patrol boat -- is now 31 miles long and 8 miles wide. ASD (PA) Pete Williams denounces deliberate spill as "indis-

26 Jan (continuing) criminate environmental war" causing catastrophic environmental damage to entire Persian Gulf region, and refutes Iraqi allegation that U.S. or coalition sabotaged facility and caused spill. U.S. is sending a team of U.S. Coast Guard, NOAA and EPA oil pollution and environmental experts to scene to assist Saudi Arabian efforts to contain the spill.

U.S. Marines stage biggest artillery attack of the war, firing a battery of 155mm howitzers at Iraqi troops six miles inside Kuwait.

Three U.S. Marines, members of the First Marine Division, were killed and seven injured when two LAV-25 Light Armored vehicles accidentally collided as the Marines were returning from a raid mission along the Saudi-Kuwaiti border. To-date, U.S. non-hostile deaths are 10, 14 are missing, and 3 have been wounded. Hostile deaths remain at 0.

Iraq fires a SCUD missile at Riyadh, Saudi Arabia, intercepted by U.S. Patriot missile. In a second attack, three SCUDs are launched at Haifa and one SCUD at Tel Aviv, Israel. All were intercepted by U.S. Patriot missiles. This latest salvo brings to 45 total SCUD launches.

U.S. troop strength has increased to 483,000 in the region.

Enemy Prisoners of War (EPW) to-date: 110, in U.S. facilities awaiting processing to Saudia Arabian EPW camp.

27 Jan DOD <u>announces that USAF F-111s attacked pipelines feeding the Sea Island Terminal with GBU-15 laser-guided bombs</u> to stem the flow of oil, now 35 miles long and 10 miles wide, into the Persian Gulf, and to ignite oil and burn off pollutants. The attack specifically targeted system of pipes that regulate oil flow from storage tanks to the terminal called manifolds. Oil flow has apparently drastically slowed, and fire should burn out in about 24 hours.

Over 22,000 sorties have been flown, including attacks on 3 SCUD missile launch sites, Republican Guard troop emplacements, bridges, lines of communications and shelters. There have been no U.S. aircraft lost in the past 48 hours.

Four Iraqi MIG-23 aircraft have been destroyed in air-to-air engagements with 2 USAF F-15s near Baghdad. Iraqi aircraft losses in air-to-air engagements to-date total 26.

USN A-6s attack and destroy an Iraqi ship, and coalition naval forces continue to hunt Iraqi patrol and mine-laying boats in the northern Arabian Gulf and near Bubiyan Island. To-date, 8 Iraqi vessels (1 oil platform service ship, 2 patrol boats, 1 tanker, and 4 unknown) are presumed destroyed, and 10 (4 mining vessels, 1 hovercraft, 3 patrol boats, and 2 unknown) have been sunk. 2 additional mines have been located and destroyed in the northern Arabian Gulf.

39 Iraqi aircraft, including 23 in the past 24 hours, have landed in Iran. Iran announces that to protect its neutrality, any warplanes landing within its borders would be confiscated and held until end of hostilities.

U.S. Patriot missiles intercept 6 Iraqi SCUD missiles aimed at Saudi Arabia and Israel. 51 SCUDs have been launched to-date.

28 Jan	DOD announces more than 24,000 sorties (about 50% attack strikes) have been flown as air campaign focuses on Iraqi command and control, counter-air ops, interdiction, airfields, SCUD sites, Republican Guard fortifications, and battlefield preparation.
	A Marine AV-8B is downed. The crewman, Captain Michael Berryman, is missing, the 15th U.S. crewman.
	The status of seven U.S. aircrewmen has been redesignated from Missing to Prisoner of War. The seven include Lieutenant Jeffrey N. Zaun, USN; Lieutenant Colonel Clifford M. Acree, and Chief Warrant Officer Guy L. Hunter, USMC.
	DOD announces that a total of 80 Iraqi aircraft have relocated to Iran. Aircraft ferrying is being characterized as "possible defections" as a consequence of air campaign that has achieved air superiority and neutralized Iraqi counterattack. Flight operations have been conducted from only 3 of Iraq's 66 airfields, numbering 30 sorties, 25 to Iran. DOD appraisal is that "Iraq is unable to offer any organized air resistance." Aircraft will be monitored to assure non-return to conflict. Iraqi aircraft relocate from central and northern Iraq, out of range of U.S. and coalition aircraft to intercept, however four were engaged on January 27 and destroyed by U.S. F-15s.
	USN A-6s have attacked Iraqi ships at Bubiyan Channel, at the Umm Qasr Naval Base, and in Kuwait harbor.
	USS SAMUEL B. ROBERTS (FFG-58) diverts the RED SEA ENERGY in the North Red Sea after an inspection team found 160 railroad cars which were inaccessible. The German-flagged freighter, enroute from Greece to Aqaba, Jordan, was diverted to another port. To-date, coalition diversions total 37, 7,020 intercepts and 837 boardings. The U.S. has conducted 490 of these boardings.
	USMC and coalition aircraft attack an Iraqi convoy inside Kuwait and destroyed 24 tanks, armored personnel carriers and trucks.
	U.S. ground forces continue to receive sporadic artillery fire along the Kuwaiti border, and have engaged in counter-battery artillery missions.
	DOD announces oil, estimated to have totalled 460 million gallons, appears to have stopped flowing from the Sea Island Terminal, however, still monitoring.
	Iraq launches one SCUD missile at Saudia Arabia. Intercepted by U.S. Patriot missile, south of Riyadh. A second SCUD fired at Tel Aviv, Israel, fell in a West Bank open field without causing injuries.
29 Jan	Over 27,000 sorties have been flown and 256 TOMAHAWK cruise missiles launched as air campaign targeting priorities continue to be command and control, airfields, SCUD locations, lines of communication, Republican Guard areas, and battlefield preparation.
	Naval forces are conducting strike operations, surface surveillance, and combat air patrols. A-6s have attacked and destroyed two Iraqi Silkworm missile launchers. Naval aircraft again attacked Iraqi ships and port facilities at Um Qasr Naval Base. F/A-18s destroyed control

29 Jan (continuing)   centers at an oil refinery at Basra.

- **In the first major ground confrontation**, Iraq mounts a four-pronged raid across Kuwaiti border. Near Al Wafra, U.S. and coalition forces engage a mechanized battalion with Cobra gunships and fixed wing aircraft, and repulse the attack, destroying 10 tanks, losing 3 light armored vehicles. North of Ras Al Khafji, at just before midnight, another Iraqi battalion crossed the border, with turned turrets--the international sign of surrender--then, attacked. U.S. AC-130s and Cobra helicopters destroyed 4 tanks, 13 vehicles. Fighting continued for control of Khafji through the night. Forty more Iraqi tanks crossed the border, and engage U.S. Marine light armored infantry. Attack was repelled, but eleven Marines were killed in action, **the first ground combat casualties of the operation.** Two Marines were wounded. A total of 33 enemy tanks and 28 APCs were destroyed.
- U.S. ground forces continue to receive sporadic artillery fire, engage in small skirmishes with Iraqi troops along the Kuwaiti border, and conducting artillery and counter-battery missions, firing hundreds of rounds and anti-tank missiles on Iraqi outposts in Kuwait.
- U.S. Marines of the 13th Marine Expeditionary Unit, deployed from USS OKINAWA (LPH-3), assault and capture Umm al Maradim Island, 12 miles off the coast of Kuwait. Marines plant the Kuwaiti flag, and destroyed anti-aircraft weapons and artillery stored on the 400 meter-by-300 meter island. **This is the second island reclaimed for the Kuwaiti government by the coalition.**
- Navy helos search Maradim Island investigating reports of Iraqis offering to surrender, and were fired upon by approximately 20 Iraqi small craft with rocket-propelled grenades and automatic weapons. Returned fire, sinking 4 boats, damaging 12. A-6s engaged fleeing boats.
- 80-90 Iraqi aircraft (35%, civilian, 65%, fighters/bombers) have now flown into Iran.
- DOD announces that the fire has been extinguished at the Sea Island Terminal, and the oil flow from the terminal has stopped. Additionally, the oil slick is breaking up.
- DOD announces that over 700,000 coalition air, ground, and naval personnel are present in the theater of operation, and over 110 coalition combatant ships are participating. U.S. troops number over 490,000.
- USCENTCOM officially begins first transfer of 36 Iraqi Enemy Prisoners of War to Saudi Arabian control.
- To-date, 200,948 National Guard and Reservists have been recalled to active duty (15,093 Navy, 22,141 USMC).

30 Jan At D+14, DOD categorically summarizes operational status:
* Targets - 26 leadership targets have been struck with 60 percent severely damaged or destroyed.
  One third of Iraq's command, control and communications facilities are destroyed or inoperative.
  Power plants and telecommunications sites have been hit. One fourth of Iraq's electrical generating facilities are inoperative, 50 percent adversely affected.
  Twenty-nine air defense systems have been hit with more than 800 sorties.
* Air-to-air combat - 29 Iraqi aircraft destroyed with no coalition losses.
* Airfields - Thirty eight of 44 targeted airfields have been bombed in over 1,300 sorties (some multiple strikes). At least nine airfields are inoperative.
  Over 70 hardened aircraft shelters have been destroyed. Forced Iraqi aircraft to hide in residential areas, moved to roads or flown to Iran. "Everytime an Iraqi airplane takes off the ground, it's running away."
* Bridges - Thirty-three of 36 targeted bridges have been bombed in over 790 sorties.
  Kuwaiti theater of operations has been isolated by strikes on railroad and highway bridges.
  Iraq's resupply efforts have been degraded from 20,000 to 2,000 tons daily. Highway traffic severely diminished.
* Strategic Locations - All 31 targeted nuclear, chemical and biological facilities have been attacked with over 535 sorties (primarily TOMAHAWK cruise missiles and precision-guided missiles). All nuclear facilities have been destroyed, including the Baghdad Nuclear Research Center. Over half of biological and chemical facilities have been heavily damaged or destroyed.
* Republican Guards - Elite forces have been target of about 300 air sorties daily. 28 B-52s dropped 470 tons. On 29 January, 21 B-52s dropped 315 tons. 178 trucks confirmed destroyed, and 55 artillery and 52 tanks have been destroyed or damaged in past 36 hours. Also, A-6s, F-16s, and F-15E air strikes are resulting in multiple secondary explosions in ammo storage revettments. 125 revettments are confirmed destroyed in northern Kuwait, along with armored personnel carriers, missiles and self-propelled artillery tubes.
* Naval operations - Navy has flown over 3,500 sorties from six carriers and have launched over 260 TOMAHAWK cruise missiles. 46 Iraqi naval vessels have been sunk or disabled and 74 enemy prisoners of war have been captured in two engagements. Iraqi naval forces operations severely degraded. Also, maritime interception operations are continuing with over 7,000 intercepts to-date.
* SCUDs - Over 1500 sorties have been flown, destroying all 30 fixed sites and all major Iraqi missile production facilities. Patriot missiles have engaged 33 SCUDs, 33 destroyed.

30 Jan (continuing) Saudi Arabian National Guardsmen and Qatari tanks engage a column of Iraqi infantry and tanks in Ras al Khafji. After a protracted battle, Iraqis are forced out of the town with help of U.S. Marine AH-1 Cobra gunships and artillery.

Navy A-6s attack three Iraqi landing craft in the vicinity of Shatt al Arab Channel, leaving 2 ships dead in the water. The other ship fled. A-6 re-attacks a patrol boat in the northern Arabian Gulf. The boat was set ablaze and left burning. A-6s attack patrol boats at a pier at Umm Qasr Naval Base, sinking one, damaging the other. In the vicinity of Bubiyan Island, Navy aircraft engage 4 military vessels, sinking 3 patrol boats and damaging a landing craft. To-date, approximately 60 enemy vessels have either been sunk or damaged.

All 18 F/A-18s aboard USS SARATOGA deliver 100,000 pounds of MK-83 one thousand pound bombs on Iraqi positions in Kuwait, **the largest amount of bomb tonnage carried in a single mission.**

USS CURTS and USS LEFTWICH rescues 20 enemy prisoners of war from an Iraqi Polnochny amphibious landing craft sunk by USN A-6 and UK Lynx helos in the northern Arabian Gulf. LEFTWICH is also primary CSAR platform in Gulf, locating and recovering downed pilots. LEFTWICH participated in 16 CSAR cases.

31 Jan DOD announces that over 32,000 sorties have been flown (2,600 today) with no losses of U.S. aircraft. Coalition air, ground and naval personnel now exceed 705,000. <u>U.S. troop strength now exceeds one half million.</u>

Republican Guard positions have been hit with over 350 tactical fighter strikes and over 10 B-52 strikes.

U.S. and coalition tactical aircraft continue to engage tactical armor and infantry positions north of the Ras al Khafji area and along the Kuwaiti Coastal Highway.

Sporadic skirmishes in Ras al Khafji between U.S., Saudi and hold-out Iraqi troops until secured at 1400. Two 6-man U.S. Marine reconnaissance teams who had been trapped in the town directing artillery strikes were recovered.

Two U.S. soldiers, one male, one female, were reported missing in Saudi Arabia. Not related to Khafji battle.

Naval combat air patrols, surface surveillance, strike and mine search operations continue. To-date, 37 mines have been located and destroyed.

USS LEFTWICH captures 15 EPWs from Khawar al Amaya oil platform.

Iraqi SCUD missile is fired at Israel, falls harmlessly in the West Bank.

1 Feb DOD announces that over 34,000 sorties have been flown (2,500 today), with 19 tactical air strikes and 5 B-52 strikes totalling 600 sorties on Republican Guard fortifications along the Saudi Arabian-Kuwaiti border. 300 sorties targeted Iraqi armor and infantry postions along the border. Also, 278 TOMAHAWK cruise missiles launched to-date.

DOD reports the destruction of another SCUD missile site. 31 January

1 Feb (continuing)   launch toward Israel was observed by 2 U.S. aircraft, and attacked site, destroying launcher, 2 trailers and 7 support vehicles.

Naval air strike operations resumed at the Uum Qasr Naval Base. At the Min al Bakir oil terminal, an A-6 attacked a patrol boat, leaving it burning. Helos picked up an additional 15 enemy prisoners of war from the Cor al Amiya oil terminal who were apparently survivors from Iraqi naval vessels engaged over the past 48 hours. Navy helos involved in EPW operation reported no oil coming from or in vicinity of oil terminal or Min al Bakir platform. Oil slick appears to be broken up, 4 miles long and 1 mile wide.

Iraqi troop and armor border movements are being observed, but not considered a "massive troop buildup" or major offensive.

Iraqi tanks have fired on an observation post along the border. Five tanks fled under fire from U.S. artillery.

DOD reports over 500 enemy prisoners of war have been captured after the siege at Ras al Khafji.

SECNAV activates 504 additional Naval Reservists from 51 units.

2 Feb   DOD announces 37,000 sorties have been flown (2,600 today), focused on targeting Republican Guard positions, strategic targets and targets of opportunity.

A USN A-6 with two crewmembers, LCDR Barry Cooke, LT Patrick Connor, from the USS THEODORE ROOSEVELT's Attack Squadron 36 and a USAF A-10 with 1 crewman has been shot down by anti-aircraft fire. The three crewmembers are listed as missing.

U.S. naval operations continue with an attack on the Al Kalia naval facility. One Iraqi Exocet-capable patrol boat was directly hit with two laser-guided bombs, while a second aircraft launched a string of 12 500-pound bombs across a second patrol boat which also went into a building on the pier generating several secondary explosions. Helos from the USS NICHOLAS engaged four Iraqi patrol boats near the Myerdam Island, destroying one, damaging two. Also, A-6s scored a direct hit with two laser-guided bombs on a patrol boat in the Kuwait City harbor. <u>35 Iraqi naval craft have been sunk or damaged to-date.</u>

<u>Senior commanders now conclude that with the destruction of all Iraqi patrol craft capable of delivering missiles, Iraqi naval forces are considered to be combat ineffective.</u>

USS SAMUEL B. ROBERTS (FFG-5) diverts 2 freighters in North Red Sea, USS HALYBURTON (FFG-40) assists with one diversion. USS BIDDLE (CG-34) diverts one freighter in the North Red Sea.

2 SCUD missiles are fired at Tel Aviv, Israel. One landed in Jordan, the other in the West Bank. No injuries, minimal damage. One SCUD was intercepted over Riyadh, S.A. by a U.S. Patriot missile. Falling debris injured 29 people.

DOD announces that one Marine has been killed and two wounded when their convoy which was returning from an artillery operation was hit by cluster bomb munitions apparently by "friendly fire."

3 Feb	DOD announces that over 41,000 sorties have been flown (2,500 today), 480 solely against Republican Guard fortifications, in addition to airfields and hardened aircraft shelters. <u>The latter targeting has resulted in the destruction of 68 additional Iraqi aircraft</u>. Also, 25-35 major bridges have been destroyed or damaged resulting in continuing resupply interdiction.
	The Navy's battleship USS MISSOURI (BB-63) fired eight 1.25-ton shells from its 16-inch guns at prefabricated concrete command and control bunkers Iraq was moving into Kuwait, destroying the bunkers. **The barrage, totalling 18,000 pounds of high explosives, marked the first combat firing of the MISSOURI's 16-inch guns since the Korean War, and was in support of Marines and coalition ground forces. This also marked the first use of a Remotely Piloted Vehicle (RPV) for gun fire spotting in a hostile environment.**
	Using its mine-avoidance sonar, USS CURTS, then, USS NICHOLAS escorted the battleship through unlighted navigational hazards steadily north in the Arabian Gulf to gain maximum tactical advantage.
	Mine explodes near USS NICHOLAS, shrapnel causes light damage.
	DOD announces that evidence concludes that a U.S. aircraft accidently hit a Light Armored Vehicle killing 7 Marines during the January 29 battle at Khafji. This "friendly fire" accident is ascribed to the mis-identification of the USMC vehicle and its close proximity to comparably-configured Iraqi armored vehicles during "very intesne, very close" combat. The four other Marine KIAs, in another LAV, are believed to have been hit by Iraqi fire.
	U.S. has lost three additional aircraft in non-combat operations, a USMC AH-1J Cobra, a USMC UH-1 Huey helo, and a USAF B-52. The two crewmen of the AH-1J, Major Eugene McCarthy and Captain Jonathan Edwards, which crashed in Saudi Arabia while returning from an armed combat escort mission on 2 February, are listed as killed in action. The 4 crewmembers of the Huey, Captain David Herr, Captain James Thorp, Corporal Albert Haddad, and Corporal Kurt Benz, are listed as killed in action. Three crewmen of the B-52, which crashed in the Indian Ocean while returning from a combat mission, have been recovered by Naval Reservists of Helicopter Squadron-75, while three other crewmen are missing.
	No hostile naval activity, reconfirming Iraqi naval capability has been neutralized.
4 Feb	DOD announces that over 44,000 sorties have been flown -- "that's approximately one bombing sortie for every minute of the DESERT STORM operation" -- (2,700 today), including 250 sorties and six B-52 strikes on Republican Guard troop positions.
	U.S. aircraft also hit targets of opportunity, including a USMC AV-8B attack with Rockeye anti-tank bombs that destroyed or damaged 25 Iraqi tanks, and a strike on a truck convoy detected moving at about 0400.
	There has been no hostile activity by Iraq's naval forces.

5 Feb DOD announces that to-date, over 47,000 sorties have been flown (2,800 today) and 284 TOMAHAWK cruise missiles launched with targeting focused on Republican Guard emplacement (400 sorties, six B-52 strikes) and logistics interdiction.
USS MISSOURI destroys Iraqi artillery emplacement.
Navy A-6s attacked Silkworm anti-ship missile sites at Uum Qasabah. Hits on two launchers and several control and support vehicles were confirmed.
USMC AV-8Bs bombed and strafed a 25-truck convoy, causing multiple secondary explosions. Strikes have also hit resupply convoys backed up attempting to cross bombed-out bridges between Baghdad and Basra.
A Navy F/A-18 is downed. The pilot, LT Robert Dwyer of the USS THEODORE ROOSEVELT's Carrier Airwing-8, is missing.
There has been no hostile activity by Iraq's air or naval forces. Iraqi ground troops continue limited probing/reconnaissance actions with some small arms fire and sporadic artillery fire.
Enemy prisoners of war to-date total about 817.
Voluntary/involuntary recall to active duty of retired Marines announced.
To-date, 211,146 National Guard and Reservists have been recalled to active duty (15,376 Navy, 22,634 USMC).

6 Feb At D+21, DOD announces that over 49,000 sorties have been flown (2,500 today), with A-6s, F-15s, F-16s and B-52s targeting Republican Guard fortifications every three hours around the clock. 650 sorties have also hit convoys and assembly areas to isolate Iraqi troops and shape the Kuwait Theater of Operations for any future engagements. Bridges, roads and railroads are being targeted and retargeted to interdict troop resupply. 42 bridges have been destroyed or extensively damaged, 70% of Iraqi supply lines have been cut.
USS MISSOURI has destroyed 4 artillery emplacements and a command bunker with another 16-inch gun barrage in support of Marines. In a second salvo, the MISSOURI fired 28 16-inch rounds against a radar control site complex, completely destroying it. 5-inch batteries also engaged. MISSOURI has fired a total of 112 16-inch shells and 12 five-inch rounds in 8 fire support missions over 48 hours.
Within two hours of relieving its sister battleship, USS WISCONSIN (BB-64) conducted its first naval gunfire support mission since the Korean War, firing an 11-round salvo with its 16-inch guns and destroying an Iraqi artillery battery in southern Kuwait. Secondary explosions reported. USS NICHOLAS escorted the battleship. USMC OV-10 called in the fire mission.
Two patrolling F-15s intercepted 4 Iraqi fighters transiting to Iran 100 feet above-ground, and shot down 2 SU-25s and 2 MIG-21s. Three other Iraqi fighters crossed into Iranian airspace before furhter engagement. 134 Iraqi planes (109 fighters, 25 transports) have flown to Iran.
Navy and Marine Corps aircraft have flown over 11,000 combat sorties

6 Feb (continuing)   during OPERATION DESERT STORM.

- USS GERMANTOWN (LSD-42) and 30 other amphibious ships arrive in the Arabian Gulf with 5th Marine Expeditionary Brigade embarked. **USS GERMANTOWN also embarked four air cushion landing craft (LCAC) for combat operations ashore, a first in Navy history.**
- Naval maritime intercept operations continue with over 7,100 merchants challenged, over 860 ships boarded, and 40 diverted.
- Marines and other troops continue ground maneuvers, and there have been numerous Iraqi reconnaissance probes. Contact has been minimal.
- To-date, there have been 35 U.S. fatalities: 12 KIA, 23 Non-Combat Fatalities; 11 WUA; 24 MIA (6 Navy, 1 USMC); 2 Missing; 8 POW (2 Navy, 2 USMC).
- U.S. troop strength is approximately 503,000, other coalition forces exceed 205,000. 32 nations have forces in place supporting OPERATION DESERT STORM (Argentina, Australia, Bahrain, Bangladesh, Belgium, Canada, China, Czechoslovakia, Denmark, Egypt, France, Germany, Greece, Hungary, Italy, Kuwait, Morocco, Netherlands, New Zealand, Niger, Norway, Oman, Pakistan, Poland, Qatar, Saudi Arabia, Senegal, Spain, Syria, United Arab Emirates, United Kingdom, United States).
- The U.S. has lost 23 aircraft (15 fixed-wing in combat, 3 fixed-wing in non-combat mishaps, 5 helicopters lost in non-combat). Coalition has lost 9 aircraft. 33 Iraqi aircraft and 3 helos have been shot down in air-to-air engagements with no U.S. losses.

7 Feb

- DOD announces that 52,000 sorties have been flown (2,600 today). Objective continues to be interdiction of Iraqi resupply, with over 600 sorties targeting bridges, highways, and railroad lines. Other air-to-ground targets are hit including Republican Guard and other Iraqi forces, command and control facilities and communication lines.
- Two USN F-14s of USS RANGER's Fighter Squadron One downed a MI-8 helo with an AIM-9M Sidewinder missile, **a combat first.**
- USN A-6s attacked and heavily damaged 2 Iraqi patrol boats in the northern gulf near the Al Faw peninsula.
- Using Remotely Piloted Vehicle (RPV) for spotting, USS WISCONSIN pounded Iraqi artillery, electronic warfare and naval sites with its 16-inch guns. 50 rounds sunk or severely damaged 15 boats, destroyed piers at Khawr al-Mufattah Marina. 19 rounds also fired at artillery and missile sites.
- USS BIDDLE (CG-34) diverts freighter in North Red Sea.
- Two F-15s intercepted 3 Iraqi SU-22s transiting to Iran, all were shot down. An A-10 downed a BO-15 helo.
- Iraq fires a SCUD missile at Riyadh, Saudi Arabia. Intercepted and destroyed by U.S. Patriot missile. No injuries or damage.
- <u>SECDEF Dick Cheney and CJCS General Colin Powell depart to Saudi Arabia for military assessment of OPERATION DESERT STORM.</u>
- SECNAV activates 528 additional Naval Reservists from 57 units.

8 Feb   DOD announces that over 55,000 sorties have been flown (2,500+ today) continuing to interdict and isolate the Kuwaiti Theater of Operations by targeting and retargeting 42 major bridges (9 attacked overnight) and SCUD launch sites. 600 sorties on planned targets and targets of opportunity (small convoys, armored vehicles). 600 tanks destroyed to-date. 150 sorties targeted around-the-clock on Republican Guard positions ("they're in their bunkers hiding").

USS WISCONSIN attacked a dozen Iraqi artillery emplacements with 36 rounds of its 16-inch guns in support of a Marine reconnaissance probe into occupied Kuwait. Using its remotely pilot vehicle to visually relay pictures and gun-firing coordinates of targets, the battleship's harassment and interdiction mission was designed to pin down and confuse Iraqi gunners during the Marine attack. Off Khafji, Saudi Arabia, WISCONSIN also blasted bunkers, troops and artillery sites.

A-6s attacked and neutralized an Iraqi training frigate collocated with a TMC-45 class patrol boar (Exocet-capable craft) at Cor Al Zubayr.

One SCUD missile is fired at Tel Aviv, Israel. Intercepted by U.S. Patriot missile. Debris caused several injuries.

13 additional Iraqi aircraft transit to Iran. Total to-date, 147 (121 fighters).

Sporadic artillery fire from counter-batteries along border continues.

Enemy prisoners of war total climbs to 943 (50+ officers) with surrender of 7 Iraqi soldiers.

To-date, 214,979 National Guard and Reservists have been recalled to active duty (15,667 Navy, 22,634 USMC).

9 Feb   DOD announces that 57,000 sorties have been flown (2,400+ today) interdicting communication lines and striking planned and on-call tactical targets throughout the KTO.

An A-6 attacked a Zouk patrol boat near Faylaka Island with a Rockeye missile, inflicting substantial damage. Naval aircraft also attacked a Silkworm site destroying three launchers and a control van with a direct hit.

A Marine AV-8B is downed. The pilot, Captain Russell Sanborn, is missing.

Bomb damage assessment confirms that 750+ tanks, 650+ artillery and 600 armored personnel carriers have been destroyed.

USS WISCONSIN continues its naval gunfire missions, responding to calls for fire from U.S. and coalition forces.

USS MISSOURI is simultaneously on patrol in the Arabian Gulf supporting Marines and coalition forces.

USS THOMAS C. HART (FF-1092) diverts a freighter in the North Red Sea.

Iraqi troops continue border probes and exchanging sporadic artillery fire with Marines and coalition ground forces.

South Korea is the 33rd coalition partner with forces in place supporting OPERATION DESERT STORM.

10 Feb   SECDEF Dick Cheney and CJCS General Colin Powell arrive back in Washington after conferring with U.S. and coalition commanders.

DOD announces that 59,000 sorties have been flown (2,800 today) with continued focus on the Republican Guards, battlefield preparation, resupply interdiction and strategic strikes in the KTO.

Naval operations, including mine countermeasures and maritime interceptions, continue. A-6s attacked two unidentified patrol boats in the northern Arabian Gulf, destroying both. Also, restrikes were made on the Uum Qasr Naval Base.

42 additional enemy prisoners of war surrendered to U.S. forces.

11 Feb   DOD announces that 62,000 sorties have been flown (2,900 today) continuing to focus on the Republican Guards (200+ sorties), battlefield preparation, strategic targets and interdicting troop resupply.

Naval operations, including mine countermeasures and maritime interceptions, continue. One mine is located and destroyed.

A B-52 strike along the border caused significant secondary explosions.

No major ground activity, only scattered border skirmishes. U.S. forces continue training exercises, redeployments.

Iraq fires SCUD missile at Saudi Arabia. Intercepted by U.S. Patriot missile. Two SCUDs are fired at Israel. One fell harmlessly in an unpopulated area after being intercepted by U.S. Patriot missile. The seond fell into a residential area, injuring 30 people and destroying several homes.

Enemy prisoners of war count rises to 1,00o+ with surrender of 75 Iraqi troops.

A 300-member contigent of Afghan Mujahedeen fighters becomes the 34th coalition partner supporting OPERATION DESERT STORM.

12 Feb   DOD announces that 65,000 sorties have been flown (2,600 today). The continuing air campaign is focusing on Republican Guard suppression (225 sorties, 6 B-52 strikes), supply interdiction and battlefield preparation (675 sorties).

USS MISSOURI, USMC aircraft/artillery, and Saudi artillery mounted a combined arms attack on multiple fixed-position targets (Iraqi troops, artillery, a hardened command bunker and tanks) in southern Kuwait. The battleship expended 60 rounds in 9 naval gunfire support missions.

6 additional Iraqis surrendered. DOD confirms for the first time that Iraqi personnel are executing would-be Iraqi deserters.

13 Feb   <u>At D+28</u>, DOD announces that the 24-hour air campaign continues with 67,000 sorties flown (2,800 today) focusing on battlefield preparation (700+ sorties), the Republican Guards (200 sorties), counter-SCUD strikes (170 sorties), and restrikes on selected strategic targets (missile propellant plants, storage facitlities, air fields, and command and control facilities).

Navy and Marine Corps aircraft have flown over 15,000 combat sorties during OPERATION DESERT STORM.

<u>USS AMERICA (CV-66) Carrier Battle Group transits Strait of Hormuz enroute Arabian Gulf redeployment.</u>

U.S. aircraft fire 2 laser-guided bombs on a Baghdad target in the residential al-Amerieh district, labeled a camouflaged fortified command and control bunker ("a legitimate military target") by DOD. Iraq claims site was a bomb shelter inhabited by civilians, claims hundreds were killed during the 0400 (local time) strike.

Naval aircraft destroyed an Exocet missile-capable Frelon helicopter on the ground. U.S. aircraft destroy 4 Iraqi transport aircraft on the ground.

Navy aircraft are assisting in the Arabian Gulf oil clean-up by providing information on the extent and movement of the spill.

Air campaign in Kuwait is complicated by smoke from over 50 oil field fires, mainly in Al-Wafra area. DOD suspects Iraq is placing charges on many wells to cloud battlefield and mask troop movements.

Marines again exchange sporadic border fire, continue patrols and counter-reconnaissance deployments.

To-date, there have been 40 U.S. fatalities: 12 KIA, 28 Non-Combat Fatalities; 10 Wia; 26 MIA (7 Navy, 2 USMC); 2 Missing; 8 POW.

U.S. troop strength is over 510,000 (80,000+ Navy, 90,000+ USMC), other coalition forces exceed 205,000.

U.S. has lost 28 aircraft (18 fixed-wing in combat, 3 fixed-wing in non-combat mishaps, 7 helicopters lost in non-combat). Coalition has lost 10 aircraft. 40 Iraqi aircraft and 4 helos have been shot down in air-to-air engagements with no U.S. losses. 136 Iraqi aircraft flown to Iran.

DOD announces 1,300 Iraqi tanks, 800 armored vehicles and 1,100 artillery pieces have been destroyed in verified bomb dfamage assessments (approximately one-third of the initial Iraqi inventory of 4,280 tanks, 1,870 APCs and 3,110 artillery pieces). Also, 25 Iraqi naval craft have been sunk or damaged, and 66 mines destroyed.

14 Feb   DOD announces that 70,000 sorties have been flown (2,800 today). Air campaign objectives remain unchanged with 24-hour focus on Republican Guards (200 sorties) and strikes in the KTO (800 sorties).

USN A-6s attacked and sank an Iraqi Osa patrol boat in Kuwait City Bay. Naval forces continue mine countermeasures and maritime interception operations. U.S. aircraft destroy 2 SCUDs/equipment.

<u>USS AMERICA Carrier Battle Group arrives in Arabian Gulf.</u>

DOD states Iraq's "military situation is precarious."

14 Feb (continuing) A USAF EF-111A crashed in Saudi Arabia. Both crewmembers were killed. This is the 19th U.S. aircraft lost in combat.

2 SCUD missiles broke up in flight over Hafr al-Batin, Saudi Arabia, showering debris on buildings, causing damage and several injuries.

15 Feb Baghdad Radio broadcasts Iraqi Revolutionary Command Council statement that Iraq is ready for negotiations "based on U.N. Security Council resolution 660 of 1990 to achieve a solution to the Gulf crisis, including its withdrawal from Kuwait. The willingness on the part of the RCC should be regarded as a guarantee from Iraq and coupled with an immediate and comprehensive cessation of all land, air and sea military operations."

President Bush announces that after initial happiness at the Iraq offer, "regrettably, the Iraq statement now appears to be a cruel hoax. Not only was the Iraq statement full of unacceptable old conditions, but Saddam Hussein has added several new conditions." The President reiterated, "They must withdraw without condition, there must be full implementation of all the Security Council resolutions, and there will be no linkage to the other problems in the area, and the legitimate rulers of Kuwait must be returned to Kuwait." President Bush stated the coalition will not end its military campaign, "until a massive withdrawal begins, with those Iraqi troops visibly leaving Kuwait."

DOD announces that 73,000 sorties have been flown (2,600 today). Objectives remain destruction of the Republican Guards (100 sorties), strategic targets in the KTO (800 sorties), restrikes, and counter-SCUD strikes (150 sorties).

DOD also announces military operations will continue until notified by higher authority of a cease fire.

Naval forces continue to support the air campaign with mine countermeasures and maritime interception operations.

The Navy has lost an additional aircraft. An A-6 sustained major damage while returning from a combat mission. The crew was recovered.

An F-15 on a counter-SCUD mission shot down a hovering Iraqi helo with a laser-guided bomb. This is the 41st Iraqi aircraft downed in air-to-air engagements.

USMC and coalition ground forces continue patrols and deployments. DOD assesses Iraqi troops in the KTO as "immobile", "hunkering down", and "confused" as a result of air campaign.

Eight additional Iraqis surrendered to U.S. forces. DOD reports 60% of EPWs have surrendered willingly. Would-be defectors may be hindered by such obstacles as minefields, execution squads and retaliations against families in Iraq.

SCUD missile fired at Saudi Arabia, breaks up in flight, impacts with no injuries. 65th SCUD fired.

SECNAV activates 993 additional Naval Reservists from 87 units.

16 Feb DOD announces that 76,000 sorties have been flown (2,600 today) as air campaign continues battlefield preparation in the KTO (700 sorties), destruction of Republican Guards, and strikes and restrikes.

Naval forces continue to support air campaign with mine countermeasures and maritime interception operations.

USMC and coalition ground forces continue to reposition to confuse Iraqi reconnaissance and exchange artillery and counter-artillery fire.

The U.S. has lost three additional aircraft. Two A-10s crashed during combat missions, both pilots are missing. An F-16 crashed in a non-combat mishap. The pilot was killed.

Two SCUD missiles were fired at Israel, both landed harmlessly.

17 Feb DOD announces that 78,000 sorties have been flown (2,600 today) with air campaign objectives continuing to focus on battlefield preparation in the KTO (800 sorties), destruction of the Republican Guards (100 sorties), and resupply interdiction.

Naval forces continue supporting the air campaign conducting air strikes, fighter cover, on-call combat search and rescue, mine countermeasures and maritime interception operations.

There have been seven significant engagements along the Kuwait and Iraq border involving USMC and coalition ground forces. In one incident, a U.S. Apache AH-64 mistakenly hit a Bradley Fighting Vehicle and an M-113 armored personnel carrier with a Hellfire missile causing 2 U.S. deaths and 6 injuries.

18 Feb DOD announces that 80,000 sorties have been flown (2,400 today) with the focus remaining on battlefield preparation in the KTO (870), 100 sorties against the Republican Guards, and strikes and restrikes on strategic targets.

Within three hours and ten nautical miles, USS TRIPOLI (LPH-10) and USS PRINCETON (CG-59) struck mines while conducting operations in the northern Arabian Gulf. USS TRIPOLI, the flagship in one of the most extensive mine-sweeping operations since the Korean War, sustained a 16X20 foot hole in forward starboard side below the waterline. Explosion caused minor flooding to six auxiliary spaces, minimized by damage control procedures. Four crewmembers were injured, and the amphibious assault ship remained fully mission capable. USS PRINCETON, underway on half power, sustained damage including a crack in her superstructure. Three crewmen were injured, one seriously, and an EOD team is enroute to assess the mission capability of the Aegis cruiser.

Naval forces continue maritime interception and mine countermeasures operations. EOD team from USS MISSOURI destroys tenth mine.

USMC Cobra helos teamed up with Saudi, Kuwaiti, and USMC observers and engaged six Iraqi armored personnel carriers. Two were destroyed, the other four returned north.

19 Feb DOD announces that 83,000 sorties have been flown (2,800 today) continuing the execution of air campaign objectives. 870 sorties have been flown in the KTO, 100 sorties against the Republican Guard, and 130 sorties against SCUD sites.

A Navy A-6 attacked and destroyed five aircraft hidden in revetments in western Iraq. Other naval forces continued to support the air campaign and conduct maritime interceptions and mine countermeasures. A minefield containing an estimated 22 mines was discovered and cordoned off in the northern Arabian Gulf. To-date, 153 mines discovered. USS BEAUFORT (ATS-2), and Naval Reserve minesweeper escort USS ADROIT (MSO 509) maneuvered through an uncharted mine field to reach USS PRINCETON.

USS TRIPOLI is operating fully mission-capable in the northern Arabian Gulf with damage control efforts stemming minor flooding. USS PRINCETON has a cracked superstructure, a jammed port rudder and leaking port shaft seal. With USS ADROIT at the point marking mines, ship is proceeding to port, towed by USS BEAUFORT, for detailed inspection. DOD says USS TRIPOLI hit a moored or floating mine, USS PRINCETON hit 2 influence mines.

USMC and coalition ground forces engage Iraqis in border skirmishes, probes and reconnaissance and counter-reconnaissance deployments. Marines exchange artillery fire with Iraqis, no casualties.

<u>DOD states for the first time that U.S. ground forces "are now ready to go to combat if the leadership decides that's what they want to do"</u>; asserts that ground troops will face a seriously-attrited although still-capable Iraqi force which "will be defeated in short order if we initiate a ground campaign."

DOD announces that 578 Iraqis have surrendered and are in Turkey's custody. Combined with 1,493 in Saudi Arabian custody, enemy prisoners of war to-date total 2,071.

Citing photographs and imagery evidence, DOD accuses Iraq of faking bomb damage at the Al Basrah Mosque to make it appear that U.S. bombs damaged the religious site.

Iraqi SCUD missile is fired at Israel, impacts with no injuries. 68th SCUD launched to-date.

20 Feb <u>At D+35,</u> DOD announces that 86,000 sorties have been flown (2,900 today), striking and restriking strategic targets, interdicting resupply, battlefield preparation (900 sorties in the KTO), destruction of Republican Guards (100 sorties), and counter-SCUD strikes (100 sorties).

Naval forces conduct air strikes and continue mine counter measures, maritime intercepts, and naval gunfire assignments. **USS AMERICA's Air Anti-Submarine Squadron 32 becomes first S-3 squadron ever to engage and destroy a hostile vessel, an Iraqi gunboat hit by three 500-pound bombs. USS VALLEY FORGE (CG-50) vectored S-3 to target.**

<u>Significant increase in contacts between U.S. forces, including Marines, and</u>

20 Feb (continuing)   Iraqi troops. A U.S. combined arms team engaged Iraqi infantry, tanks and artillery along the border. One U.S. servicemember was killed, seven wounded. In one day-long engagement 100-kilometers above the border, U.S. artillery and tactical aircraft attacked 300 vehicles in revetted positions, destroying 28 tanks and 28 vehicles.

Three additional U.S. aircraft have been lost. An Army helo crashed during combat, killing both pilots. A USMC CH-46 helo and an F-16 were non-combat losses.

No Iraqi aircraft have flown in ten days.

To-date, there have been 55 U.S. fatalities: 17 KIA, 38 Non-Combat Fatalities; 25 WIA; 27 MIA (7 Navy, 2 USMC); 2 Missing; 9 POW (2 Navy, 2 USMC).

U.S. troop strength is over 527,000 (82,000+ Navy, 94,000 USMC), other coalition forces exceed 205,000.

To-date, 219,858 National Guard and Reservists have been called to active duty (17,198 Navy, 28,359 USMC).

U.S. has lost 36 aircraft (28 fixed wing in combat, 5 fixed wing in non-combat mishaps, 8 helicopters lost in non-combat). Coalition has lost 11 aircraft. 42 Iraqi aircraft and 6 helos have been shot down in air-to-air engagements with no U.S. losses. 137 Iraqi aircraft flown to Iran.

21 Feb   **Iraq accepts Soviet-brokered eight-point peace proposal. U.S. expresses "serious" reservations.**

DOD announces that 88,000 sorties have been flown (2,400 today) with air campaign focus on battlefield preparation in the KTO (800+ sorties), destruction of the Republican Guards (100 sorties), interdiction of communication lines, and strikes and restrikes on strategic targets.

Naval forces conduct air strikes and combat operations including mine countermeasures and maritime intercepts. USS SPRUANCE (DD-963) diverts a freighter in the North Red Sea.

Marine Attack Squadron-331 AV-8Bs conducted first of 243 sorties off the flight deck of the USS NASSAU (LHA-4). This is the first time in history that USMC AV-8Bs have conducted combat missions from a Landing Helicopter Assault ship. 256 tons of ordnance on targets.

Two Navy aircraft have been lost in non-combat mishaps. A SH-60 helo's engine failed taking off from USS HALYBURTON (FFG-40), made emergency water landing. 3 crewmen rescued, helo lost. CH-46 helo from USS SEATTLE (AOE-3) crashed in the North Red Sea. 3 crewmen rescued, another is missing.

Firing 50 rounds from off Khafji, USS WISCONSIN destroys command complex. RPVs spotted targets and provided coastline reconnaissance.

Throughout the border region, a continued increase in engagements, reconnaissance and counter-reconnaissance probes between U.S. forces, including Marines, and Iraqi troops involving artillery, attack helos, and tactical air strikes. A USMC unit exchanged small arms and stagger missile fire with Iraqi troops.

21 Feb (continuing) 4 SCUD missiles impacted harmlessly in King Khalid Military City, and coastal Saudi Arabia. 72 SCUDs fired to-date.

DOD has authorized awarding of National Defense Service Medal to all U.S. service personnel on active duty after 2 August 1990 in special recognition of "outstanding performance during OPERATIONs DESERT SHIELD and DESERT STORM."

22 Feb **After consultations with coalition partners, President Bush rejects Iraqi peace plan, declares ground campaign will not be initiated if before 1200 (EST) on 23 February Iraq publicly agrees to: begin large-scale immediate withdrawal; complete withdrawal within one week; within 48 hours, leave Kuwait City and allow prompt return of the legitimate government of Kuwait; withdraw from all prepared defenses along the Saudi-Kuwait and Saudi-Iraq borders, from Bubiyan and Warbah Islands, and from Kuwait's Rumaila oil fields; return troops to Iraqi positions of 1 August 1990; cooperate with International Red Cross and release all POWs and 3rd country civilian prisoners and remains of servicemen within 48 hours; remove all explosives or booby traps and provide data on location and nature of any land or sea mines; cease all combat air fire, aircraft flights over Iraq and Kuwait except for transport aircraft carrying troops out of Kuwait; cease all destructive action against Kuwaiti citizens and property, and release all Kuwaiti detainees. U.S. and coalition agrees not to attack retreating Iraqi forces and will exercise restraint as long as withdrawal proceeds within these guidelines. Any breach of these terms will bring an instant and sharp response from coalition in accordance with U.N. Security Council Resolution 678.**

DOD announces that 91,000+ sorties have been flown (2,700+ today) refocusing on battlefield preparation in the KTO (1,000 sorties), destruction of the Republican Guards (100 sorties), strike and restrike of selected strategic targets, and counter-SCUD (100 sorties).

To-date, USS JOHN F. KENNEDY (CV-67) has launched nearly 80 direct bombing/missile strike missions with over 800 sorties in direct attacks.

Naval forces are conducting strike operations, surface surveillance, combat air patrols, mine countermeasures and maritime intercept operations.

One Marine has been killed and seven wounded by Iraqi artillery fire during three separate border engagements. Marines destroyed 18 Iraqi tanks, 15 vehicles, and captured 87 enemy prisoners of war.

1st Marine Division task forces secretly move 10 miles into Kuwait.

Ground forces are continuing an aggressive and active recon patrolling along and throughout the border area. Marines are also dropping napalm in oil-filled Iraqi trenches to ignite oil, clear a path for assault forces.

<u>An estimated one hundred oil wells have been destroyed in Kuwait, along with oil tanks, export terminals and other installations.</u> President Bush states Iraq has "launched a scorched-earth policy destroying the entire oil production system of Kuwait." DOD states oil wells were rigged with explosives and "systematically and deliberately destroyed".

23 Feb	DOD announces that 94,000 sorties have been flown (2,900 today) re-focusing on battlefield preparation in the KTO (1,200 sorties), destruction of the Republican Guard (100 sorties), attacks and re-attacks on selected strategic targets, counter-SCUD (300 sorties), and interdiction of communications.
	Naval forces are conducting combat air patrols, naval gunfire support, mine countermeasures and maritime intercept operations.
	<u>USS MISSOURI destroyed targets on Faylaka Island, off the coast of Kuwait City.</u>
	Ground forces continue to engage Iraqi forces with artillery, attack helos and tactical aircraft throughout the border area. A Marine patrol engaged 12 Iraqi tanks, destroying four with TOW missile fire. Other tanks fled, were engaged by air and artillery fire. Marines captured 143 enemy prisoners of war. 2100+ EPWs captured to-date.
	DOD announces that 1,685 Iraqi tanks (39% of known inventory), 925 armored vehicles (32% of known inventory) and 1,450 artillery pieces (48% of known inventory) have been destroyed to-date.
	200 of Kuwait's 950 oilwells are burning creating thick smoke, and wellheads, oil facilities and shipping terminals are being destroyed by Iraq.
	DOD reports as many as 10,000 Kuwaitis are being rounded up and summarily executed. Other atrocities are reported including systematic murders of previously-tortured Kuwaitis.
	1 SCUD missile is fired at Saudi Arabia, broke up in flight. A second SCUD was intercepted by U.S. Patriot missiles over Israel.
	Iraq does not comply with deadline (1200 EST) to meet coalition demands. Iraq announced "We will never surrender. A lot of Americans will die."
	At 2000 (EST), President Bush announced he's directed General Norman Schwarzkopf, in conjunction with coalition forces, "to use all forces available, including ground forces, to eject the Iraqi army from Kuwait.... <u>The liberation of Kuwait has entered a final phase.</u>"
	Following President Bush's statement, SECDEF Dick Cheney announced commencement of "large ground offensive." Cheney reports "units are on the move".
24 Feb	CINCCENTCOM announces that forces of the U.S., Saudi Arabia, UK, France, United Arab Emirates, Bahrain, Qatar, Oman, Syria and Kuwait are proceeding in a major ground, naval and air offensive.
	At 0400 (Desert Time), assault elements of 1st Marine Division (1st Battalion, 5th & 7th Marines, supported by 3rd Tank Battalion) and 2nd Marine Division (6th Marines and armor) launched attack, easily breeching Iraq's vaunted defense lines of minefields, barbed wire, bunkers and berms. Marines spearheaded attack, with USA paratroopers, air assault forces, special forces, and ground forces of the UK, Saudi Arabia, Kuwait, Egypt and Syria. Within 9 hours, Marines destroyed numerous Iraqi tanks and bunkers, seized the Burgan oil field and Al Jabbir Airfield, and captured thousands of Iraqi troops.
	Amphibious feint attacks under naval gunfire are launched in Arabian Gulf.

24 Feb (continuing) At 10+ hours into ground offensive, <u>U.S. casualties have been "remarkably light"</u>, offensive is "progressing with dramatic success", no reported use of chemical weapons by Iraq, and more than 5,500 enemy prisoners of war have been captured.

With the exception of one engagement between Marine task force and an Iraqi armor unit, resulting in Iraqi tanks and troops retreating, only light contact with Iraqi forces. Iraqi troops are reported to be retreating, not engaging and surrendering. Some contact with Republican Guard troops.

U.S. Navy, along with UK, Saudi and Kuwaiti naval forces are conducting carrier air, minesweeping, and amphibious missions along the east coast of Kuwait. USS MISSOURI and USS WISCONSIN fired at targets in occupied Kuwait in support of ground offensive.

USMC AV-8B is downed. Pilot, Captain James N. Wilbourn, is missing.

Maritime intercept operations also continue with USS SAMUEL B. ROBERTS recording 100th interception.

Two Iraqi aircraft flew to Iran.

25 Feb <u>At G+2</u>, DOD announces ground offensive continues, is achieving success, operation is running ahead of schedule, and U.S./coalition forces are encountering only light-to-moderate resistance from Iraqi forces. U.S. forces have engaged the Republican Guards with reported success.

<u>Over eighteen thousand enemy prisoners of war have been captured</u>.

In several engagements, Marines attacked an Iraqi force, destroying 50-60 tanks. Reserve Company "B", 4th Tank Battalion alone destroyed/stopped 34 tanks. In joint operations with USA, Marines captured 20 T-62 tanks, 40 armored personnel carriers and 400+ EPWs, and also engaged a 150 armored vehicle formation. Marines fight their way to outskirts of Kuwait City. Coalition forces have destroyed 270+ Iraqi tanks since commencement of ground offensive.

<u>U.S. ground casualties remain extrememly light: 4 KIA, 21 WIA</u>.

Over 97,000 sorties have been flown. Today, Navy, Marine and other aircraft have flown 3,000 sorties. 1,300 sorties have been directed at the KTO, 700 on close air support of ground forces.

USS JOHN F. KENNEDY records 10,000th arrested landing during this deployment, and aircraft of Carrier Airwing Three (embarked) have delivered 3 million+ pounds of ordnance.

A USMC AV-8B and USMC OV-10 are downed. Harrier pilot is rescued. Major Joseph J. Small and Captain David Spellacy are missing.

Naval forces, including USS WISCONSIN and USS MISSOURI, are continuing naval gunfire support and other operations. MISSOURI alone fires 133 rounds or 125 tons of ordnance on targets. Minesweepers cleared additional fire support areas for the battleships.

HMS GLOUCESTER, escorting USS MISSOURI in Arabian Gulf, destroys an incoming Iraqi Silkworm missile aimed at MISSOURI with two Sea Dart missiles. A second Silkworm missile was fired but fell in the gulf. USN aircraft destroyed the missile launch site.

25 Feb (continuing)   Iraqi SCUD missile is fired at Dhahran, Saudi Arabia, breaks up in flight scattering debris over a U.S. housing compound in suburban Al Khobar, killing 27 U.S. Army Reserve personnel, wounding 100 others. A SCUD missile fired at Qatar impacts harmlessly.

DOD reports 600 fires are now burning in the KTO, including 517 oil wellheads.

At 1735 (EST), Baghdad Radio announced that Iraq's "Foreign Minister informed the Soviet ambassador....which constitutes a practical compliance with U.N. Security Council Resolution 660", and Iraqi President Saddam Hussein had ordered his troops to make a fighting withdrawal from occupied Kuwait and return to the positions they occupied before the 2 August 1990 invasion of Kuwait.

The White House responds, stating there is "no evidence to suggest the Iraqi army is withdrawing. In fact, Iraqi units are continuing to fight.... We continue to prosecute the war. We have heard no reason to change that.... And because the announcement from Baghdad referred to the Soviet initiative, Saddam Hussein must personally and publicly accept explicitly all relevant U.N. Security Council resolutions."

Navy implements third "stop loss" action, applying to Navy (Regular and Reserve) cryptologic technician interpreters who are Arabic linguists, and whose effective dates of retirement or separation fall on or after 2 March 1991.

26 Feb   On Baghdad Radio, President Saddam Hussein announced Iraqi troops have begun withdrawing from Kuwait and will be completed today. In the 25-minute speech, Hussein maintained that Kuwait is a part of Iraq which was separated from it in the past, and current circumstances are such that armed forces are forcing us to withdraw.... It should be borne in mind that Constantinople was not conquered in the first battle; the result was achieved in other battles."

President Bush reacted calling Hussein's speech "an outrage. He is not withdrawing. His defeated forces are retreating. He is trying to claim victory in the midst of a rout, and he is not voluntarily giving up Kuwait. He is trying to save the remnants of power and control in the Middle East by every means possible and here, too, Saddam Hussein will fail. Saddam is not interested in peace, but only to regroup and fight another day, and he does not renounce Iraq's claim to Kuwait. To the contrary -- he makes clear that Iraq continues to claim Kuwait.... He still does not accept UN Security Council resolutions or the coalition terms of 22 February, including the release of our POWs, all POWs, third country detainees, and an end to the pathological destruction of Kuwait. The coalition will continue to prosecute the war with undiminished intensity.... It is time for all Iraqi forces to lay down their arms. And that will stop the bloodshed..... **The liberation of Kuwait is close at hand.**"

At G+3, DOD announces that U.S. and coalition forces are engaging, outflanking, out-maneuvering and destroying armed and fully retreating

26 Feb (continuing)   Iraqi troops throughout the KTO as ground offensive continues; 21 Iraqi divisions have been destroyed or rendered combat-ineffective; Marine recon unit is the first U.S. force to enter Kuwait City, re-takes control of U.S. Embassy. Marines comb neighborhoods for Iraqis.

Pockets of resistance remain, including Republican Guard units and at Kuwait International Airport, where Marines engaged Iraqi tanks.

<u>30,000+ enemy prisoners of war have been captured, 400+ tanks destroyed</u>.

Naval forces and Marine amphibious forces operated all along the Kuwaiti coast executing feints to make Iraqis think an amphibious landing was occurring. Marine Light Attack Squadron-269 helos conducted a "wake-up call" on Faylaka Island defenders, while simultaneously, Marine Medium Helicopter Squadrons-263 and 365 and Marine Heavy Helicopter Squadron-461 simulated a heliborne landing on Bubiyan Island. 13th MEU pulled a feint attack south of Kuwait City.

Using Remotely Piloted Vehicles and Marine spotters ashore to zero-in on targets, including artillery, mortar and missile positions, ammunition storage facilities and a Silkworm missile site, battleships <u>USS WISCONSIN and USS MISSOURI have fired more than 1,000 rounds of 16" ammunition in support of ground operations. USS MISSOURI alone fired more than one million pounds of ordnance</u>. USS WISCONSIN's RPVs provided on-site reconnaissance support from 11 nautical miles out for advancing Marines.

<u>DOD announces over 100,000 sorties have been flown.</u> Coalition forces, including the U.S. Navy and Marine Corps, flew 3,000 sorties today. 1,400 sorties have been directed at the KTO, 700 on close air support.

Navy A-6Es of USS RANGER's VA-155 and Marine aircraft bombed Iraqi troops fleeing Kuwait City to Basra in "bumper to bumper" convoys along two multi-lane highways. Numerous tanks, armored vehicles, jeeps, cars, ambulances, and tractor-trailers were destroyed.

<u>U.S. ground casualties are 4 KIA, 21 WIA, 2 MIA.</u>

Overall total: 55 KIA, 155 WIA, 30 MIA, 9 POW.

USS BIDDLE, assisted by Spanish vessel, diverts freighter in North Red Sea.

27 Feb   <u>At D+42/G+4</u>, CINCCENTCOM announces U.S. and coalition forces engaged in a climatic "classic tank battle", supported by attack aircraft, with approximately 3 divisions of Republican Guard forces in Iraq near Euphrates Valley. These remnants of Iraq's forces were "boxed in" by a "solid wall" of U.S. forces on their eastern flank, and U.S. and coalition forces, including U.S. Marines, on their southernn flank. Battle ended with loss of 200 Iraqi tanks, 50 armored vehicles and 20 artillery pieces.

<u>29 Iraqi divisions have been destroyed or rendered combat-ineffective.</u>

<u>Over fifty thousand enemy prisoners of war have been captured.</u> (48,000+ between 24 - 27 February)

<u>U.S. casualties are 28 KIA, 89 WIA, 5 MIA since start of ground offensive.</u>

Overall total: 79 KIA, 213 WIA, 35 MIA, 9 POW.

To-date, 3,008 Iraqi tanks (4,230 initial inventory), 1,856 armored vehicles

27 Feb (continuing) (2,870 initial inventory), and 2,140 artillery pieces (3,110 initial inventory) have been destroyed.

General Norman Schwarzkopf details battle plan of OPERATION DESERT STORM. Outnumbered 2-1, with fewer tanks/artillery, facing a heavily-dug in force, preliminary tactics were devised consisting of:

* Initial alignment of ground forces - Deliberately deployed forces near King Khalid Military City directly aligned on Iraqi positions to present frontal defensive line.
* Naval threat - Continual naval and Marine amphibious force presence in Arabian Gulf served as a major deterrent by forcing Iraq to keep thousands of troops deployed along the coastline to defend against a possible large-scale amphibious landing. Conducted a number of amphibious rehearsals, including Operation Imminent Thunder, forcing Iraq to concentrate forces to defend against landing or raids.
* Air campaign - Utilized U.S. Navy (carrier-based), U.S. Marine and U.S. and coalition ground air forces to isolate KTO, destroyed bridges and supply lines running north or south in Iraq, interdicted reinforcement and resupply, bombed troops to weaken and attrite number (front line Iraqi troops attritted to 50% or below, second level attritted to 50-75%), destroyed Iraqi Air Force, and neutralized Iraqi reconnaissance capability. Once blinded, allowed U.S./coalition forces to shift to the west ("the Hail Mary play") without opposition or counter-attack.
* Logistics - Troops flanking westward were equipped with fuel, ammo, spare parts, water and food to be self-sustained for 60 days.
* Special operations - Special forces were inserted into Iraq providing strategic reconnaissance/targeting.

After G-Day, the next two days, simultaneous sea and ground operations ensued: special forces conducted mine countermeasures in Arabian Gulf, threatened coastal flanks with amphibious operations; carrier and ground-based air strikes and restrikes prevented bridge rebuilding; U.S. and coalition forces deployed to block a Republican Guard avenue of egress out of Kuwait; set up a flanking guard position preventing attack from any force; with naval gunfire support, began attacks to the east to engage remnants of Republican Guard tank units; 1st Marine Division engaged and seized Kuwaiti International Airport; 2nd Marine Division encircled and cut off avenue of egress out of Kuwait City.

<u>General Schwarzkopf declares massive destruction of Iraqi army; states Iraq is no longer a regional military threat, "unless someone chooses to rearm them in the future."</u>

At 2100 (EST), President Bush addresses the nation, declares <u>"Kuwait is liberated. Iraq's army is defeated."</u> The President announces that at 2400 (EST), "exactly 100 hours since ground operations commenced and six weeks since the start of Operation Desert Storm, all U.S. and coalition forces will suspend further offensive combat operations."

Terms of the cease fire are:

27 Feb (continuing)
- Immediate release of all coalition POWs, third-country nationals and the remains of all who have fallen.
- Iraq must release all Kuwaiti detainees.
- Iraq must inform Kuwait of the location and nature of all land/sea mines.
- Iraq must comply fully with all relevant U.N. Security Council resolutions.

After United Nations formally requests compliance, Iraq delivers letter to U.N. stating intention to comply with cease-fire terms.

U.S. and coalition air strikes and sporadic ground attacks continued until 2400 (EST) deadline. 103,000 sorties have been flown (3,000 today) focusing on battlefield air interdiction and close air support.

<u>Navy and Marine Corps pilots have flown over 26,000 combat sorties to-date.</u>

USMC AV-8B is downed. Pilot, Captain Reginald Underwood, is killed.

While off Kuwaiti coast, to assist ground forces to secure and enter Kuwait City, USS WISCONSIN's Remotely Piloted Vehicle detects 2 small boats fleeing Faylaka Island. Navy A-6s were called in and destroyed the boats, believed to be carrying Iraqi secret police.

USS AVENGER (MCM-1) with Explosive Ordnance Disposal Mobile Unit 6, Det. 12 finds, identifies and neutralizes a live bottom influence mine in combat. Considered invisible to sonar, this is a naval first.

Maritime intercept operations continue with over 7,500 merchants challenged, over 940 ships boarded, and 47 diverted.

SECNAV activates 1,959 additional Naval Reservists from 87 units.

28 Feb

<u>DOD announces temporary cease fire is holding with U.S. and coalition forces in defensive positions,</u> conducting combat air patrols and reconnaissance operations. However, there have been several incidents of Iraqi troops firing on U.S./coalition forces, attributed to isolated Iraqis cut off from communications unaware of ceasefire.

Over 110,000 sorties have been flown by U.S. and coalition forces.

<u>DOD reports 42 Iraqi divisions have been destroyed or rendered combat-ineffective.</u> An additional division of Iraqi troops has been able to avoid capture or destruction, and flee to safety.

USS NIMITZ (CV-68) and USS FORRESTAL (CV-59) Carrier Battle Groups will depart on 5 and 7 March 1991 for overseas deployment. The battle groups will provide operational and maintenance flexibility for carrier battle groups in support of OPERATION DESERT STORM and ensure maximum readiness and deployment stability of naval forces in that area.

Iraq agrees to meeting to work out cease-fire issues.

1 March

DOD announces cease-fire remains in effect, only one minor violation. U.S./coalition forces remain on alert, in strong defensive positions.

DOD reports Marines captured, destroyed, or damaged, 1,060 tanks, 608 armored personnel carriers, 432 artillery pieces, five FROG launchers and 2 SCUD transporter erector launchers during 100 hours of offensive combat. Marine sweeps also uncovered a bunker containing chemical artillery shells.

1 March (continuing) Navy, Marine and other aircraft are conducting defensive, counter-air, reconnaissance, SCUD reaction, and resupply operations.

Naval forces are conducting maritime interception and minesweeping operations. 125 mines have been destroyed to-date.

Hundreds of Iraqi soldiers waving white flags on Faylaka Island surrendered to the battleship USS MISSOURI's Remotely Piloted Vehicle flying overhead after their trenchline was bombarded.

<u>The U.S., British, French and Canadian Embassies are open in Kuwait City</u> and fully functioning. Kuwaiti International Airport is operational.

2 March

By 11-1 vote, U.N. Security Council approves Resolution 686, outlining conditions Iraq must meet prior to a formal cease-fire. Conditions include release of all POWs, release of all Kuwaiti hostages, provide locations of all mines in Kuwait, and compliance with all previous U.N. resolutions.

DOD announces cease-fire remains in effect. U.S./coalition forces remain on alert in defensive positions.

Navy, Marine and other aircraft are flying reconnaissance, resupply and combat air patrol missions.

Naval forces are conducting continuing maritime interception and minesweeping operations.

USS WISCONSIN's RPV gathered intelligence on Faylaka Island's defenses prior to evacuation of Iraqi EPWs.

Marine LAV strikes a land mine, killing one Marine, wounding three others. Mine-clearing operations continue.

Over a thousand additional enemy prisoners of war surrender at Talil Airfield. To-date, over 50,000 EPWs in custody.

3 March

CINCCENTCOM General Norman Schwarzkopf and Joint Forces Commander General Prince Khalid bin Sultan bin Abdul Aziz meet 7 Iraqi military officials, led by Deputy Chief of Staff LTGeneral Sultan Hasheem Ahmad, at Safwan Airfield in occupied Iraq. After two hour meeting, Iraqi military formally accepted all demands for a permanent cease-fire. Iraq agrees to immediate release of a small number of POWs as a token of good faith, and to safety measures to ensure that military forces do not accidentally engage each other with hostile fire.

DOD announces defensive air reconnaissance and combat air patrol operations continue.

Naval forces continue defensive counter-air, reconnaissance, maritime interception and minesweeping operations.

Navy CH-46 helos with loudspeakers rounded-up 1405 surrendering Iraqi troops on Faylaka Island. EPWs were ferried by helo to the USS OGDEN (LPD-5) for further transport to Saudi EPW facilities.

62,000+ EPWs in custody to-date.

Twenty Iraqi aircraft, including F-1s, MIG-21s, and 8 helos, were captured in bunkers at Talil Airfield.

4 March   Iraq releases ten Prisoners of War (6 Americans, 3 of whom were designated MIA), including Navy LT Jeffrey Zaun, LT Robert Wetzel, and LT Lawrence Slade. No Marines repatriated. POWs were turned over to U.S. officials by the International Committee of the Red Cross near the Jordanian border station of Ruwayshid, then transferred to the hospital ship USNS MERCY (T-AH 19) for medical treatment.

DOD announces establishment of a demarcation zone in southern Iraq between U.S./coalition forces and Iraqi forces to prevent engagements between forces.

Iraqis have provided information on location of land and sea mines.

Naval forces are conducting defensive counter-air, mine removal, reconnaissance, and maritime interception operations.

Air reconnaissance operations continue, including over Baghdad.

DOD revises U.S. casualty data: 98 KIA, 308 WIA, 35 MIA, 6 POW (reflects release of 6 Americans).

Enemy prisoners of war total 63,000+ in Saudia Arabia, 37,000 in U.S. facilities, 3,000+ in Turkey.

6,661 Naval Reservists are currently serving in the Arabian Gulf theater.

5 March   Iraq releases thirty five Prisoners of War (15 Americans, 9 of whom were designated MIA) to the International Red Cross, including USMC Lieutenant Colonel Clifford Acree, Chief Warrant Officer Guy Hunter, Jr., Captain Michael Berryman, Captain Russell Sanborn, and Major Joseph Small III. No Navy personnel released.

DOD announces minor repositioning of forces in the KTO, continued defensive posture.

Naval forces are conducting counter-air, reconnaissance, maritime interception operations and mine removal. To-date, 140 mines destroyed.

USS SAMUEL B. ROBERTS diverts freighter in N. Red Sea.

Over 114,000 sorties have been flown by U.S. and coalition forces.

DOD revises U.S. casualty data: 115 KIA, 65 Non-Combat Fatalities, 330 WIA, 37 MIA, 6 POW.

Based on the end of hostilities with Iraq, USS FORRESTAL (CV-59) Carrier Battle Group will not deploy on March 7 as previously announced. The eight ships and embarked air wing will be ready to deploy should circumstances warrant.

Sealift update: 247 ships in support, 211 under MSC operational control; 450 offloads completed (18.3 billion pounds of fuel and equipment involving 2,000+ tanks, 2,200 armored vehicles, 1,000 assorted helos, aircraft, trucks and other combat equipment for the Marines and Air Force, hundreds of self-propelled Howitzers for the Army, and equipment for three Navy Fleet Hospitals).

6 March   At D+49, in a prisoner exchange, 35 released Prisoners of War transit from Baghdad to Riyadh, 294 Iraqi Enemy Prisoners of War transit to Baghdad. U.S. POWs are transferred to USNS MERCY for medical treatment.

6 March (continuing)   DOD announces cease-fire is holding, no incidents. Information exchange on location of land and sea mines continues. Mine clearing and equipment-collecting sweeps continue. <u>To-date, 3,700 Iraqi tanks, 2,400+ armored personnel carriers, and 2,600+ artillery pieces have been destroyed, damaged or captured.</u>

Elements of 1st Marine Division withdraw from Kuwait to defensive positions in Saudi Arabia, 2d Marine Division shifts into 1st Marine Division's former positions.

Naval forces continue to conduct defensive counter-air operations to protect U.S. fleet, combat air patrols, maritime interceptions and minesweeping to clear Al Ashwaba and other mined Kuwaiti ports. USS NEW ORLEANS (LPH 11), an embarked mine countermeasures squadron and four mine countermeasures ships, are leading minesweeping activities, aided by ships from UK, Holland and Belgium.

<u>USS WISCONSIN</u> redeploys for home.

Marine AH-1J Cobra helo is lost in a non-combat mishap. Both crewmembers were injured. U.S. aircraft losses to-date: 57 (35 fixed-wing-27 in combat, 8 in non-combat-and 22 helos-5 in combat, 17 in non-combat). To-date, 116,000+ sorties have been flown.

DOD revises U.S. casualty data: <u>115 KIA, 2 (Died from combat wounds), 78 Non-combat fatalities, 338 WIA, 26 MIA (5 Navy, 2 USMC), 0 POW.</u>

President Bush addresses joint session of Congress: "I can report to the nation: Aggression is defeated. The war is over."

<u>DOD announces list of units in initial redeployment to home stations:</u>

U. S. NAVY

Medical staff (USNS MERCY, USNS COMFORT, Fleet Hospital Five (1,742 pers) - to arrive in CONUS 8 March at various destinations via Norfolk, Travis/Andrews AFB.
Naval Special Warfare Trng Grp 1 (115 pers) - to NAB Coronado.
Naval Beach Group ONE (210 pers) - to NAS North Island.
Amphibious Medical Support Unit (95 pers) - to Philadelphia.
303 Security Unit (15 pers) - to Andrews AFB.

U.S. MARINE CORPS

7th Marine Expeditionary Brigade (100 pers) - MCB, 29 Palms.
1st Battalion, 5th Marines (900 pers) - MCB, Camp Pendleton.
Regimental Combat Team 7 Det B (750 pers) - MCB, 29 Palms.
Surveillance, Recon Intell Grp 7 (150 pers) - MCB, Camp Pendleton.
Marine Air Grp 70 (150 pers) - MCB, Camp Pendleton.
Brigade Svc Support Grp7 Det A (200 pers) - MCB, Camp Pendleton.
Brigade Svc Support Grp 7 Det B (50 pers) - MCB, Camp Pendleton.
3rd Battalion, 3rd Marines (600 pers) - MCAS, Kaneohe Bay.

7 March   Naval forces execute on-going defensive counter-air and other operations.
<u>Navy ships in the region:</u> Six aircraft carriers (SARATOGA, JOHN . F. KENNEDY, THEODORE ROOSEVELT, MIDWAY, RANGER and AMERICA; two battleships (WISCONSIN - deploying enroute home - and MISSOURI); two command ships (BLUE RIDGE AND

7 March (continuing)	LASALLE); twelve cruisers; eleven destroyers; ten frigates; four mine warfare ships; thirty-one amphibious ships; thirty-two auxiliaries. Additionally, two hospital ships (MERCY and COMFORT) are in the region and other military sealift ships. USS FORRESTAL Battle Group is enroute to the region.
	Maritime interception operations continue with 7,766 merchants challenged, 945 ships boarded, 48 diverted. The Navy has conducted 547 of the boardings. USS MOOSBRUGGER diverts freighter in N. Red Sea.
	Navy ships are also assisting commercial vessels navigate through northern Arabian Gulf waters made potentially dangerous by mines.
8 March	Naval forces continue conducting defensive counter-air, surface surveillance, maritime interceptions and minesweeping operations. After two weeks of non-stop minesweeping operations, the port of Kuwait City is safe enough to reopen.
	The Federal Republic of Germany is sending minesweepers to the Arabian Gulf to assist the Navy in clearing Iraqi mines from Kuwaiti waters.
	Marine ground forces continue to redeploy to defensive positions.
	Two Marine F/A-18 jets collided in mid-air over Saudi Arabia without injury to either pilot. Both pilots ejected and landed safely by parachute.
	First Navy personnel from Arabian Gulf theater arrive in CONUS.
	Due to changes in operational requirements, the activation of 321 Marine Reservists has been cancelled.
9 March	Naval forces continue defensive counter-air, surface surveillance, maritime interceptions and minesweeping operations.
	Marine ground forces continue retrograde to defensive positions.
	First USMC personnel from Arabian Gulf theater arrive in CONUS.
10 March	<u>**COMUSNAVCENT declares R-Day**</u>, the initial surge force reduction of naval forces commencing in accordance with the CINCCENT redeployment plan.
	Naval forces continue defensive counter-air, surface surveillance, maritime interceptions and minesweeping operations.
	Marine ground forces continue retrograde to defensive positions.
	21 repatriated American POWs, including LT Jeffrey Zaun, LT Robert Wetzel, LT Randolph Slade (Navy), LTCOL Cliff Acree, Captain Michael Berryman, CWO Guy Hunter, Jr., Captain Russell Sanborn, and Major Joseph Small (USMC), arrive in CONUS.
11 March	<u>USS SARATOGA and USS MIDWAY Carrier Battle Groups commence redeployments to their respective homeports.</u> USS SARATOGA transits the Suez Canal enroute Mayport, Florida; USS MIDWAY departs the Arabian Gulf enroute Yokosuka, Japan.
	Naval forces continue defensive counter-air, combat air patrols, surface surveillance, maritime interceptions and minesweeping operations.

11 March (continuing) With helo from USS BIDDLE providing air cover, the 1,000th boarding of a freighter is completed in the N. Red Sea. The Cypriot-flagged DIMIS is allowed to proceed after inspection of cargo.

Marine ground forces continue retrograde to defensive positions.

Status of Marine Captain Reginald C. Underwood, missing since 24 February combat downing of his AV-8B, changed to Killed In Action.

DOD revises U.S. casualty data: 121 KIA, 2 (Died from combat wounds), 81 Non-combat fatalities, 23 MIA (5 Navy, 1 USMC), 0 POW.

USNS MERCY (T-AH 19) ordered to stand down. At end of 210-day deployment, hospital ship with crew of 1,200, including 265 Naval Reservists, has treated 6,050+ outpatients from sea and land-based units, admitted 650+ patients, performed 290+ surgeries, created 900 pairs of glasses, filled 16,000 prescriptions, took 5,500+ x-rays, and conducted 21,000 laboratory procedures. Dental staff treated 2,000+ patients; physical therapy department treated 2,000 patients. 1,300+ helos landed on the ship.

USNS COMFORT (T-AH 20) ordered to stand down. At end of seven month deployment, hospital ship with crew of 1,200, admitted 700+ patients and treated 8,000+ patients. With 750 personnel redeployed to CONUS, skelton crew of 380 got underway from Bahrain anchorage at 1314 (EST) as part of the 15-ship Atlantic Amphibious Task Force led by USS NASSAU (LHA 4).

Fleet Hospitals Five and Six ordered to stand down. At end of deployment, Fleet Hospital Five has treated more than 32,000 patients, including all coalition forces, ex-patriots, EPWs and refugees, admitted 4,250 patients, performed 600 surgeries, treated 3,100+ dental patients, and filled 22,000 perscriptions.

12 March DOD announces cease fire is holding, troop demobilization continues. To-date, 16,000 troops have returned home (approximately 4,000 Navy, 4,000 USMC).

USS JOHN F. KENNEDY (CV-67), accompanied by USS SAN JACINTO, USS MISSISSIPPI, USS SAMUEL B. ROBERTS USS PREBLE, USS MOOSBRUGGER and USS THOMAS S. GATES, transits the Suez Canal enroute to the Mediterranean.

There are 73 Navy ships in the Arabian Gulf, Gulf of Oman and Northern Arabian Sea, 19 Navy ships in the Red Sea, and 15 Navy ships in the Mediterranean.

Command ship USS LASALLE, HMS CATTISTOCK and two tankers reopen major Kuwaiti port of Ash Shuaybah, steamed through a channel cleared of mines by a hundred U.S. and coalition divers, bringing in potable water and supplies to assist the reconstruction of Kuwait. **First U.S. Navy warship to make port visit to newly-liberated Kuwait.**

Naval forces continue on-going counter air-defensive and other operations.

Marine ground forces continue retrograde to defensive positions.

DOD revises U.S. casualty data: 126 KIA, 2 (Died from combat wounds), 82 Non-combat fatalities, 357 WIA, 22 MIA (5 Navy, 0 USMC), 0 POW).

12 March (continuing) Status of Marine Captain David M. Spellacy, missing since 25 February combat downing of his OV-10, changed to Killed in Action.

President Bush proclaims 5-7 April as "National Days of Thanksgiving" for victory over Iraq.

13 March Naval forces continue on-going counter air-defensive and other operations.

Marine ground forces continue holding defensive positions.

DOD reports over 514,000 U.S. personnel are in the theater (74,000+ Navy, 89,500+ Marines). To-date, 26,000 personnel have redeployed to the U.S. (11,000 Navy, 4,500 Marines).

<u>DOD revises U.S. casualty data: 125 KIA, 2 (Died from combat wounds), 93 Non-combat fatalities, 357 WIA, 21 MIA (4 Navy, 0 USMC), 0 POW.</u>

Iraq returns the remains of 12 coalition dead (4 U.S., 8 UK).

Status of Navy LT William T. Costen, missing since 18 January combat downing of his A-6E, changed to Killed in Action.

President Bush signs Executive Order establishing a Southwest Asia Service Medal for outstanding performance of members of the U.S. Armed Forces who deployed to Southwest Asia or in surrounding contiguous waters or air space on or after 2 August 1990 and participated in Operations DESERT SHIELD and DESERT STORM.

14 March <u>At D+56</u>, Naval forces continue on-going counter air-defensive and other operations.

Marine ground forces maintain defensive positions.

DOD announces 37,000+ U.S. troops (18,000 Navy, 5,500 USMC) have redeployed. 503,000+ (67,000+ Navy, 88,500+ USMC) remain in theater.

There are 64 Navy ships in the Arabian Gulf, Gulf of Oman and Northern Arabian Sea, 9 Navy ships in the Red Sea, and 22 Navy ships in the Mediterranean.

USS MOOSBRUGGER (DD-980) detaches from redeploying USS JOHN F. KENNEDY battle group to undergo required maintenance in the Mediterranean.

To-date, 7,954 merchants have been intercepted, 1,003 boardings, and 51 diversions. The Navy has conducted 555 boardings.

The Emir of Kuwait returns from exile.

15 March Naval forces continue counter air-defensive, combat air patrol and mine-sweeping operations. 166 mines destroyed to-date.

Marine forces redeploy and maintain defensive positions.

DOD announces 51,000+ U.S. personnel (27,000 Navy, 6,500 USMC) have redeployed. 489,000+ (58,000+ Navy, 87,500+ USMC) remain in theater. Total coalition forces in theater total 694,000+.

Air Anti-Submarine Squadron 30 departs USS JOHN F. KENNEDY.

<u>DOD revises U.S. casualty data: 125 KIA, 2 (Died from combat wounds), 95 Non-combat fatalities, 357 WIA, 21 MIA (4 Navy, 0 USMC), 0 POW.</u>

16 March	Naval forces continue counter air-defensive, combat air patrols and minesweeping operations. Marine forces maintain defensive positions. 81 crewmembers of USS LEADER (MSO 490), whose minesweeping efforts enabled the battleships USS MISSOURI and USS WISCONSIN to safely transit mine-infested waters for close-in gunfire support, return from six-month deployment in the Arabian Gulf to NAVBASE Charleston SC. Ship remains overseas, manned by crew of USS EXULTANT, as part of crew rotation policy for minesweepers.
17 March	Naval forces continue counter air-defensive, combat air patrols and minesweeping operations. Marine ground forces hold defensive positions. U.S./coalition military officials meet with 10 Iraqi military officers at Safwan Airfield, rejects Iraqi request to move aircraft around the country. Iraq warned that any Iraqi warplanes that fly would be shot down. Crew of USS TRIPOLI (LPH-10) awarded Combat Action Ribbon for being endangered by enemy mine attack on 18 February. USS TRIPOLI remains in Bahrain port undergoing repairs.
18 March	Naval forces continue counter air-defensive, combat air patrols and minesweeping operations. USS NORMANDY (CG-60) diverts a freighter in the N. Red Sea, and assists USS WILLIAM V. PRATT (DDG-44) with diversion of a second freighter in the North Red Sea. Marine ground forces hold defensive positions. DOD reports over 468,000 U.S. personnel are in the theater (56,000+ Navy, 74,500 USMC). To-date, 71,500 + personnel have redeployed to the U.S. (29,000 Navy, 19,500 USMC). **USS SYLVANIA (AFS-2) arrives in Norfolk VA homeport, the first return of a ship supporting OPERATION DESERT STORM.** During seven-month deployment, the combat stores ship delivered 19,000+ pallets of cargo (equaling 20,500 tons of supplies), answered 30,000+ requisitions, and delivered spare parts and food sustaining 35,000+ sailors aboard 150 ships. Helicopter Combat Support Squadron Six (HC 6) Det. Four, embarked on USS SYLVANIA, provided vertical replenishment service, logging 700+ accident-free hours, transferring 5,000 tons of supplies, 915 passengers, 31,000 pounds of mail, and 10 emergency medevacs.
19 March	Naval forces continue counter air-defensive, combat air patrols and minesweeping operations. Elements of 2d Marine Division hold defensive positions in Kuwait. DOD reports majority of 1st Marine Division is preparing to redeploy. DOD reports over 461,500 U.S. personnel are in the theater (56,000+ Navy, 72,500+ USMC). To-date, 78,500+ personnel have rededployed to the U.S. (29,000 Navy, 21,500 USMC).

19 March (continuing) DOD announces remains of 4 U.S. personnel returned 13 March by Iraq have been identified. They include Navy LT W. Thompson Costen and LT Charles J. Turner.

DOD revises U.S. casualty data: 124 KIA, 2 (Died from combat wounds), 97 Non-combat fatalities, 357 WIA, 21 MIA (4 Navy, 0 USMC), 0 POW.

A USMC AV-8B conducting night training operations from the USS NASSAU (LHA-4) crashed into the Red Sea. The uninjured pilot was rescued by a small boat from the USS MANITOWOC (LST-1180).

20 March   One of a flight of two Iraqi SU-22 Fitter jets was shot down, near Takrit, Iraq. The other aircraft landed on its own after the engagement. DOD states the Iraqi attempt to fly these two fighter aircraft is a violation of terms agreed upon with Iraqi military officials during the 3 March military-to-military talks at Safwan.

Naval forces continue counter air-defensive, combat air patrols and minesweeping operations.

Marine ground forces hold defensive positions.

DOD reports over 454,500 U.S. personnel are in the theater (55,500+ Navy, 70,500+ USMC). To-date, 85,500+ personnel have redeployed to the U.S. (29,500 Navy, 23,500 USMC).

Navy modifies "stop loss" policy allowing medical personnel and CTI Arabic linguists involuntarily retained to be separated or retired on 1 April 1991, but not later than 1 June 1991.

U.S. Marine Corps demobilizes 1,424 Reservists.

21 March   At D+63, Naval forces continue counter air-defensive, combat air patrols, minesweeping and maritime interception operations. 8,122 intercepts, 1,032 boardings and 52 ships diverted to-date.

There are 51 Navy ships in the Arabian Gulf, Gulf of Oman and Northern Arabian Sea, 22 Navy ships in the Red Sea, and 13 Navy ships in the Mediterranean.

USNS MERCY departs Arabian Gulf, enroute Oakland homeport.

Marine ground forces hold defensive positions.

DOD reports over 450,000 U.S. personnel are in the theater (55,500+ Navy, 70,000+ USMC). To-date, 90,000+ personnel have redeployed to the U.S. (29,500 Navy, 24,000 USMC).

Approximately 200 Naval Reservists have been demobilized to-date.

DOD revises U.S. casualty data: 124 KIA, 2 (Died from combat wounds), 102 Non-combat fatalities, 357 WIA, 21 MIA (4 Navy, 0 USMC), 0 POW.

Navy Cargo Handling and Port Group and Naval Reserve Cargo Training Battalion arrives at Naval Supply Center, Williamsburg VA. During seven month deployment, the cargo handlers offloaded and backloaded over 75 Maritime Prepostioning Ships and breakbulk ships with supplies ranging from ammunition to heavy vehicles. The "combat stevedores" offloaded one ship every three days.

22 March An Iraqi SU-22 Fitter, one of a flight of two aircraft, was shot down near Kirkuk. The second aircraft, a PC-7 propeller-driven, single engine trainer was not engaged, but the pilot ejected after the Fitter was shot down. This is the second breach of agreed terms.

Naval forces continue counter air-defensive, combat air patrols, minesweeping and maritime interception operations.

Marine ground forces hold defensive positions.

DOD reports over 445,000 U.S. personnel are in the theater (55,500+ Navy, 67,500+ USMC). To-date, 95,000+ personnel have redeployed to the U.S. (29,500 Navy, 26,500 USMC).

Fast Sealift Ship USNS BELLATRIX departs Saudi Arabia enroute to Savannah GA with first cargo on-load of equipment returning to CONUS. Load consists primarily of equipment from U.S. Army's 24th (Mechanized) Infantry Division. Eight other MSC ships are loaded out, scheduled to depart.

USS MACDONOUGH (DDG-39) and USS NICHOLAS (FFG-47) arrives at NAVBASE Charleston SC homeport, the first Navy surface combatants to return to CONUS. During six-month deployment to the Arabian Gulf, both ships enforced United Nations resolutions by challenging over 600 commercial ships and boarding many ships in search of contraband; escorted and protected numerous ships and planes returning from raids in Iraq and Kuwait; and conducted at-sea rescues of downed pilots. As the northern-most ship in the coalition task force, USS NICHOLAS and embarked helos conducted the first surface attack on Iraqi anti-aircraft sites and captured the first enemy prisoners of war.

Helicopter Anti-Submarine Squadron (Light) 44, Detachment Eight, arrives at NAVSTA Mayport FL homeport. During six-month embark aboard USS NICHOLAS, squadron saw considerable action against Iraqi forces and executed the first helicopter missile attack, captured the first enemy prisoners of war, rescued a downed pilot in the Arabian Gulf, discovered/destroyed mines, and conducted hundreds of merchant vessel identifications and/or challenges enforcing United Nations trade sanctions.

23 March Naval forces continue counter air-defensive, combat air patrols, minesweeping and maritime interception operations.

Marine ground forces hold defensive positions.

USS YELLOWSTONE (AD-41) arrives at NAVBASE Pearl Harbor homeport. During eight-month deployment to the Mediterranean and Red Seas, the destroyer tender provided repair, supply, logistics and personnel support including the completion of over 10,000 repair jobs on 30 U.S. and coalition ships, as well as the first time transportation of aircraft and transferring missiles.

24 March Naval forces continue counter air-defensive, combat air patrols, minesweeping and maritime interceptions operations.
USS MISSOURI, USS SACRAMENTO, and USS FORD redeploy.
Navy's Atlantic Fleet Amphibious Task Force -- USS NASSAU, USS IWO JIMA, USS GUAM, USS SHREVEPORT, USS TRENTON, USS RALEIGH, USS SAGINAW, USS LA MOURE COUNTY, USS MANITOWOC, USS SPARTANBURG, USS PORTLAND, USS PENSACOLA and USS GUNSTON HALL -- transits the Suez Canal enroute CONUS. USS COMFORT accompanies task force.
Marine ground forces hold defensive positions.
LT Mark D. Jackson, NR MSCO Mideast 106 Norfolk, dies of injuries sustained in an automobile accident in Dhahran, Saudi Arabia. **First death of a Naval Reservist recalled to active duty in OPERATION DESERT STORM.**
Elements of Reserve Naval Mobile Construction Battalion 23 return to CONUS. During a four-month deployment, battalion detachments were assigned to sites in Guam, Okinawa, Korea, Japan, Midway Island, and Adak, Alaska and continued and completed construction projects started by active duty Naval Mobile Construction Battalions 7 and 40, who had been redeployed to then OPERATION DESERT SHIELD. The remainder of the battalion remains deployed in Guam and outlying areas to continue work on critical projects.

25 March Naval forces continue counter air-defensive, combat air patrols, maritime interception and minesweeping operations.
While actively sweeping for mines in the Arabian Gulf, USS LEADER (MSO-490) deployed its magnetic acoustic influence combination sweep which detonated a suspected mine approximately 600 yards behind the ship. No injuries, crankshaft cracked in the #1 main propulsion unit. Ship continued mission, then proceeded to Bahrain shipyard under its own power for scheduled maintenance.
Marine ground forces hold defensive positions.
USS WORDEN (CG-18) arrives at NAVBASE Pearl Harbor homeport. During a one-month deployment in the Arabian Gulf, the guided missile cruiser provided air defense coverage for three carrier battle groups and coalition ships, identifying over 15,000 aircraft returning from strike missions and challenging and identifying over 50 vessels transiting the Iranian coast.

26 March Naval forces continue counter air-defensive, combat air patrols, minesweeping, and maritime interceptions operations.
To-date, 8,379 merchants have been challenged, 1,055 boarded, and 53 diverted. The Navy has conducted 571 boardings.
There are 48 Navy ships in the Arabian Gulf, Gulf of Oman, and Northern Arabian Sea, 8 Navy ships in the Red Sea, and 28 Navy ships in the Mediterranean.
Marine ground forces hold defensive positions.

26 March (continuing) DOD reports over 411,500 U.S. personnel are in the theater (43,000+ Navy, 60,500+ USMC). To-date, 128,500 personnel have redeployed to the U.S. (42,000 Navy, 33,500 USMC)
To-date, 393 Naval Reservists have been demobilized.
<u>DOD revises U.S. casualty data: 124 KIA, 2 (Died from combat wounds), 107 Non-combat fatalities, 357 WIA, 21 MIA (4 Navy, 0 USMC), 0 POW.</u>

27 March Naval forces continue counter air-defensive, combat air patrols, mine sweeping, and maritime interceptions operations.
USS HALYBURTON (FFG-40) diverts a freighter in the N. Red Sea.
Marine ground forces hold defensive positions.
Fast Sealift Ship USNS ALTAIR departs Saudi Arabia for CONUS with equipment. 23 other MSC ships are loaded out and underway.
The first Navy air combatants to return to CONUS, Carrier Air Wing 3 and Carrier Air Wing 17, embarked on USS KENNEDY and USS SARATOGA (respectively), arrive at homeports:

NAS, Oceana VA	Attack Squadron 75
	Fighter Squadron 14
	Fighter Squadron 32
NAS, Norfolk VA	Carrier Airborne Early Warning Squadron 126
NAS, Cecil Field FL	Attack Squadron 46
	Attack Squadron 72

Carrier Air Wing 3 flew more than 11,000 sorties, totalling nearly 33,000 flight hours, during the seven and a half-month deployment. Squadrons flew nearly 3,000 combat missions totalling 11,000+ combat hours, and delivered 3.5 million pounds of ordnance on enemy targets in Iraq and Kuwait. The air wing had no aircraft or personnel losses during combat operations.

NAS, Oceana VA	Attack Squadron 35
	Fighter Squadron 74
	Fighter Squadron 103
NAS, Norfolk VA	Carrier Airborne Early Warning Squadron 125
NAS, Cecil Field FL	Strike Fighter Squadron 81
	Strike Fighter Squadron 83

Carrier Air Wing 17 flew 12,500 sorties and 33,500 flight hours during the nearly eight-month deployment. Squadrons flew 2,694 combat missions and delivered 4,047,000 pounds of ordnance on enemy targets. The air wing scored the Navy's only air-to-air enemy aircraft kills of the conflict, but had three of its aircraft shot down.

28 March <u>At D+70</u>, naval forces continue counter air-defensive, combat air patrols, minesweeping, and maritime interception operations.
USS WILLIAM V. PRATT (DDG-44) diverts a freighter in the N. Red Sea.
Marine ground forces hold defensive positions.

28 March (continuing) The first Navy carrier battle groups to return to CONUS, USS JOHN F. KENNEDY and USS SARATOGA, arrive at homeports:

Norfolk VA:

USS JOHN F. KENNEDY (CV-67), the 4th carrier deployed, departed with just five days notice, leading a seven-and-a-half month battle group deployment that maintained a close watch on shipping in the Red Sea and launched 11,000+ combat sorties against Iraq. Aircraft from USS JOHN F. KENNEDY conducted the first war-time use of the Stand-off Land Attack Missile (SLAM), and battle group ship USS SAN JACINTO fired the first TOMAHAWK cruise missile against Iraq. During the 226 day deployment, USS JOHN F. KENNEDY was underway for 196 days, travelled 50,000 miles, and made the first-ever aircraft carrier Red Sea port visits to Jeddah, Saudi Arabia and Hurghada, Egypt.

USS MISSISSIPPI (CGN-40) conducted operations as part of the Maritime Intercept Force Red Sea escort unit. During a seven-and-a-half month deployment, the cruiser's crew boarded 73 merchant ships to enforce U.N. sanctions and fired TOMAHAWK cruise missiles on Iraqi targets.

USS SAN JACINTO (CG-56) conducted maritime intercept operations preventing cargo shipments to or from Iraq and served as the anti-warfare commander protecting the Red Sea battle force from preemptive Iraqi or terrorist attacks. On 16 January, USS SAN JACINTO made naval history by firing the first TOMAHAWK cruise missile in combat to support air strikes by USS JOHN F. KENNEDY and USS SARATOGA. The AEGIS cruiser completed its seven-and-a-half month deployment protecting the battle force from any Iraqi air strikes.

USS THOMAS S. GATES (CG-51) conducted operations in the Maritime Intercept Force, and under the command of Destroyer Squadron 36, the Red Sea escort cruiser played a decisive role in maritime interceptions during OPERATION DESERT SHIELD and DESERT STORM.

Newport RI:

USS SAMUEL B. ROBERTS (FFG-58) conducted operations with the Red Sea Maritime Interception Force working cooperatively with an international force of ships to enforce U.N. sanctions against Iraq. The frigate alone conducted over 100 boardings of merchant ships to prevent cargo shipments to or from Iraq.

Colts Neck NJ:

USS SEATTLE (AOE-3), a fast combat support ship, provided the ships of the USS JOHN F. KENNEDY Battle Group with fuel, ammunition and stores during the seven-and-a-half month deployment.

28 March (continuing) Mayport FL:

- USS SARATOGA (CV-60), the 3rd carrier deployed, led a high-speed transit of the Atlantic to the gulf region, making the normally ten-day voyage in seven days -- the fastest Atlantic crossing since World War II. On station, the battle group units were strategically positioned to guard the northern and southern Red Sea entrances, then conducted the most successful maritime interdiction operation ever undertaken by the U.S., challenging 1,500+ merchants ships, intercepting and boarding 242, and diverting 13 from delivering contraband cargo. Following the tragic drownings of 21 crewmembers during a holiday port visit to Haifa, Israel, the carrier launched around-the-clock strikes on targets in Iraq and occupied Kuwait, registering 12,664 sorties, 11,700 launchings, 217 days underway, and only 20 days in port.

- USS PHILIPPINE SEA (CG-58) escorted the USS SARATOGA across the Atlantic and through the Suez Canal -- eventually becoming the first Navy ship to ever transit the Suez Canal six times -- to join the Maritime Interception Force in the Gulf of Aqaba. On two occasions while enforcing U.N. sanctions, USS PHILLIPINE SEA fired warning shots from its five-inch batteries and .50 caliber machine guns to stop vessels seeking to elude the quarantine. With the onset of hostilities, the guided missile cruiser, fired its TOMAHAWK cruise missiles at targets in Iraq before assuming operational duties.

- USS SPRUANCE (DD-963) conducted assignments ranging from good-will visits to submarine hunting to firing its TOMAHAWK cruise missiles against targets in northern Iraq to assisting in the evacuation of the American Embassy in Beirut. In addition the destroyer operated as a member of the Maritime Interception Force, boarding three merchants and diverting one before completing its nearly eight-month deployment.

- USS SAMPSON (DDG-10) performed the final Adams class guided missile destroyer deployment as a unit of the Maritime Interception Force, conducting the first boarding and search of a merchant during OPERATION DESERT SHIELD and the first diversion of a ship with prohibited cargo. After conducting the first-ever exercise ASROC shot in the Red Sea, USS SAMPSON operated with ships of various NATO navies conducting surveillance and protection of shipping in the approaches to the Suez Canal.

- USS ELMER MONTGOMERY (FF-1082) fired the first warning shots by U.S. forces during an interception and was the first ship in theater to conduct 100 boardings. The fast frigate also diverted 6 merchants with prohibited cargo, supported by embarked Helicopter Squadron (Light) 36, Detachment 9, before assuming anti-air warfare defense of the Suez Canal and Mediterranean.

28 March (continuing) Norfolk VA:
- USS BIDDLE (CG-34) conducted 36 boardings and diverted 8 merchant ships--the highest percentage of the Navy's maritime interceptions force--assisted by embarked Helicopter Detachment One's 375 anti-sub and anti-surface warfare sorties. The guided missile cruiser then assumed anti-aircraft defenses for the combined battle force in the Red Sea, coordinating 850+ aircraft interceptions with carrier-based combat air patrols.
- USS THOMAS C. HART (FF-1092) conducted 43 boardings and over 300 interrogations of merchant vessels near the Gulf of Aqaba, in the Northern Red Sea. Her 131 days in the Red Sea made the ground offensive easier by choking off supplies to Saddam Hussein's war machine.
- USS SOUTH CAROLINA (CGN-37) spearheaded maritime interceptions in the Red Sea, boarding 26 merchant vessels before shifting to anti-air warfare commander for the Mediterranean Sea, protecting and identifying hundreds of coalition aircraft transiting to and from air strikes.

Colts Neck NJ:
- USS DETROIT (AOE-4), a fast combat support ship, replenished 250+ ships, including USS JOHN F. KENNEDY, USS SARATOGA and USS AMERICA battle groups and 52 coalition ships, with 70 million gallons of diesel and jet fuel, and thousands of tons of ammunition and general stores by the end of deployment.
- **USS WISCONSIN (BB-64), the first battleship to return to CONUS, arrived at Norfolk VA homeport.** Braving mine fields and enemy fire in the Arabian Gulf, USS WISCONSIN fired her 16-inch guns 324 times during 34 naval gunfire support missions, accounting for some 874,800 pounds of high explosives on enemy targets including command posts, infantry bunkers, missile and artillery sites and communication bunkers in occupied Kuwait. The battleship's barrages were so deadly, hundreds of Iraqis surrendered to the Remotely Piloted Vehicle -- the unmanned drone aircraft -- that was the spotter for the guns, a first in history.
- Tactical Electronic Warfare Squadron 130 of Carrier Air Wing 3 (embarked on USS JOHN F. KENNEDY) arrives at Whidbey Island WA homeport.
- Tactical Electronic Warfare Squadron 132 of Carrier Air Wing 17 (embarked on USS SARATOGA) arrives at Whidbey Island WA homeport.

29 March
- Naval forces continue counter air-defensive, combat air patrols, minesweeping and maritime interception operations.
- Marine ground forces hold defensive positions.
- USS FRANCIS HAMMOND (FF-1867), USS SHASTA (AE-33), USS NIAGRA FALLS (AFS-3) and coalition ships, assists burning Sri Lankan merchant vessel MERCS-HORANA in Arabian Gulf.
- Status of LT Charles J. Turner, missing since 18 January downing of his A-6, was changed to Killed in Action.

30 March   Naval forces continue counter air-defensive, combat air patrols, minesweeping and maritime interception operations.
Marine ground forces hold defensive positions.
USS PRINCETON (CG-59) and crew awarded Combat Action Ribbon in recognition of the superior and arduous work the crew put in to keep the ship in war-fighting status following the 18 February mining of the ship. USS PRINCETON continues to undergo repairs.

31 March   Naval forces continue counter air-defensive, combat air patrols, minesweeping and maritime interception operations.
Marine ground forces hold defensive positions.
USS KALAMAZOO (AOR-6) transits Suez Canal enroute CONUS.

1 April   Naval forces continue counter air-defensive, combat air patrols, minesweeping and maritime interception operations.
Marine ground forces hold defensive positions.
USS MARVIN SHIELDS (FF-1066), the first West coast ship to return to CONUS, arrives at San Diego CA homeport. During a six-and one-half month deployment, the frigate participated in merchant intercept operations in support of U.N. resolutions, acted as an escort/screen ship for the combined battle force, and assisted in training Kuwaiti Naval Forces as the coalition force prepared for possible hostilities.

2 April   Naval forces continue counter air-defensive, combat air patrols, minesweeping and maritime interception operations.
To-date, 8,598 merchants have been challenged, 1,110 boarded and 58 diverted. Navy has conducted 581 boardings.
Marine ground forces hold defensive positions.
DOD reports over 373,000 U.S. personnel are in the theater (42,500+ Navy, 54,500+ USMC). To-date, 167,000+ have redeployed to the U.S. (42,500 Navy, 39,500 USMC).
There are 44 Navy ships in the Arabian Gulf, Gulf of Oman, and Northern Arabian Sea. There are 13 Navy ships in the Red Sea. There are 25 Navy ships in the Mediterranean.
<u>DOD revises U.S. casualty data: 139 KIA, 2 (Died from combat wounds), 111 Non-combat fatalities, 357 WIA, 6 MIA (3 Navy, 0 USMC).</u>
196,495 National Guard and reservists are on active duty (18,038 Navy, 27,670 USMC).
To-date, 1,081 Naval and 2,878 Marine Reservists have been demobilized.
USS CHICAGO (SSN-721) arrives at San Diego CA homeport. During a six-month deployment, the attack submarine worked with U.S. and coalition forces deployed to the Southwest Asia area of operations.
A total of 13 Navy submarines conducted surveillance and reconnaissance operations in support of OPERATION DESERT SHIELD and DESERT STORM. Two, USS LOUISVILLE (SSN-724) and USS PITTSBURGH (SSN-720), conducted submarine-launched TOMAHAWK cruise missile attacks against Iraq.

3 April	By 12-1 vote, U.N. Security Council approves Resolution 687 to formally end Gulf War. Terms, which become effective when Iraq agrees, are:

* Iraq must give up weapons of mass destruction. U.N. will inspect and monitor the destruction and removal of chemical, biological and nuclear weapons. Iraq forbidden from using, developing or acquiring any additional weapons.
* Iraq must compensate Kuwait for war damages, including environmental.
* Establishment of a demilitarized zone extending 6 miles into Iraq, 3 miles into Kuwait. U.N. observer unit will monitor.
* Recognizes and guarantees 1963 borders between Iraq and Kuwait.
* Requires Iraq to condemn and renounce terrorism, halt support for international terrorism, forbids terrorist organizations from operating on Iraqi territory.

Naval forces continue counter air-defensive, combat air patrols, minesweeping and maritime interception operations.

Marine ground forces hold defensive positions.

USS AMERICA (CV-66), USS NORMANDY (CG-60), and USS WILLIAM V. PRATT (DDG-44) transit Suez Canal enroute CONUS.

VADM Stanley R. Arthur, Commander U.S. Naval Forces Central Command/Commander Seventh Fleet, RADM Raynor A.K. Taylor, Commander Middle East Force and RADM Robert Sutton, Commander U.S. Naval Logistics Support Force are awarded the Order of Bahrain, First Degree by the Amir of Bahrain for their outstanding professional contributions during OPERATION DESERT STORM.

4 April

At D+77, naval forces continue counter air-defensive, combat air patrols, minesweeping and maritime interception operations. To-date, 8,645 merchant ships have been challenged, 1,116 boarded and 59 diverted. The Navy has conducted 582 boardings.

There are 42 Navy ships in the Arabian Gulf, Gulf of Oman and Northern Arabian Sea. There are 10 Navy ships in the Red Sea. There are 21 Navy ships in the Mediterranean.

Marine ground forces hold defensive positions, continue redeployments.

DOD reports there are 365,000+ U.S. personnel in the theater (42,500+ Navy, 52,000+ USMC). To-date, 175,000+ have redeployed to the U.S. (42,500 Navy, 42,000 USMC).

To-date, 1,081 Naval and 4,245 Marine Reservists have been demobilized; 18,038 Naval and 26,303 Marine Reservists are on active duty.

DOD revises U.S. casualty data: <u>139 KIA, 2 (Died from combat wounds), 113 Non-combat fatalities, 357 WIA, 6 MIA (3 Navy, 0 USMC), 0 POW.</u>

<u>Sealift update:</u> To-date, 33 MSC ships have loaded out (totalling 135,000 tons of cargo and equipment) or have been turned around are underway to CONUS. This includes Fast Sealift Ships USNS BELLATRIX, USNS ALTAIR, and USNS REGULUS plus 12 Ready Reserve Force ships, two Prepositioning Ships, 15 charters and one ship under MSC charter. 36 MSC ships are loading or waiting to load.

5 April	Naval forces continue counter air-defensive, combat air patrols, minesweeping and maritime interception operations. Marine ground forces hold defensive positions, redeploy. Helicopter Anti-Submarine Squadron (Light) 42, Detachment 6, arrives at NAVSTA Mayport FL homeport. During six month embarkation aboard USS MOOSBRUGGER, squadron conducted 100+ merchant vessel identifications and/or challenges enforcing United Nations trade sanctions.
6 April	**Iraq accepts United Nations terms for a formal cease-fire in the Persian Gulf War.** Naval forces continue counter air-defensive, combat air patrols, minesweeping and maritime interception operations. USS TRIPOLI returns to duty following successful repairs and sea trials. Marine ground forces hold defensive positions, redeploy. USS MOOSBRUGGER (DD-980) arrives at NAVBASE Charleston SC homeport. During a seven-and-a-half month deployment, the destroyer conducted 67 searches and boardings of merchant ships, including the first boarding of a vessel, confronted a Soviet ship carrying personal and household items for the Iraqi military, carried the Navy SEAL Insertion Forces used to board uncooperative vessels, and escorted convoys transporting troops to Saudi Arabia.
7 April	Naval forces continue counter air-defensive, combat air patrols, minesweeping and maritime interception operations. Marine ground forces hold defensive positions, redeploy. USS HALYBURTON diverts a freighter in the N. Red Sea. **Fast Sealift Ship USNS BELLATRIX arrives at Savannah GA port with first cargo-load of equipment from Persian Gulf War.**
8 April	Naval forces continue counter air-defensive, combat air patrols, minesweeping and maritime interception operations. Marine ground forces hold defensive positions, redeploy. USS BUNKER HILL (CG-52) arrives at NAVBASE Yokosuka JA homeport. During four month deployment, the AEGIS guided missile cruiser served as the anti-air warfare command ship -- "Zulu Whiskey" -- in the Arabian Gulf, directing 23 ships and 200+ fighters from six nations in excess of 65,000 combat sorties in the air war over the gulf. USS BUNKER HILL also played an important role in launching multiple TOMAHAWK cruise missiles against enemy targets ashore from the gulf.
9 April	**U.N. Security Council approves Resolution 689 establishing a United Nations-Iraq-Kuwait Observer Mission (UNIKOM) to monitor permanent cease-fire.** Naval forces continue counter air-defensive, combat air patrols, minesweeping and maritime interception operations.

9 April (continuing) Marine ground forces hold defensive positions, redeploy.
DOD reports there are 326,000+ U.S. personnel in the theater (34,500+ Navy, 43,000+ USMC). To-date, 214,000 have redeployed to the U.S. (50,500 Navy, 51,000 USMC).

10 April Naval forces continue counter air-defensive, combat air patrols, minesweeping and maritime interception operations.
Marine ground forces hold defensive positions, redeploy.
USS HALEAKALA (AE-25) arrives at Apra Harbor GUAM homeport. During a one-month deployment, the combat logistics force ship replenished 15 ships while underway, and delivered cargo supporting Marine units ashore.
Ready Reserve Force cargo ship SS CAPE INSCRIPTION arrives in Houston TX with redeployment cargo.

11 April At D+84, naval forces continue counter air-defensive, combat air patrols, minesweeping and maritime intercept operations.
To-date, 553 mines have been discovered and destroyed.
To-date, 8,770 merchants have been intercepted, 1,117 boarded, and 61 diverted. The Navy has conducted 590 boardings.
There are 41 Navy ships in the Arabian Gulf, Gulf of Oman and Northern Arabian Sea, including USS RANGER. There are 8 Navy ships in the Red Sea, including USS THEODORE ROOSEVELT. There are 10 Navy ships in the Mediterranean.
Marine ground forces hold defensive positions, redeploy.
DOD reports there are 310,000+ U.S. personnel in the theater (33,000+ Navy, 38,500+ USMC). To-date, 230,000+ have redeployed to the U.S. (52,000 Navy, 55,500 USMC).
To-date, 2,386 Naval and 4,970 Marine Reservists have been demobilized; 16,733 Naval and 25,578 Marine Reservists are on active duty.
DOD revises casualty data: 139 KIA, 2 (Died from combat wounds), 118 Non-combat fatalities, 357 WIA, 6 MIA (3 Navy, 0 USMC), 0 POW.
Sealift update: To-date, 41 MSC ships have loaded out or have turned around and are underway to CONUS (totalling 168,000 tons of cargo and equipment). 36 ships are loading or waiting to load.
USS LEFTWICH (DD-984) with Helicopter Anti-Submarine Squadron 3 Detachment 5 embarked, arrives at NAVSTA Pearl Harbor homeport. During a five-and-a-half month deployment, the destroyer conducted 200+ merchant ship interceptions and one boarding, was one of the first ships to fire TOMAHAWK cruise missiles, was the first combatant to conduct a wartime reload of TOMAHAWKs for continued operations, with embarked helos and SEALs captured the first Iraqi territory repatriated in the war and enemy prisoners of war, and conducted 16 combat search and rescue cases.

U.N. Security Council declares formal cease-fire ending Persian Gulf War.

APPENDIX B

PARTICIPATING NAVAL UNITS

SHIPS PARTICIPATING IN DESERT SHIELD/STORM

USNAVCENT Data as of 24 April 1991

Ship	Dates
A.J. HIGGINS TAO-190	09 SEP - TBD
ACADIA AD-42	18 OCT - 12 MAR
ADROIT MSO-509	SEP 90 - TBD
ALGOL TAKR-287	24 OCT - 20 APR
ALTAIR TAKR-291	SEP 90 - 26 MAR
AMERICA CV-66	15 JAN - 03 APR
ANCHORAGE LSD-36	12 JAN - TBD
ANTIETAM CG-54	05 AUG - 03 NOV
AVENGER MCM-1	SEP 90 - TBD
BARBEY FF-1088	31 JUL - 03 NOV
BARBOUR COUNTY LST-1195	12 JAN - TBD
BEAUFORT ATS-2	29 JAN - TBD
BELLATRIX TAKR-288	SEP 90 - 26 MAR
BIDDLE CG-34	22 AUG - 21 SEP/23 OCT - 09 DEC/09 JAN - 13 MAR
BLUE RIDGE LCC-19	28 AUG - TBD
R.G. BRADLEY FFG-49	28 JUL - 12 NOV
TATTNALL DDG-19	19 AUG - 24 AUG
BUNKER HILL CG-52	28 OCT - 10 MAR
BREWTON FF-1086	05 AUG - 04 NOV
CAPE COD AD-43	26 FEB - TBD
CAPELLA TAKR-293	SEP 90 - APR 91
CARON DD-970	14 JAN - TBD
CAYUGA LST-1186	05 SEP - 08 NOV/12 JAN - 13 MAR
CHAUVENET TAGS-29	SEP 90 - TBD
CHICAGO SSN-721	07 FEB - 07 MAR
CIMMARON AO-177	05 AUG - 04 NOV
COMFORT TAH-20	30 AUG - 23 MAR
CONCORD AFS-5	18 SEP - 25 SEP
CURTISS TAVB-4	10 SEP - 09 APR
CURTS FFG-38	02 NOV - 14 MAR
DENEBOLA TAKR-289	17 OCT - 05 MAR
DENVER LPD-9	12 JAN - TBD
DETROIT AOE-4	24 AUG - 21 SEP/07 NOV - 16 DEC/06 JAN - 06 MAR
DUBUQUE LPD-8	09 SEP - 13 OCT
DURHAM LKA-114	05 SEP - 08 NOV/12 JAN - 13 MAR
EISENHOWER CVN-69	08 AUG - 24 AUG
ENGLAND CG-22	31 JUL - 03 NOV
FIFE DD-991	30 OCT - 14 MAR
FLINT AE-32	05 AUG - 04 NOV

Ship	Dates
FORD FFG-54	26 JAN - 24 MAR
FORT McHENRY LSD-43	05 SEP - 08 NOV/12 JAN - 13 MAR
FREDERICK LST-1184	12 JAN - TBD
GATES CG-51	14 SEP - 12 MAR
GERMANTOWN LSD-42	12 JAN - TBD
GOLDSBOROUGH DDG-20	05 AUG - 04 NOV
GUAM LPH-9	08 SEP - 23 MAR
GUNSTON HALL LSD-44	03 SEP - 23 MAR
H.W. HILL DD-986	13 JAN - 12 MAR
HALEAKALA AE-25	09 FEB - 14 MAR
HALYBURTON FFG-40	18 JAN - 09 APR
HAMMOND FF-1067	23 JAN - 21 APR
HASSAYAMPA TAO-145	08 SEP - 14 MAR
HAWES FFG-53	14 JAN - TBD
HORNE CG-30	24 JAN - 20 APR
IMPERVIOUS MSO-449	SEP 90 - TBD
INDEPENDENCE CV-42	05 AUG - 04 NOV
IWO JIMA LPH-7	08 SEP - 23 MAR
J. RODGERS DD-983	19 AUG - 24 AUG
J. HUMPHREYS TAO-188	15 JAN - 23 APR
J.F. KENNEDY CV-67	14 SEP - 12 MAR
J.L. HALL FFG-32	08 AUG - 24 AUG
JARRETT FFG-33	24 JAN - 20 APR
JASON AR-8	12 JAN - 04 APR
JOUETT CG-29	05 AUG - 04 NOV
JUNEAU LPD-10	12 JAN - TBD
KALAMAZOO AOR-6	15 JAN - 30 MAR
KANSAS CITY AOR-3	13 JAN - 19 APR
KIDD DDG-993	01 FEB - TBD
KILAUEA TAE-26	03 SEP - 08 MAR
KISKA AE-35	02 NOV - 14 MAR
LA MOURE COUNTY LST-1194	08 SEP - 14 MAR
LASALLE AGF-3	HOME PORT
LEADER MSO-490	SEP 90 - TBD
LEFTWICH DD-984	04 DEC - 08 MAR
LEYTE GULF CG-55	14 JAN - TBD
LOUISVILLE SSN-724	18 JAN - 30 JAN
MACDONOUGH DDG-39	17 OCT - 24 FEB
MANITOWAC LST-1180	08 SEP - 23 MAR
MARS AFS-1	21 DEC - 22 MAR
McINERNEY FFG-8	05 FEB - 12 JUN
McKEE AS-41	03 MAR - TBD
MERCURY TAKR-10	OCT 90 - 18 MAR
MERCY TAH-19	15 SEP - 21 MAR
MIDWAY CV-41	02 NOV - 14 MAR
MISSISSIPPI CGN-40	14 SEP - 12 MAR

Ship	Dates
MISSOURI BB-63	01 JAN - 24 MAR
MOBILE BAY CG-53	30 OCT - 14 MAR
MOBILE LKA-115	12 JAN - TBD
MONTGOMERY FF-1082	24 AUG - 09 JAN
MOOSBRUGGER DD-980	03 OCT - 27 NOV/21 DEC - 12 MAR
MOUNT HOOD AE-29	01 FEB - 13 MAR
MOUNT VERNON LSD-39	12 JAN - TBD
NASSAU LHA-4	06 SEP - 23 MAR
NEOSHA TAO-143	08 AUG - 23 AUG
NEW ORLEANS LPH-11	12 JAN - TBD
NEWPORT NEWS SSN-750	MEDITERRANEAN
NIAGARA FALLS AFS-3	15 JAN - TBD
NICHOLAS FFG-47	17 OCT - 24 FEB
NITRO AE-32	16 JAN - 10 APR
NORMANDY CG-60	15 JAN - 03 APR
O'BRIEN DD-975	13 AUG - 09 DEC
OGDEN LPD-5	05 SEP - 08 NOV/12 JAN - 13 MAR
OKINAWA LPH-3	05 SEP - 08 NOV/12 JAN - 13 MAR
OLDENDORF DD-972	02 NOV - 14 MAR
OPPORTUNE ARS-41	26 NOV - 31 MAR (MED)
P.F. FOSTER DD-964	13 JAN - 19 APR
PASSUMPSIC TAO-107	24 JAN - 25 MAR
PENSACOLA LSD-38	06 SEP - 14 MAR
PEORIA LST-1183	12 JAN - TBD
PHILADELPHIA SSN-690	MEDITERRANEAN
PHILIPPINE SEA CG-58	22 AUG-21 SEP/25 OCT- 09 DEC/06 JAN - 09 FEB
PITTSBURGH SSN-720	MEDITERRANEAN
PLATTE AO-186	14 JAN - 13 APR
POLLUX TAKR-290	OCT 90 - MAR 90
PONCHATOULA TAO-148	12 JAN - 16 MAR
PORTLAND LSD-37	03 SEP - 23 MAR
PRATT DDG-44	15 JAN - 03 APR
PREBLE DDG-46	15 JAN - 12 MAR
PRINCETON CG-59	13 JAN - 29 APR
PUGET SOUND AD-38	18 FEB - TBD
R.K. TURNER CG-20	14 JAN - 20 APR
RALEIGH LPD-1	08 SEP - 14 MAR
RANGER CV-61	13 JAN - 19 APR
D.R. RAY DD-971	09 JUN - 18 SEP
REASONER FF-1063	05 AUG - 04 NOV
REGULUS TAKR-292	OCT 90 - MAR 90
REID FFG-30	27 APR - 09 SEP
S.B. ROBERTS FFG-58	05 SEP - 12 MAR
SACRAMENTO AOE-1	01 JAN - 24 MAR
SAGINAW LST-1188	06 SEP - 23 MAR
SAMPSON DDG-10	24 AUG - 21 SEP/01 NOV - 16 DEC

Ship	Dates
SAN JACINTO CG-56	14 SEP - 12 MAR
SAN JOSE AFS-7	24 SEP - 13 MAR
SAN BERNADINO LST-1189	09 SEP - 13 OCT
SAN DIEGO AFS-6	14 JAN - 06 APR
SANTA BARBARA AE-28	15 JAN - TBD
SARATOGA CV-60	22 AUG - 21 SEP/23 OCT - 09 DEC/06 JAN - 11 MAR
SAVANNAH AOE-4	08 OCT - 13 OCT
SCHENECTADY LST-1185	09 SEP - 10 OCT
SCOTT DDG-995	08 AUG - 24 AUG
SEATTLE AOE-3	14 SEP - 11 MAR
SHASTA AE-33	13 JAN - 29 APR
SHIELDS FF-1066	30 OCT - 15 FEB
SHREVEPORT LPD-12	03 SEP - 23 MAR
SIRIUS TAFS-8	17 NOV - 23 NOV/10 FEB - 03 APR
SOUTH CAROLINA CGN-37	23 OCT - 11 DEC
SPARTANBURG COUNTY LST-1192	03 SEP - 23 MAR
SPICA TAFS-9	11 OCT - 14 MAR
SPRUANCE DD-963	08 FEB - 11 MAR
SURIBACHI AE-21	08 AUG - 22 AUG
SYLVANIA AFS-2	08 OCT - 13 OCT/12 JAN - 17 FEB
TAYLOR FFG-50	28 JUL - 12 NOV
T. ROOSEVELT CVN-71	14 JAN - 20 APR
T.C. HART FF-1092	24 AUG - 11 DEC/15 JAN - 11 MAR
TARAWA LHA-1	12 JAN - TBD
TICONDEROGA CG-47	08 AUG - 24 AUG
TRENTON LPD-14	03 SEP - 23 MAR
TRIPOLI LPH-10	12 JAN - TBD
VALLEY FORGE CG-50	13 JAN - 19 APR
VANCOUVER LPD-2	12 JAN - TBD
VANDERGRIFT FFG-48	27 APR - 09 SEP
VIRGINIA CGN-38	15 JAN - 03 APR
VREELAND FF-1068	18 JAN - TBD
VULCAN AR-5	23 JAN - 15 FEB
W.S. DIEHL TAO-193	30 OCT - 13 MAR
WHITE PLAINS AFS-4	17 AUG - 15 OCT
WISCONSIN BB-64	18 AUG - 13 MAR
WORDEN CG-18	28 OCT - 15 FEB
WRIGHT TAVB-3	SEP 90 - TBD
YELLOWSTONE AD-41	25 SEP - 13 OCT/08 JAN - 27 FEB

AIRCRAFT SQUADRONS PARTICIPATING IN DESERT SHIELD/STORM

HC-11	DET 4	02 NOV - 14 MAR
	DET 7	01 JAN - 24 MAR
	DET 8	13 JAN - 19 APR
	DET 11	05 AUG - 04 NOV
HC-1	DET 6	28 AUG - TBD
HC-6	DET 1	15 JAN - TBD
	DET 4	08 OCT - 13 OCT/12 JAN - 17 FEB
	DET 5	15 JAN - 13 MAR
	DET 7	17 NOV - 23 NOV/10 FEB - 03 APR
HC-8	DET 1	08 OCT - 13 OCT
	DET 2	24 AUG - 21 SEP/07 NOV-16 DEC/06 JAN-06 MAR
	DET 5	14 SEP - 11 MAR
	DET 4	14 JAN - 06 APR
HM-14	DET 1	ABU DHABI
HS-11		15 JAN - 03 APR
HS-12		02 NOV - 14 MAR
HS-14		13 JAN - 19 APR
HS-3		22 AUG - 21 SEP/23 OCT-09 DEC/06 JAN-11 MAR
HS-7		22 AUG - 21 SEP/23 OCT-09 DEC/06 JAN-11 MAR
HS-8		05 AUG - 04 NOV
HS-9		14 JAN - 20 APR
HSL-32	DET 7	24 AUG - 11 DEC/15 JAN - 11 MAR
HSL-33	DET 7	27 APR - 09 SEP
	DET 9	05 AUG - 04 NOV
HSL-34	DET 1	22 AUG - 21 SEP/23 OCT-09 DEC/09 JAN-13 MAR
	DET 5	01 FEB - TBD
HSL-35	DET 7	31 JUL - 03 NOV
HSL-36	DET 8	18 JAN - TBD
HSL-37	DET 6	02 NOV - 14 MAR
HSL-42	DET 1	14 SEP - 12 MAR
	DET 3	14 JAN - TBD
	DET 6	03 OCT - 27 NOV/21 DEC - 12 MAR
	DET 7	28 JUL - 12 NOV
	DET 8	05 FEB - 12 JUN
	DET 9	28 JUL - 12 NOV
HSL-43	DET 8	27 APR - 09 SEP
HSL-44	DET 5	14 JAN - 20 APR
	DET 6	18 JAN - 09 APR
	DET 7	15 JAN - 03 APR
	DET 8	17 OCT - 24 FEB
	DET 9	14 SEP - 12 MAR
HSL-46	DET 7	22 AUG - 21 SEP/25 OCT-09 DEC/06 JAN-09 FEB

HSL-48	DET 1	08 FEB - 11 MAR
	DET 2	14 JAN - 19 APR
	DET 3	14 JAN - TBD
VA-115		02 NOV - 14 MAR
VA-145		13 JAN - 19 APR
VA-155		13 JAN - 19 APR
VA-185		02 NOV - 14 MAR
VA-196		05 AUG - 04 NOV
VA-35		23 OCT - 09 DEC/06 JAN - 11 MAR
VA-36		14 JAN - 20 APR
VA-46		14 SEP - 12 MAR
VA-65		14 JAN - 20 APR
VA-72		14 SEP - 12 MAR
VA-75		14 SEP - 12 MAR
VA-85		15 JAN - 03 APR
VAQ-130		14 SEP - 12 MAR
VAQ-131		13 JAN - 19 APR
VAQ-132		23 OCT - 09 DEC/06 JAN - 11 MAR
VAQ-136		02 NOV - 14 MAR
VAQ-137		15 JAN - 03 APR
VAQ-139		05 AUG - 04 NOV
VAQ-141		14 JAN - 20 APR
VAW-113		05 AUG - 04 NOV
VAW-115		02 NOV - 14 MAR
VAW-116		13 JAN - 19 APR
VAW-123		15 JAN - 03 APR
VAW-124		14 JAN - 20 APR
VAW-125		23 OCT - 09 DEC/06 JAN - 11 MAR
VAW-126		14 SEP - 12 MAR
VF-1		13 JAN - 19 APR
VF-102		15 JAN - 03 APR
VF-103		23 OCT - 09 DEC/06 JAN - 11 MAR
VF-14		14 SEP - 12 MAR
VF-154		05 AUG - 04 NOV
VF-2		13 JAN - 19 APR
VF-21		05 AUG - 04 NOV
VF-32		14 SEP - 12 MAR
VF-33		15 JAN - 03 APR
VF-41		14 JAN - 20 APR
VF-74		23 OCT - 09 DEC/06 JAN - 11 MAR
VF-84		14 JAN - 20 APR
VFA-113		04 AUG - 04 NOV
VFA-15		14 JAN - 20 APR
VFA-151		02 NOV - 14 MAR
VFA-192		02 NOV - 14 MAR
VFA-195		02 NOV - 14 MAR

VFA-25	05 AUG - 04 NOV
VFA-81	23 OCT - 09 DEC/06 JAN - 11 MAR
VFA-82	15 JAN - 03 APR
VFA-83	23 OCT - 09 DEC/06 JAN - 11 MAR
VFA-86	15 JAN - 03 APR
VFA-87	14 JAN - 20 APR
VP-19	28 AUG - 02 FEB
VP-23	02 OCT - 10 NOV
VP-4	10 NOV - 10 MAR
VP-40	06 FEB - 10 MAR
VP-46	26 JAN - 10 MAR
VP-8	05 DEC - 10 MAR
VP-91	09 FEB - 23 FEB
VPMAU	12 FEB - 24 FEB
VPU-1	25 JAN - 10 MAR
VPU-2	12 SEP - 10 MAR
VRC-50 (FUJAIRAH)	PROVIDED DETS FOR DURATION
VS-22	14 SEP - 12 MAR
VS-24	14 JAN - 20 APR
VS-30	23 OCT - 09 DEC/06 JAN - 11 MAR
VS-32	15 JAN - 03 APR
VS-37	05 AUG - 04 NOV
VS-38	13 JAN - 19 APR
VRC-30	13 JAN - 19 APR
VRC-40	14 JAN - 20 APR
VP-11	10 NOV - 09 DEC
VQ-1	08 AUG - 10 MAR
VQ-2	06 DEC - 10 MAR

OTHER UNITS PARTICIPATING IN DESERT SHIELD/STORM

Unit	Dates
COMNAVSPECWARCOM	12 AUG - 29 SEP
COMNAVSPECWARGRU ONE	12 AUG - TBD
COMSPECBOATRON ONE	12 AUG - 03 APR
SPECBOATU TWELVE	12 AUG - 03 APR
SPECBOATU THIRTEEN	12 AUG - 03 APR
SPECBOATU ELEVEN	12 AUG - 03 APR
SEAL TEAM THREE	12 AUG - 03 APR
SEAL TEAM ONE	12 AUG - 12 MAR
SEAL TEAM FIVE	12 AUG - TBD
SDV TEAM ONE	15 JAN - 03 APR
COMNAVSPECWARU TWO	09 AUG - 02 APR
SEAL TEAM TWO	09 AUG - 02 MAR
SEAL TEAM FOUR	09 AUG - 02 MAR
SEAL TEAM EIGHT	09 AUG - 17 APR
SDV TEAM TWO	03 AUG - 25 AUG
COMSPECBOATRON TWO	09 AUG - 02 MAR
SPECBOAYU TWENTY	13 AUG - TBD
NAVSPECWARUNIT TWO	20 JAN - 16 MAR

STAFFS PARTICIPATING IN DESERT SHIELD/STORM

C7F	28 AUG - TBD
CCDG-12	14 JAN - TBD
CCDG-2	15 JAN - 03 APR
CCDG-5	24 JAN - 24 APR
CCDG-8	23 OCT - 09 DEC/06 JAN - 11 MAR
CCG-1	05 AUG - 04 NOV
CCG-2	15 JAN - 22 APR
CCG-5	02 NOV - 14 MAR
CCG-6	23 OCT - 09 DEC/06 JAN - 11 MAR
CCG-7	13 JAN - 19 APR
CCG-8	14 JAN - 20 APR
CDS-14	15 JAN - 03 APR
CDS-15	02 NOV - 14 MAR
CDS-17	29 OCT - 15 FEB
CDS-22	14 JAN - TBD
CDS-23	05 AUG - 04 NOV
CDS-24	23 OCT - 09 DEC/06 JAN - 11 MAR
CDS-32	23 OCT - 09 DEC/06 JAN - 11 MAR
CDS-35	01 FEB - 20 APR
CDS-36	02 DEC - 12 MAR
CDS-7	13 MAR - 19 APR
COMUSNAVCENT	28 AUG - TBD
CPG-2	06 SEP - 24 MAR
CPG-3	12 JAN - TBD
CPR-1	12 JAN - TBD
CPR-5	12 JAN - 13 MAR
CPR-6	08 SEP - 24 MAR

APPENDIX C

ALLIED PARTICPATION AND CONTRIBUTIONS

Theater Coalition Ships

(Total ships in theater on the date specified)

Country	22 Aug	18 Sep	21 Oct	12 Nov	21 Jan
Argentina				2	2
Australia					3
Belgium	3	3	3	3	6
Canada	3	3	3	3	3
Denmark		1	1	1	1
France	7	14	14	15	14
Germany	6	-	-	7	5
Greece		1	1	1	1
Italy	2	3	4	3	10
Netherlands	2	2	3	3	3
Norway		1	1	-	1
Poland			1	-	1
Portugal			1	1	1
Spain	3	3	3	3	4
Turkey					2
U.S.	45	45	55	65	100
UK	7	-	12	16	18
USSR		2	2	4	4
Total	78	78	104	127	179

Sources: Time, August 27, 1990, January 28, 1991.
New York Times, September 18, October 21, November 12, 1990.
Washington Post National Weekly Edition, January 21-27, 1991.

Theater Coalition Troops

(Total troops in theater on the date specified, in thousands)

Country	26 Aug	18 Sep	21 Oct	12 Nov	21 Jan
Bangladesh			2.0	2.0	6.0
Canada					1.7
Czechoslovakia				0.2	0.2
Egypt	5.0	5.0	14.0	29.0	35.0
France	8.5	13.1	8.0	5.0	10.0
Gulf Cooperation Council	3.0	3.0	3.0	3.0	3.0
Honduras					0.2
Hungary (Medics)					0.1
Kuwait	7.0	7.0	7.0	7.0	7.0
Morocco	1.0	1.2	2.0	2.0	2.0
Niger					0.5
Pakistan		2.0	5.0	2.0	5.0
Saudi Arabia	45.0	45.0	45.0	45.0	45.0
Senegal					0.5
Syria	1.2	4.0	19.0	19.0	20.0
Turkey (on Iraqi border)	70.0	100.0	95.0	95.0	100.0
U.S.	40.0	140.0	200.0	210.0	450.0
UK		6.0	6.0	11.0	35.0
Total	180.7	326.3	406.2	430.2	721.2

Sources: New York Times, August 26, September 18, October 21, November 12, 1990.
Time, September 26, 1990, March 4, 1991.
Washington Post National Weekly Edition, January 21-27, 1991.

Allied Contributions

By February 1, 1991, 32 countries had joined the United States in the coalition against Iraq and had pledged enough money to fund 80 percent of the war effort. In all, 13 countries and the Afghan Mujahedeen had committed combat forces.

Country	Personnel	Equipment	Money
Afghan Mujahedeen	2,000 troops		
Argentina		2 ships, 2 transport aircraft	
Australia	medical/surgical team	3 ships	
Bangladesh	3,000 troops		
Belgium	50 medical	4 transport aircraft 2,800 hospital beds 3 minesweepers 1 frigate 18 Mirage-5 aircraft	
Bulgaria	1 unit army engineers		
Canada	medical/surgical team	CF-18 fighters 3 ships air defense aircraft transport aircraft	
Czechoslovakia	400 medical		
Denmark		1 corvette	
Egypt	30,000 troops		
France	11,500 ground troops 2,500 transport/support 4,500 extra ground, stationed in Dijbouti	3 frigates 3 destroyers 1 patrol boat 2 tankers 1 support ship 1 transport 54 combat aircraft	
Germany	580 soldiers to operate air defense systems in Turkey	Minesweepers & other ships 18 Alpha jets in Turkey	$9B ($3.5B paid $5.5B pledged)
Greece		1 frigate	
Hungary	medical personnel		

Country	Personnel	Equipment	Money
Italy		3 frigates 2 corvettes 8 fighter aircraft	
Japan			$11B pledged
Kuwait	7,000 ground troops	35 combat aircraft	$21B ($2.5B paid $18.5B pledged)
Morocco	1,700 troops		
Netherlands		2 frigates 1 fast combat ship 1 emergency hospital 2 squadrons Patriot missiles to Turkey 2 squadrons Hawk air defense missiles 2 P-3 Orion aircraft $33M in ammunition	
New Zealand	medical/surgical team	aircraft	
Niger	400 troops		
Norway		1 coast guard ship	
Pakistan	11,000 troops		
Philippines	medical personnel		
Poland		military field hospital 1 hospital ship	
Portugal		1 naval supply ship	
Romania	medical team and anti-chemical warfare specialists		

Country	Personnel	Equipment	Money
Saudi Arabia	65,000 troops	117 combat aircraft	$14.6B ($1.6B paid $13B pledged) including offer to pay for all food, water, petroleum and transportation for Allied forces
Senegal	500 troops		
Sierra Leone	30 medical personnel		
Singapore	medical team		
South Korea			$280M ($60M paid $220M pledged)
Soviet Union		1 destroyer on patrol	
Spain		1 frigate 2 corvettes	
Sweden	field hospital and medical personnel		
Syria	20,000 troops		
Turkey	120,000 troops	Access to Turkish bases for Allied aircraft	
United Arab Emirates			$1.66B ($660M paid $1B pledged)
United Kingdom	31,000 ground troops	5 destroyer/frigates 5 minesweepers 10 support ships 75 combat aircraft	

Source: *Defense News*, February 4, 1991.
New York Times, March 24, 1991.
Office of Navy Surgeon General, April 2, 1991.

APPENDIX D

AIRCRAFT SORTIE COUNT

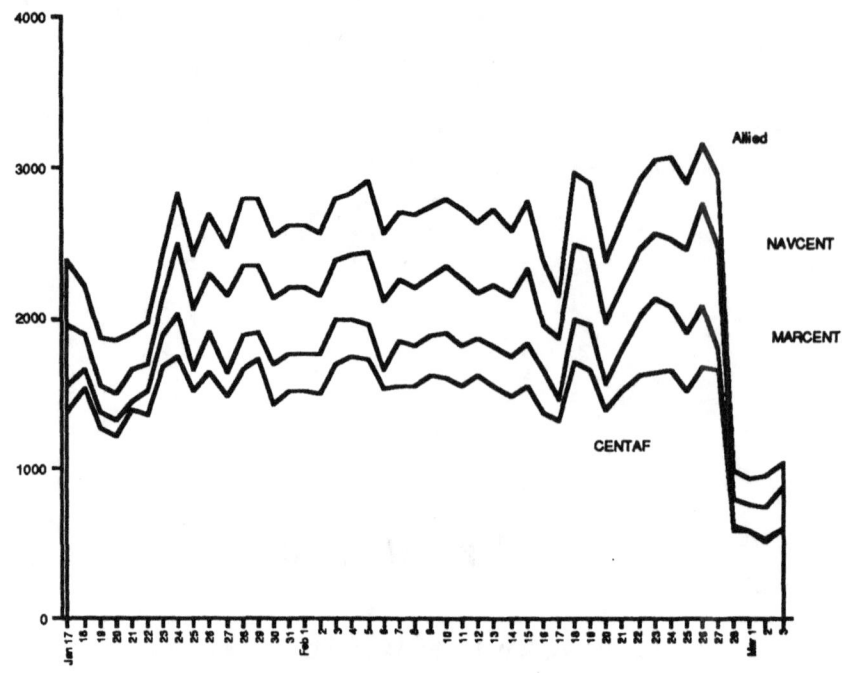

Date	CENTAF	MARCENT	NAVCENT	Allied	Total Flown	Cum Flown
Jan 17	1381	169	415	423	2388	*
18	1529	122	233	316	2200	*
19	1275	108	178	302	1863	*
20	1223	98	175	346	1842	8323
21	1394	50	217	246	1907	10230
22	1362	149	189	282	1982	12212
23	1679	216	238	291	2424	14636
24	1741	278	455	337	2811	17447
25	1526	138	396	347	2407	19854
26	1635	266	403	368	2672	22526
27	1471	169	502	331	2473	24999
28	1670	223	452	430	2775	27774
29	1723	176	447	437	2783	30557
30	1421	262	454	401	2538	33397
31	1520	237	449	403	2609	36006
Feb 1	1522	238	447	398	2605	38611
2	1492	263	398	411	2564	41175
3	1689	301	379	407	2776	43951
4	1734	266	420	397	2817	46768
5	1729	234	470	472	2905	49673
6	1537	125	453	445	2560	52233
7	1543	308	405	434	2690	54934
8	1547	275	379	475	2676	57610
9	1619	266	393	455	2733	60343
10	1600	305	430	450	2785	63128
11	1543	272	450	446	2711	65839
12	1616	247	299	459	2621	68460
13	1542	266	416	478	2702	71162
14	1468	279	396	433	2576	73738
15	1543	284	491	451	2769	76507
16	1382	271	309	416	2378	78885
17	1320	146	397	280	2143	81028
18	1718	283	475	481	2957	83985
19	1655	303	484	440	2882	86867
20	1399	164	417	405	2385	89252
21	1511	257	435	424	2627	91879
22	1614	402	445	445	2906	94785
23	1643	484	436	478	3041	97826
24	1648	436	442	536	3062	100888
25	1518	382	556	425	2881	103769
26	1673	405	664	417	3159	106928
27	1651	147	671	471	2940	109868
28	575	30	187	200	992	110860
Mar 1	592	0	167	173	932	111792
2	515	17	215	217	964	112756
3	597	4	278	168	1047	113803

D-2

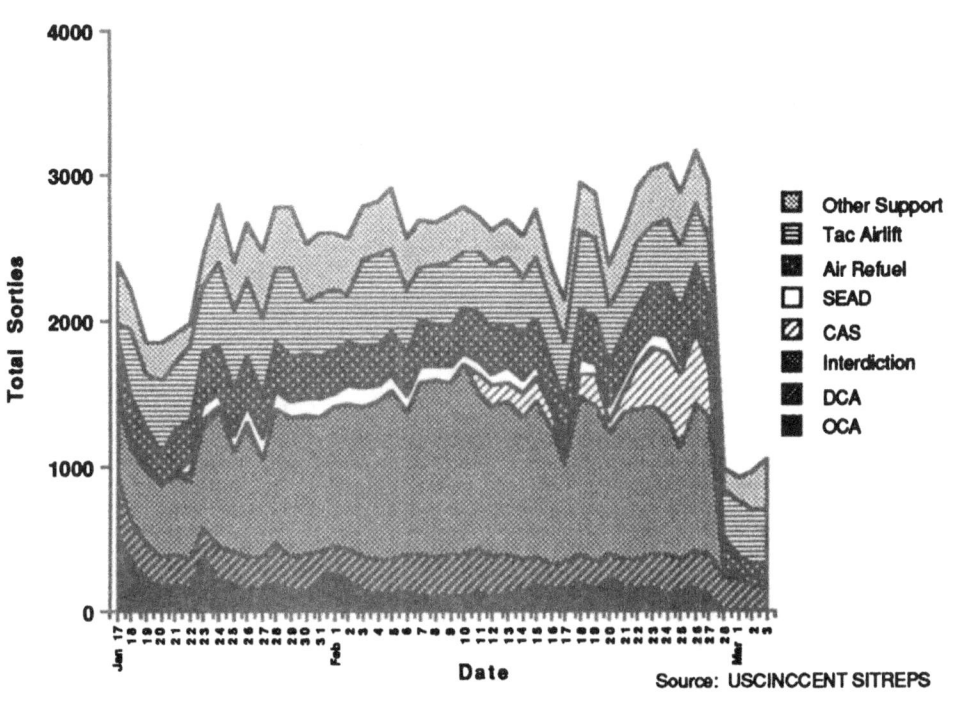

Source: USCINCCENT SITREPS

Date	OCA	DCA	Interdiction	CAS	SEAD	Air Refuel	Tac Airlift	Other Support	Total Flown	Cum Flown
Jan 17	518	415	531	67	0	362	85	420	2388	*
18	362	272	487	72	0	298	460	269	2200	*
19	216	266	497	43	0	264	346	231	1863	*
20	180	205	487	16	0	196	510	256	1842	8323
21	196	198	552	3	0	298	450	210	1907	10230
22	163	200	554	50	81	276	510	148	1982	12212
23	375	200	723	28	118	328	467	189	2424	14636
24	211	234	957	2	115	318	556	418	2811	17447
25	194	234	674	0	114	312	537	342	2407	19854
26	144	240	917	5	132	319	522	393	2672	22526
27	153	232	684	0	140	291	515	458	2473	24999
28	202	257	940	0	122	320	512	422	2775	27774
29	139	240	964	0	113	300	604	423	2783	30557
30	148	252	954	18	100	302	350	414	2538	33397
31	212	212	932	0	112	293	421	427	2609	36006
Feb 1	271	186	955	0	98	293	406	396	2605	38611
2	223	220	999	0	116	309	311	386	2564	41175
3	149	229	1043	0	120	288	589	358	2776	43951
4	131	226	1093	0	102	288	622	355	2817	46768
5	127	234	1161	0	115	289	559	420	2905	49673
6	141	247	1000	0	102	281	445	344	2560	52233
7	122	292	1176	0	95	325	366	314	2690	54934
8	114	266	1215	4	87	295	399	296	2676	57610
9	118	272	1201	0	92	287	434	329	2733	60343
10	122	272	1302	0	99	304	368	318	2785	63128
11	130	303	1077	130	94	310	422	245	2711	65839
12	109	262	1034	149	88	303	447	229	2621	68460
13	124	272	1056	132	100	297	454	260	2702	71162
14	140	222	994	160	79	314	387	280	2576	73738
15	184	199	1068	164	87	326	417	324	2769	76507
16	156	184	931	128	46	270	405	258	2378	78885
17	156	186	682	58	87	289	409	276	2143	81028
18	199	196	1097	146	110	338	538	333	2957	83985
19	155	188	1086	196	74	322	532	329	2882	86867
20	229	184	819	83	90	299	388	293	2385	89252
21	163	197	1024	138	87	309	366	343	2627	91879
22	160	202	1038	287	100	301	460	358	2906	94785
23	155	255	998	403	94	343	412	381	3041	97826
24	132	270	932	453	100	363	447	365	3062	100888
25	142	216	770	504	83	347	434	385	2881	103769
26	153	266	1026	477	75	390	400	372	3159	106928
27	110	303	920	361	83	364	418	381	2940	109868
28	0	228	34	31	2	208	319	170	992	110860
Mar 1	0	216	44	8	0	108	392	164	932	111792
2	6	181	39	17	0	92	376	253	964	112756
3	0	162	36	30	0	92	394	333	1047	113803

Statistics of Carrier Fixed-wing Flight Operations During Desert Storm

During Operation Desert Storm (from 17 January to 28 February), the six U.S. aircraft carriers deployed to the theater flew a total of 18,117 fixed-wing aircraft sorties. Of these sorties, 16,899 were combat or direct combat-support missions. The remaining 1,218 sorties included logistics flights, functional check flights for newly arrived or repaired aircraft, or other indirect support activities.

Table 1 shows the combat and combat-support sorties flown by all the carriers according to an analysis of carrier launch and recovery logs, air plans, and steam catapult logs. The number of sorties is broken out into the eight mission categories reported in the daily Central Command situation reports. These mission categories include offensive counterair (OCA), defensive counterair (DCA), interdiction, close air support (CAS), suppression of enemy air defenses (SEAD), aerial refueling, tactical airlift, and other support, including electronic support measures (ESM), electronic countermeasures (ECM), airborne early warning (AEW) and other support activities. Figure 1 shows the daily distribution of Navy sorties by mission area. Figure 2 depicts the same data in terms of the percentage of the total sorties flown in a given mission category each day.

Because the breakdown given in table 1 does not include all Navy fixed-wing sorties, and because the definition of mission categories imperfectly reflects Navy operations, table 2 employs a different set of mission categories to obtain another view of carrier activity. This set of missions includes OCA and DCA missions as defined in table 1. The theater strike mission includes interdiction, CAS, and sorties that were capable of both SEAD and strike. Maritime strike missions include armed surface combat air patrol (SUCAP) and armed reconnaissance missions (which attacked not only ships at sea but some coastal targets as well). The SEAD/EW mission includes not only SEAD missions (those armed with HARM or other air-to-surface weapons targeted against surface air defenses) but both ESM and ECM missions as well. Combat support is equivalent to the category other support in table 1. The general support category in table 2 includes logistics and other missions. A small number of sorties could not be categorized based on the information available at the time of publication. These sorties are listed as unknown. Figures 3 and 4 show the sortie breakdown in terms of numbers and percentages in a manner similar to figures 1 and 2.

Table 1. CV fixed-wing combat and combat support sorties

	17-Jan	18-Jan	19-Jan	20-Jan	21-Jan	22-Jan	23-Jan	24-Jan	25-Jan	26-Jan	27-Jan	28-Jan	29-Jan	30-Jan	31-Jan
OCA	68	39	79	50	26	45	36	46	42	30	45	75	10	13	18
DCA	122	144	54	106	93	77	94	105	103	70	97	99	94	86	99
Interdiction	91	75	74	78	79	75	82	119	91	70	89	96	106	144	139
CAS	0	0	0	0	0	1	0	0	0	0	0	0	0	5	13
SEAD	78	18	12	4	13	16	10	9	22	8	7	22	4	5	10
Aerial refuel	85	101	71	71	64	72	67	81	81	74	88	98	74	77	83
Tac airlift	0	0	0	0	0	0	0	0	0	0	0	0	0	0	0
Other support	104	58	51	54	52	68	57	74	56	54	56	62	43	52	60
Total	548	435	341	363	327	354	346	434	395	306	382	452	331	382	422

	1-Feb	2-Feb	3-Feb	4-Feb	5-Feb	6-Feb	7-Feb	8-Feb	9-Feb	10-Feb	11-Feb	12-Feb	13-Feb	14-Feb	15-Feb
OCA	19	17	28	12	34	22	31	23	29	29	44	32	35	19	25
DCA	98	72	80	102	95	65	71	74	73	73	74	59	60	73	74
Interdiction	168	102	110	141	187	106	131	124	130	145	164	112	143	141	159
CAS	2	0	0	0	0	0	0	0	0	0	0	0	0	0	0
SEAD	1	0	3	4	6	14	7	8	6	8	8	5	17	10	4
Aerial Refuel	83	66	52	57	51	49	60	62	66	61	69	48	47	53	65
Tac Airlift	0	0	0	0	0	0	0	0	0	0	0	0	0	0	0
Other support	67	54	52	60	56	57	66	62	53	58	68	78	57	59	68
Total	438	311	325	376	429	313	366	353	357	374	427	334	359	355	395

	16-Feb	17-Feb	18-Feb	19-Feb	20-Feb	21-Feb	22-Feb	23-Feb	24-Feb	25-Feb	26-Feb	27-Feb	28-Feb
OCA	39	17	41	29	22	28	22	34	60	40	49	36	6
DCA	52	86	84	85	91	91	90	36	72	75	80	100	86
Interdiction	105	117	193	206	180	197	152	198	196	261	311	293	98
CAS	0	0	0	0	0	0	0	0	0	0	0	0	0
SEAD	5	9	7	8	4	0	12	0	0	12	6	8	0
Aerial Refuel	34	50	56	56	43	53	52	50	59	75	74	66	38
Tac Airlift	0	0	0	0	0	0	0	0	0	0	0	0	0
Other support	46	48	75	76	61	72	65	66	58	61	78	74	54
Total	281	327	456	460	401	441	393	384	445	524	598	577	282

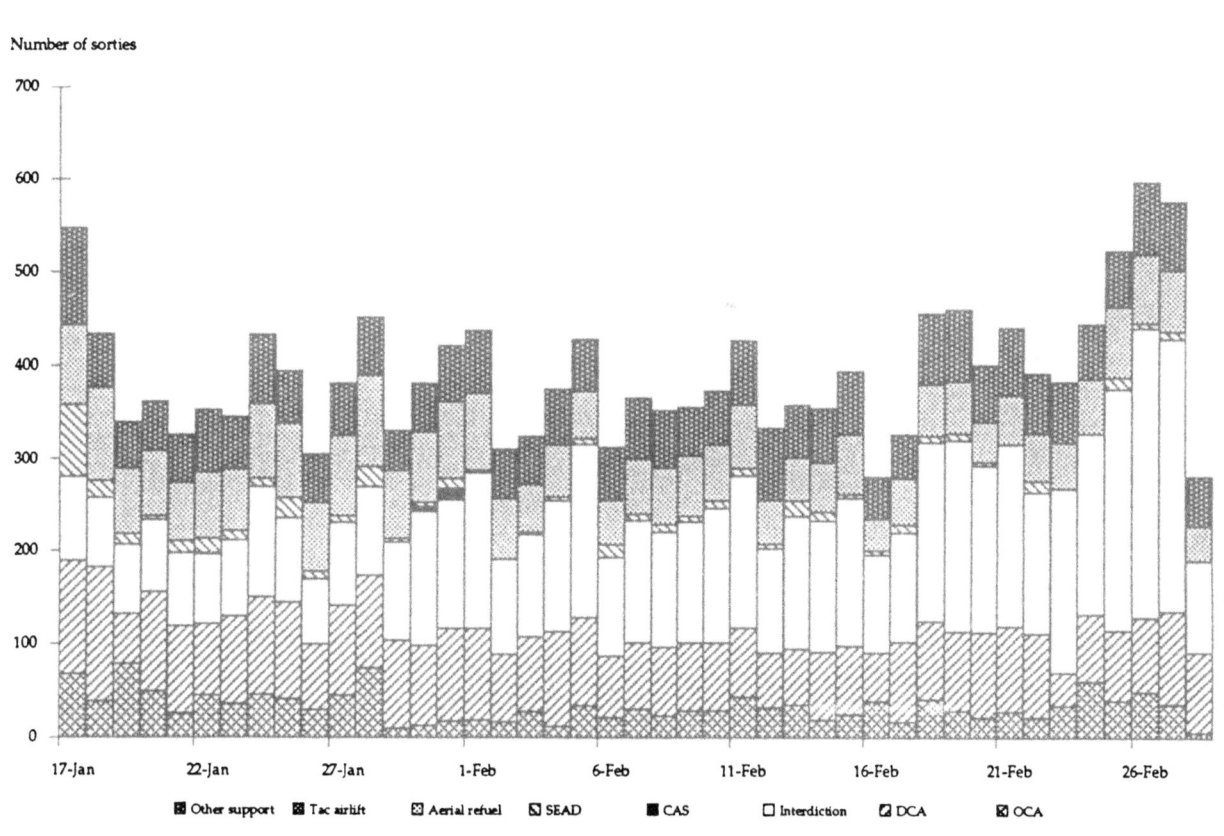

Figure 1. CV fixed-wing combat and combat-support sorties

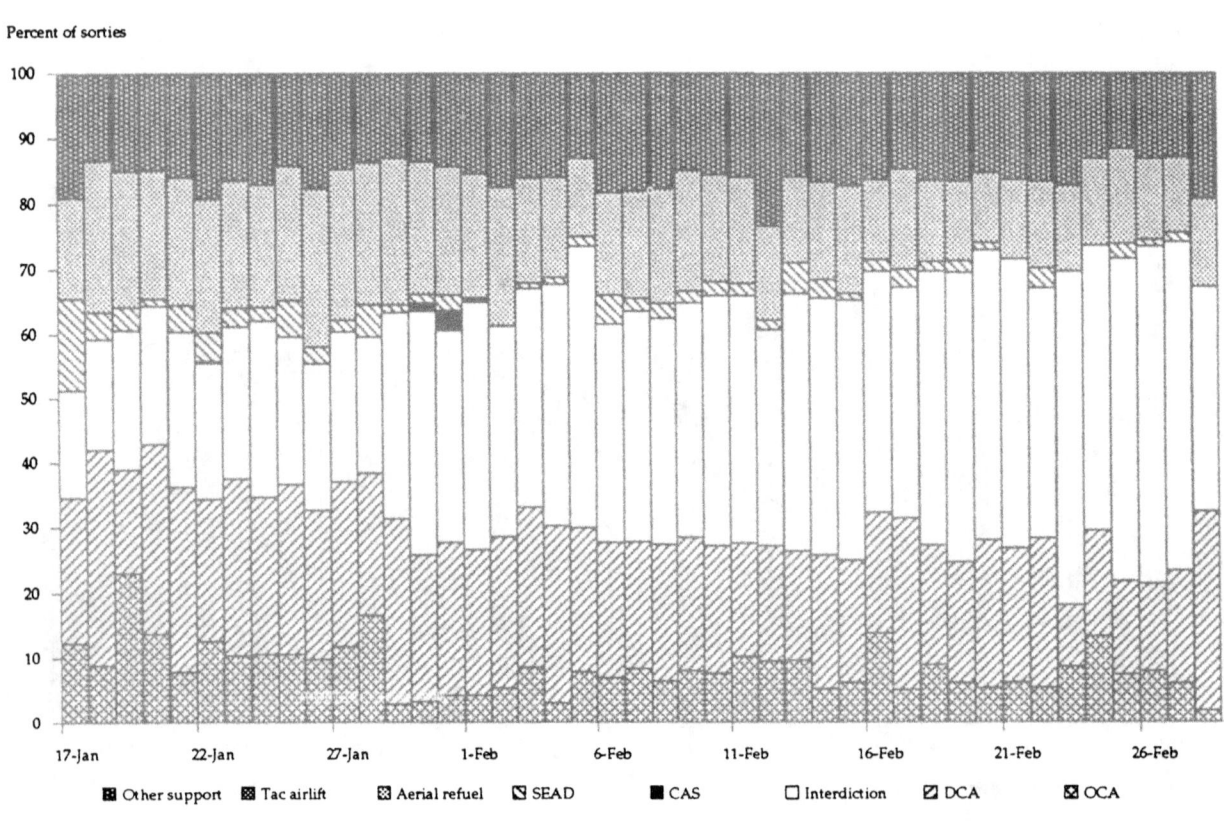

Figure 2. CV fixed-wing combat and combat-support sorties, percentiles

Table 2. Total CV fixed-wing sorties

	17-Jan	18-Jan	19-Jan	20-Jan	21-Jan	22-Jan	23-Jan	24-Jan	25-Jan	26-Jan	27-Jan	28-Jan	29-Jan	30-Jan	31-Jan
OCA	68	39	79	50	26	45	36	46	42	30	45	75	10	13	18
DCA	122	144	54	106	93	77	94	105	103	70	97	99	94	86	99
Theater strike	69	67	61	49	41	54	49	82	56	41	48	63	65	117	116
Maritime strike	22	12	20	32	38	22	33	37	35	29	41	33	41	32	36
SEAD/EW	113	37	31	26	35	41	28	34	35	24	22	41	20	23	31
Tanking	85	101	71	71	64	72	67	81	81	74	88	98	74	77	83
Combat support	69	39	32	32	30	43	39	49	43	38	41	43	27	34	39
General support	73	64	11	10	5	14	6	13	12	5	6	18	34	26	11
Unknown	8	7	2	7	5	4	4	6	35	14	14	10	6	15	9
Total	629	506	354	380	337	372	356	453	442	325	402	480	371	423	442

	1-Feb	2-Feb	3-Feb	4-Feb	5-Feb	6-Feb	7-Feb	8-Feb	9-Feb	10-Feb	11-Feb	12-Feb	13-Feb	14-Feb	15-Feb
OCA	19	17	28	12	34	22	31	23	29	29	44	32	35	19	25
DCA	98	72	80	102	95	65	71	74	73	73	74	59	60	73	74
Theater strike	136	65	81	115	159	82	104	91	102	127	145	95	123	126	143
Maritime strike	34	37	31	26	28	24	27	33	28	18	19	17	20	15	16
SEAD/EW	26	17	22	26	30	39	40	32	30	34	36	28	45	37	40
Tanking	83	66	52	57	51	49	60	62	66	61	69	48	47	53	65
Combat support	42	37	33	38	32	32	33	38	29	32	40	55	29	32	32
General support	26	12	18	12	17	11	11	18	15	7	58	56	18	15	32
Unknown	10	6	13	3	12	6	9	2	2	3	9	5	9	8	15
Total	474	329	356	391	458	330	386	373	374	384	494	395	386	378	442

	16-Feb	17-Feb	18-Feb	19-Feb	20-Feb	21-Feb	22-Feb	23-Feb	24-Feb	25-Feb	26-Feb	27-Feb	28-Feb
OCA	39	17	41	29	22	28	22	34	60	40	49	36	6
DCA	52	86	84	85	91	91	90	36	72	75	80	100	86
Theater strike	85	87	163	181	154	172	126	176	171	244	279	271	74
Maritime strike	20	30	30	25	26	25	26	22	25	17	32	23	26
SEAD/EW	26	25	45	44	32	28	41	34	26	34	37	38	21
Tanking	34	50	56	56	43	53	52	50	59	75	74	66	38
Combat support	25	32	37	40	33	44	36	32	32	39	47	44	33
General support	10	25	14	8	10	15	29	19	14	22	22	16	26
Unknown	6	2	12	3	2	9	12	10	5	11	8	13	3
Total	297	354	482	471	413	465	434	413	452	569	628	606	311

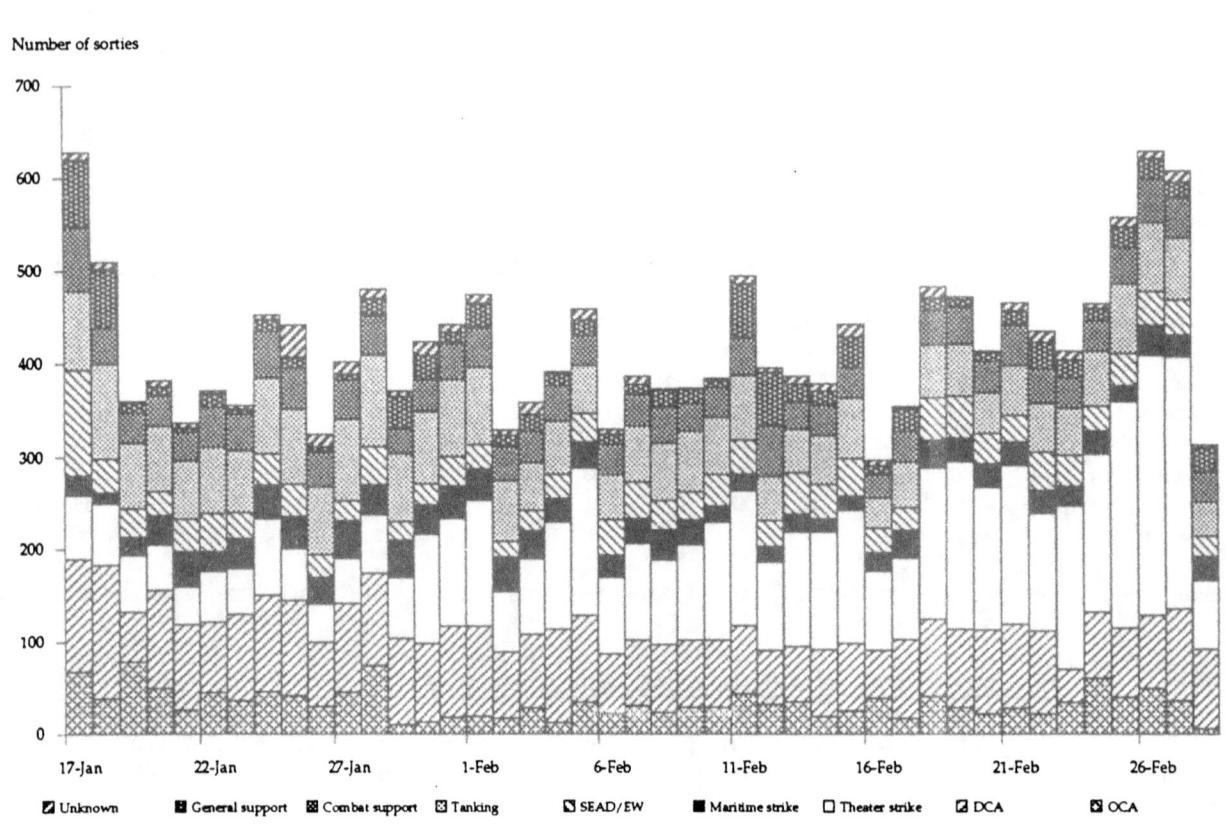

Figure 3. Total CV fixed-wing sorties

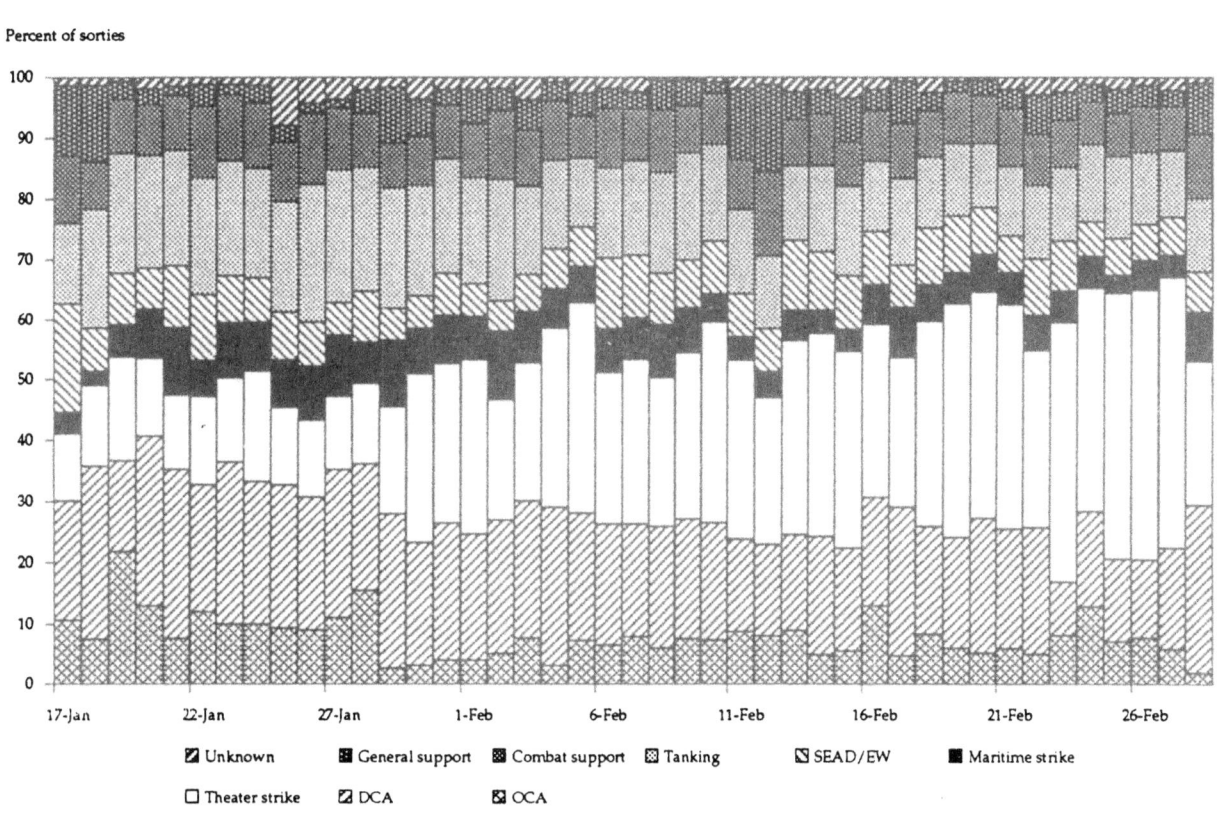

Figure 4. Total CV fixed-wing sorties, percentiles

APPENDIX E

AIRCRAFT READINESS RATES

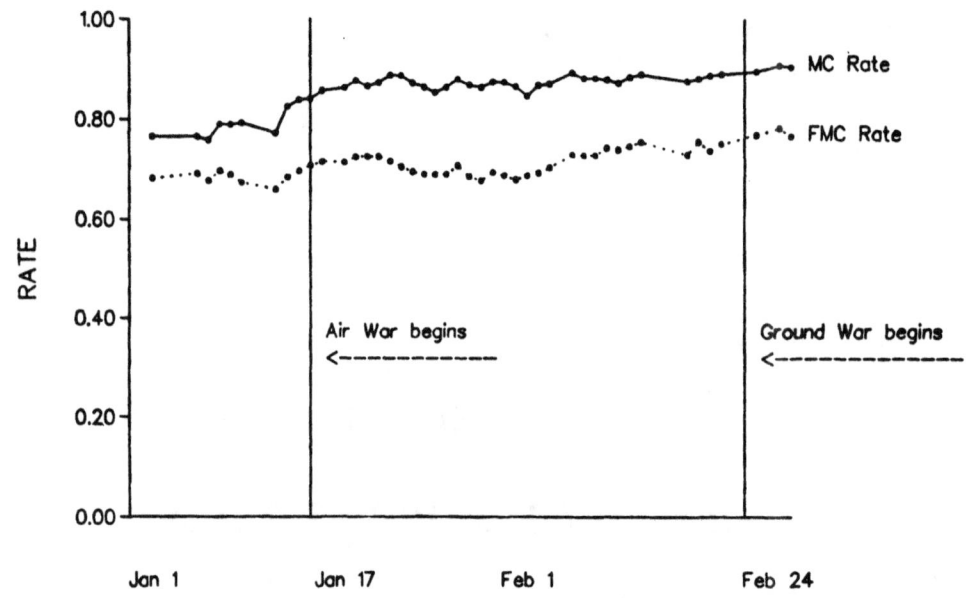

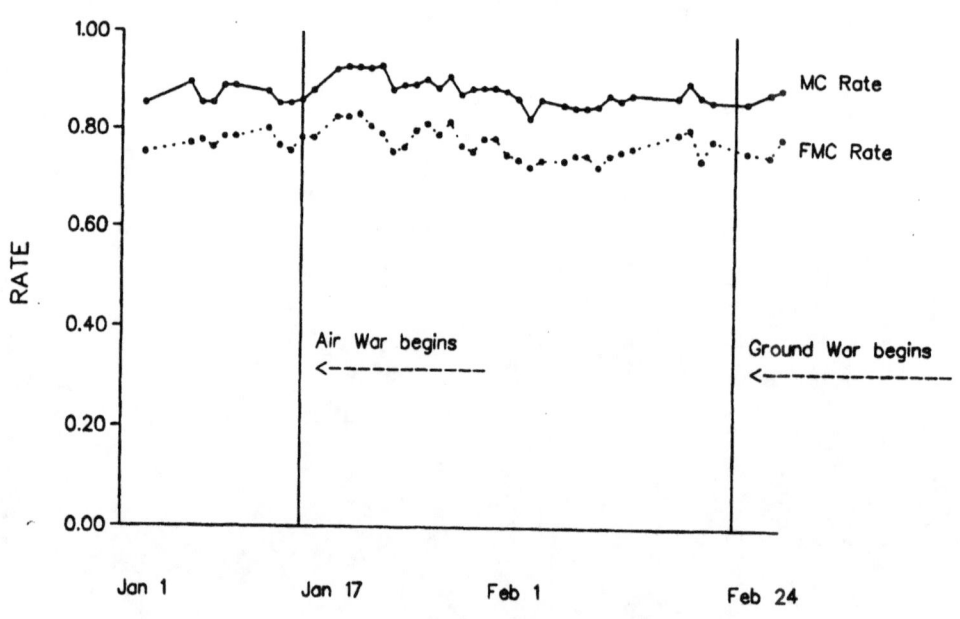

APPENDIX F

AIRCRAFT AND PERSONNEL LOSSES

OPERATION DESERT STORM AIRCRAFT LOSSES
7 Combat, 4 Non-Combat

17 Jan	1. U.S. Navy F/A-18 Hornet MIA: LCDR Michael S. Speicher
18 Jan	2. U.S. Navy A-6E Intruder POW: LT Jeffrey N. Zaun (Repatriated 4 March 1991) POW: LT Robert Wetzel (Repatriated 4 March 1991) 3. U.S. Navy A-6E Intruder KIA: LT William T. Costen KIA: LT Charles J. Turner
20 Jan	4. U.S. Navy A-6E Intruder Loss due to extensive damage. Aircraft recovered safely onboard aircraft carrier. Crew safe.
21 Jan	5. U.S. Navy F-14A Tomcat POW: LT Lawrence R. Slade (Repatriated 4 March 1991) One crewmember (LT Devon Jones) recovered safely.
26 Jan	6. U.S. Navy F/A-18 Hornet (Non-Combat) One pilot recovered safely.
2 Feb	7. U.S. Navy A-6E Intruder MIA: LCDR Barry T. Cooke KIA: LT Patrick K. Connor
5 Feb	8. U.S. Navy F/A-18 Hornet (Non-Combat) KIA: LT Robert J. Dwyer
15 Feb	9. U.S. Navy A-6E Intruder (Non-Combat) Two crewmembers recovered safely.
21 Feb	10. U.S. Navy SH-60 Seahawk (Non-Combat) No injuries. 11. U.S. Navy H-46 Sea Knight (Non-Combat) Killed: PO3 James F. Crockford

Notes: (1) MIA/KIA status as of 1 May 1991

APPENDIX G

NAVAL GUNFIRE SUPPORT

BATTLESHIP NAVAL GUNFIRE SUPPORT (NGFS) IN OPERATION DESERT STORM

The battleships WISCONSIN and MISSOURI contributed significantly to DESERT STORM in providing naval gunfire support for troops ashore. Their unmanned aerial vehicles (UAVs) gave them unique reconnaissance capabilities that were extensively used. The two battleships delivered over 2.1 million pounds of ordnance -- the equivalent of 542 A-6 missions. Battle damage assessment (BDA) was available for 41 of 80 missions and indicated that 68% of the targets received heavy damage or worse.

NGFS Data

Number of 16-inch missions fired:
WISCONSIN 33
MISSOURI <u>47</u>
Total 80

Number of 16-inch round fired:
WISCONSIN 324
MISSOURI <u>759</u>
Total 1083

Total ordnance delivered:
    2,166,000 pounds (approximate)
    4,322 Mk 82 bomb equivalents
    542 A-6 mission equivalents

Spotter services:
    41 (52%) missions were spotted by organic UAV.
    8 (10%) missions were spotted by ground or air spotter.
    31 (38%) missions were pre-planned/not spotted.

Calls for fire:
    (18%) missions were called for by ground forces.
    (82%) missions were pre-planned or self-determined.

Battle damage assessment (BDA):
BDA was not available for 39 missions due to lack of spotter or smoke and/or haze. BDA was available for 41 missions (68 targets):

light to moderate damage	32%
heavy damage	26%
target neutralized	10%
target destroyed	32%

Types of targets in NGFS missions:

artillery targets	17	command/observation posts	4
small boats (in port)	13 (1 mission)	troops in the open	4 (events)
AAW sites	10	logistics sites	3
bunkers	10	tanks	3
infantry in trenches	8 (events)	buildings	2
ammo storage sites	6	mine fields	2
SAM/SSM/rocket launchers	5	pier	1
radar/comm/ESM/SIGINT sites	5	trucks	1

APPENDIX H

SURFACE WARFARE

DESERT STORM U.S. Navy Surface Warfare Operations

This timeline includes selected items of U.S. Navy surface warfare force operations or participation as they appeared in the daily CNO SITREPS from 17 JAN 90 to 4 MAR 91. It is not all-inclusive and generally does not include Maritime Interception Force (MIF) operations or aircraft operations conducted from carriers. It's purpose is to portray "what the U.S. Navy surface warfare forces were doing" during the air and ground campaigns. Since it is comprised of initial daily information, inaccuracies may appear that do not reflect the real story after further review of events, correlation of sources and later battle damage assessment (BDA.) Information is as of 0600 local on the listed date. A summary of significant operations conducted by the surface warfare forces is also presented.

17 JAN 91 (D-DAY)
- Operation DESERT STORM commenced at 170000Z with cruise missile launches. USS *San Jacinto* launched first TLAM.
- Initial assessment has 51 of 52 TLAM's successfully launched.
- USS *Spruance* and USS *Virginia* have been placed under CINCCENT OPCON.

18 JAN 91 (D+1)
- Current assessment has 100 of 106 TLAM's successfully launched.
- Combat forces Yankee (TF-155) and Zulu (TF-154) conducted TLAM strikes on Iraqi targets.

19 JAN 91 (D+2)
- Combat forces Yankee (TF-155) (Red Sea) and Zulu (TF-154) (Persian Gulf) conductedTLAM strikes on Iraqi targets.
- VQ-2 EP-3 tasked to provide I&W to USS *Virginia* and USS *Spruance* during evacuation of US Embassy in Beirut. All embassy personnel departed safely, without incident.

20 JAN 91 (D+3)
- Combat forces Yankee (TF-155) and Zulu (TF-154) continued to conduct TLAM strikes (34) on Iraqi targets.
- *Nicholas* with AHIPS (Army helo) and Kuwait gunboat attacked enemy personnel on Dorra oil field platforms. Total of 9 platforms neutralized. Up to 23 POW's captured.
- *Leyte Gulf* entered Arabian Gulf late 19 JAN.

23 JAN 91 (D+6)
- Exercise Sea Soldier IV continues. An amphibious demonstration is scheduled 23 JAN using LCAC and helo's.

24 JAN 91 (D+7)
- Exercise Sea Soldier IV preparation continues. Landings scheduled 22-24 JAN with practice D-Day landings 26 JAN.
- Navy priorities: Seek out/destroy Iraqi naval units. Monitor oil platforms and attack when Iraqi military presence detected.

26 JAN 91 (D+9)
- Navy intentions: Seek out and destroy Iraqi naval units.
- Amphibious rehearsal (Sea Solder IV) continues. D-Day rehearsal landing scheduled for a.m. 26 JAN.

27 JAN 91 (D+10)
- Navy intentions: Seek out and destroy Iraqi naval units.
- Conducted amphibious assault rehearsal landing in Oman as part of Sea Soldier IV. Maneuvers ashore continue through 2 FEB.

30 JAN 91 (D+13)
- Navy and Marine forces engaged approx. 20 Iraqi small boats west of Maradin Island. Several boats reported destroyed.

4 FEB 91 (D+18)
- *Missouri* with *Curts*, *Nicholas* and two RSNF escorts are operating near the Saudi-Kuwaiti border.
- *Missouri* destroyed a communications bunker with seven 16-inch rounds.

5 FEB 91 (D+19)
- TF-156 completed Sea Soldier IV backload, hot wash up and lessons learned being applied to Desert Saber amphibious assault planning.
- *Missouri* will continue NGFS to MARCENT. NAVCENT may rotate *Wisconsin* into area after *Missouri* departs.

6 FEB 91 (D+20)
- *Missouri* continued NGFS for MARCENT, attacking gun emplacements, a radar control site and a SIGINT site. NAVCENT will rotate *Wisconsin* into area today.
- NAVCENT intends to reposition *America* and seven supporting ships to Gulf of Oman/North Arabian Sea NLT 13 FEB.

7 FEB 91 (D+21)
- TF-156 is scheduled to commence amphibious training today (through 14 FEB) at Al Hamra, UAE.
- *Missouri* (joined by *Wisconsin*) continued NGFS for MARCENT, hitting targets north of Khafji.

8 FEB 91 (D+22)
- TF-156 is conducting resupply, maintenance and practice amphibious training today (through 14 FEB) at Al Hamra, UAE.
- *Wisconsin* relieved *Missouri* and continued NGFS for MARCENT, hitting an artillery emplacement north of Khafji.
- TF-151 will continue full-time NGFS off Kuwait until 9 FEB.
- *Spruance* (48 TLAM) transits Suez Canal today enroute NRS replacing *Philippine Sea* (15 TLAM.)

9 FEB 91 (D+23)
- An OPORD has been issued by CINCCENT to NAVCENT to prepare for amphibious operations. Establishment of an Amphibious Objective Area (AOA), pre-assault planning, mine countermeasures (MCM), naval gunfire support (NGFS) ordered. AOA recommendations due to CINCCENT by 8 FEB.
- U.S. Navy SEALS conducted underwater recon of area west of Maradin Island and will recon to confirm SCUD decoys.
- USS *Wisconsin* fired NGF in support of USMC near Khafji and fired 24 16-inch rounds on patrol boats in Mina Saud harbor. Boats sunk- (8),

damaged- (5), one pier destroyed. Expended 24 rounds against artillery, command post and infantry.

11 FEB 91 (D+25)
- *America* BG chopped from TF-155 to TF-154, ETR Hormuz 14 FEB.

12 FEB 91 (D+26)
- Iraq's one remaining OSA PTG is located at Umm Qasr Naval Base. All five TNC-45 and FPB57 Exocet-capable PB's are assessed as destroyed.
- *Missouri* returns to fire support area near Al Khafji to support MARCENT ops 12 FEB.

13 FEB 91 (D+27)
- In support of MARCENT, *Missouri* destroyed command bunker and antenna complex.
- TF-156 and TF-158: Conducted ashore training in UAE including live firing. Making final prep for amphibious landing, if ordered.
- JCS has modified CONUS CV readiness posture, rescinding requirement for 3 additional CV's to be in increased readiness posture.

14 FEB 91 (D+28)
- No enemy naval activity.
- *America* BG enroute Arabian Gulf, transiting strait of Hormuz.
- TF-156/158 (amphibs) commenced backload from UAE training area.
- *Wisconsin* assumed NGFS in support of MARCENT. *Missouri* on seven hour tether.
- USN elements conducted recon of Kuwaiti coast using rubber duck insertion. Assisted by MH-53's.

15 FEB 91 (D+29)
- No enemy air or naval activity. Enemy coastal radars have been more active in past two days, suggesting fear of amphibious attack.
- TF-156/158 (amphibs): Faylaka Island raid planning/rehearsal to commence 15 FEB.
- TF-151: *Tripoli* and mine warfare ships enroute Northern Arabian Gulf for MCM ops in support of possible amphibious ops. NGFS BB's on seven hour tether.

16 FEB 91 (D+30)
- Enemy naval activity further reduced following heavy patrol craft attrition vicinity of Faylaka Island on 13 FEB.
- TF-156 departed training area for ATF Box, preparing for amphibious raid on Faylaka Island, if ordered.
- TF-151 to commence MCM ops in Faylaka FSA.

17 FEB 91 (D+31)
- TF-156 standing by to execute Faylaka Island raid if ordered.

18 FEB 91 (D+32)
- USS *Princeton* struck a suspected moored mine in NAG at 180417Z. Three personnel with injuries transferred to HMS *Argus*. No danger of sinking. Survey teams from salvage ship USS *Beaufort* aboard.
- USS *Tripoli* struck a mine in NAG at 180135Z. No personnel injuries. Some flooding forward (contained.) No damage above water line. Ship

reports no stability problems and is underway on own power. Survey teams from USS *Beaufort* aboard.

19 FEB 91 (D+33)
- Damage sustained by USS *Princeton* indicates detonation of influence type mine as opposed to direct contact mine.
- USS *Princeton* enroute Jebel Ali, UAE under tow of USS *Beaufort*.
- USS *Tripoli* reports fully mission capable with several flooded compartments. She has resumed duty as MCM/NGFS Commander.

20 FEB 91 (D+34)
- Large minefield located on sonar by *Adroit*. Estimate lane clear for BB to enter Faylaka FSA in two to three days.
- *Wisconsin* remains within seven hours of MARCENT NGFS area.

21 FEB 91 (D+35)
- More than 40 mines reported detected in NAG by MCM forces in the past 36 hours.
- USS *Princeton* diverted to Bahrain due to increasing sea state.

22 FEB 91 (D+36)
- Marines flew 20 sorties against targets in the KTO, marking the first time that AV-8 combat air sorties have ever been launched from the deck of an LHA (*Nassau*.)
- *Tripoli* damage appears to be more severe than originally estimated. Hole size revised to 20 by 30 feet.

23 FEB 91 (D+37)
- TF-154 (*Midway, Ranger, Roosevelt, America*) attacked Faylaka Island destroying communication facility, AAA site and bunkers. Attacks included seven AV-8 sorties from *Nassau*.

24 FEB 91 (D+38) (G-DAY)
- Commenced the ground offensive "G" day 24 FEB, "H" hour 0100Z.
- TF-154 (*Midway, Ranger, Roosevelt, America*) continued attacks on Faylaka Island in preparation for ground offensive.
- *Tripoli* scheduled to remain on station until 241400Z to crossdeck AMCM helo's and equipment to *New Orleans*.

25 FEB 91 (D+39) (G+1)
- *Missouri* sighted missile inbound, while 12 miles off Kuwait City. Possible Silkworm, but no ESM detected. Target engaged and destroyed by two Sea Darts from HMS *Gloucester*.
- Anticipate *Princeton* ready for tow to Jebel Ali, UAE today.
- *Tripoli* enroute Jubayl ETA today, to cross deck AMCM helo's and equipment to *New Orleans*. Estimate resumption of AMCM ops 4 MAR.

26 FEB 91 (D+40) (G+2)
- *Wisconsin* and *Missouri* will conduct dual BB NGFS in NAG today.
- *La Salle* replaced *Tripoli* as AMCM support and C2 platform until arrival of *New Orleans*. Until that time *Tripoli's* AMCM helo's will stage and sortie from Jubayl.
- CTG 156.2 (CPG3) still offloading 5th MEB at Al Mishab for chop to MARCENT.

27 FEB 91 (D+41) (G+3)
- TF-156 executed deceptive amphibious helo operations toward Bubiyan beach.
- TF-151 continued combined AMCM operations with Royal Navy.

28 FEB 91 (D+42) (G+4)
- President Bush directed a cessation of offensive operations for USCENTCOM forces effective 280800 in the KTO.
- NAVCENT tasking as of 280500Z includes: protect the fleet, support CENTCOM tasking, continue mineclearing ops, prepare for logistics over the shore, assess capability of, and time to prepare Ash Shuaybah, Kuwait as operational logistics port.
- *Princeton* arriving Jebel Ali for mine damage assessment.
- Completion of TF-158 offload of 5th MEB elements at Ras Al Mishab now projected for 1 MAR.
- *Avenger* discovered Italian Manta bottom influence mine in vicinity of *Princeton/Tripoli* mine explosions. Mine destroyed. Estimate Iraq had approx. 150 Manta's.

1 MAR 91 (D+43)
- *La Salle* has temporarily replaced *Tripoli* as AMCM support and C2 platform until arrival of *New Orleans*.

2 MAR 91 (D+44)
- TF-156 4th MEB prepared to continue amphib ops and began backload of 5th MEB units 1 MAR.
- TF-151 with RN and RSNF continues combined AMCM and ship MCM. Top priority is to sweep a lane into Ash Shaybah.
- Naval missions: maintain naval superiority, blockade Kuwait coast to prevent small vessels from escaping, continue MCM ops, plan for Faylaka EPW evacuation.

3 MAR 91 (D+45)
- Naval missions: ops include NAG mine searches, and surface surveillance.
- TF-156 and TF-158 (afloat MAGTAF) will conduct evacuation of EPW's from Faylaka Island on 3 MAR and reconnaissance of other islands to determine presence of Iraqi forces.

4 MAR 91 (D+46)
- TF-156 conducted evacuation of 1405 EPW's (one BG, three COL, 86 officers) from Faylaka Island. No resistance.
- DESERT STORM total 16-inch ordnance fired by *Wisconsin* and *Missouri* was 1083, equal to 4322 Mk-82 bombs or 542 A-6 missions. BDA for 41 missions were classified as "heavy, neutralized, or destroyed" for 68% of targets.
- MCM ops to clear route to Ash Shuaybah will be completed by 5 MAR.

A summary of significant surface warfare operations or participation:

1. TLAM strikes on Iraqi targets in the first moments of the war.
2. Successful evacuation of U.S. Embassy in Beirut, no casualties.
3. Nine oil platforms at Dorra neutralized, 23 EPW's taken.
4. Exercise Sea Soldier IV amphibious assault exercise.
5. Approx. 20 Iraqi small boats west of Maradin Island engaged, several sunk.
6. *Missouri* NGFS destroyed Iraqi communications bunker with seven 16-inch rounds.
7. TF-156 practiced amphibious assault training.
8. *Wisconsin* joined *Missouri* provided NGFS north of Khafji.
9. Preparation for amphibious assault operation.
10. SEALs conducted underwater recon in area west of Maradin Island.
11. *Wisconsin* conducted NGFS for Marines near Khafji, sunk small boats, damaged a pier, and hit bunkers and communication facilities.
12. *Missouri* returned to provide NGFS near Khafji, hit command bunker and antenna complex.
13. U.S. Navy elements conducted recon of Kuwaiti coast using rubber duck insertion.
14. TF-156/158 practiced assault of Faylaka Island.
15. TF-151 mine warfare ships in northern Arabian Gulf for MCM operations.
16. *Princeton* and *Tripoli* struck mines.
17. *Adroit* located large minefield, cleared path for battleships to attack Faylaka Is.
18. First ever combat AV-8 sorties launched from an LPH (Nassau.)
19. Faylaka Island attacked.
20. CTG 156.2 offloaded 5th MEB at Al Mishab for chop to MARCENT.
21. TF-156 conducted deceptive amphibious helo assault toward Bubiyan Beach.
22. TF-151 conducted combined MCM operations with the Royal Navy.
23. *Avenger* discovered Italian-made bottom influence mine.
24. Blockaded Kuwaiti coast to prevent escape of Iraqi small boats.
25. Conducted massive MCM operation to clear a path into Ash Shaybah.
26. Evacuated over 1400 EPW's from Faylaka Island.
27. Conducted reconnaissance of other islands searching for Iraqi troops.

APPENDIX I

UNMANNED AERIAL VEHICLES

UNMANNED AERIAL VEHICLES IN DESERT SHIELD/STORM

Unmanned Aerial Vehicles (UAVs) performed superbly during DESERT SHIELD/STORM. Their uses included targeting, "real time" battle damage assessment, artillery and naval gunfire adjustment, reconnaissance and advanced warning, and coordination of ground and air operations. UAVs elicited very positive feedback from DESERT STORM commanders.

UAV Data

522 Sorties/1641 hours flown (at least 1 UAV airborne at all times during DESERT STORM):

Unit	Sorties	Hours
Navy		
VC-6 Det 1 (USS WISCONSIN)	100	342.9
(Embarked 7 Aug 90)		
VC-6 Det 2 (USS MISSOURI)	64	209.7
(Embarked 3 Nov 90)		
Marine Corps		
1st RPVCO	94	330.3
(Commenced ops 26 Sep 90)		
2nd RPVCO	69 (Thru 1 Mar)	226.6
(Commenced ops 27 Nov 90)		
3rd RPVCO	147 (Thru 24 Feb)	380.6
Army		
USA UAVPLT	48	150.8
(Commenced ops 1 Feb 91)		
Total	**522**	**1640.9**

12 UAVs destroyed:
- 1 hostile fire
- 3 electromagnetic interference (EMI)
- 2 operator error
- 6 engine/general/airframe failure

11 UAVs damaged during DESERT STORM (repairable):
- 2 EMI
- 6 operator error
- 3 engine/general failure

3 UAVs suffered minor damage due to small arms fire.

APPENDIX J

MARITIME INTERCEPTION OPERATIONS

OPERATION DESERT STORM
CHRONOLOGICAL SHIP DIVERSIONS SUMMARY

DIVERTED SHIP (FLAG)	DATE	LOC	DIVERTING SHIP(S)
1. *HENG CHUNG HAI* (CHINA)	18 Aug 1990	ARABIAN GULF	USS ENGLAND (warned, boarded, anchored-proceeded) (enroute Iraq to Qing Dao, China)
2. *DONGOLA* (CYPRUS)	18 Aug	N. RED SEA	USS SCOTT (diverted without boarding) (enr Sudan to Aqaba)
3. *KOTA WIRAMA* (BAHAMAS)	28 Aug	N. ARABIAN SEA	USS SAMPSON (enr Jeddah to Iraq w/porcelain)
4. *ZANOOBIA* (IRAQ)	04 Sep	N. ARABIAN SEA	USS GOLDSBOROUGH (enr Sri Lanka to Umm Qasr w/tea)
5. *ARI* (LIBERIA)	12 Sep	N. RED SEA	USS BIDDLE (enr Jeddah to Aqaba w/wood and steel)
6. *HAUL TRIBUTE* (PHILIPPINE)	20 Sep	N. RED SEA	USS MONTGOMERY (enr Pireaeus to Aqaba w/military equip)
7. *RED SEA ENSIGN* (GERMANY)	29 Sep	N. RED SEA	USS MONTGOMERY (enr Jeddah to Aqaba w/chem and steel)
8. *BLUE NILE* (SUDAN)	04 Oct	N. RED SEA	USS S. B. ROBERTS (enr U.K. to Aqaba with chem and steel)
9. *TADMUR* (IRAQ)	08 Oct	N. ARABIAN SEA	USS GOLDSBOROUGH HMS BRAZEN HMAS DARWIN (enr Aqaba to Iraq with/rice, flour, cooking oil)
10. *BAR'ZAN* (QATAR)	12 Oct	N. RED SEA	USS S. B. ROBERTS (enr Port Suez to Aqaba with/pump, rice, flour)
11. *LEPANTO* (HONDURAS)	12 Oct	N. RED SEA	USS S. B. ROBERTS (enr Jeddah to Aqaba w/nuts, beans, seeds)

DIVERTED SHIP (FLAG)	DATE	LOC	DIVERTING SHIP(S)
12. *AL WATTYAH* (UAE)	20 Oct	N. RED SEA	USS S. B. ROBERTS (div 21st/enr Jeddah to Aqaba w/chems, elect)
13. *OLANDIA* (GERMANY)	28 Oct	N. RED SEA	USS PHILIPPINE SEA (one container-Iraq/Jordan shipping) (enr Italy to Aqaba w/spare parts)
14. *BLUE NILE* (SUDAN)	28 Oct	N. RED SEA	USS MOOSBRUGGER (potassium labelled "cotton", no consignee) (enr Port Sudan to Aqaba)
15. *WLADYSLAW JAGIELLO* (POLAND)	01 Nov	N. RED SEA	USS BIDDLE (4 diesel generators-w/o papers) (enr Sweden to Aqaba)
16. *RED SEA EUROPA* (GERMANY)	02 Nov	N. RED SEA	USS BIDDLE (chemicals not on manifest) (enr Greece to Aqaba)
17. *NIKOLAY SABITSKIY* (RUSSIA)	15 Nov	N. RED SEA	USS MOOSBRUGGER (household goods manifest/Iraq) (enr Russia to Aqaba)
19. *PREMIER* (GERMANY)	22 Nov	N. RED SEA	USS BIDDLE (many changes on manifest) (enr Cyprus to Aqaba w/ball bearings,) (milling machine, 2 heavy containers)
23. *TILIA* (CYPRUS)	13 Dec	N. RED SEA	USS GATES USS MISSISSIPPI (motor vehicles from Kuwait for Yemen) (enr Aqaba to Hodeida-returned)
24. *DONGOLA* (CYPRUS)	13 Dec	N. RED SEA	USS SAMPSON (256 Kuwait m/v's, one with Kuwaiti-flag) (enr Aqaba to Port Sudan-returned)
25. *TILIA* (CYPRUS)	15 Dec	N. RED SEA	USS MISSISSIPPI (cars not listed properly on manifest) (enr Aqaba to Hodeida-returned)

DIVERTED SHIP (FLAG)	DATE	LOC	DIVERTING SHIP(S)
26. *TILIA* (CYPRUS)	16 Dec	N. RED SEA	USS MISSISSIPPI SNS DIANA (improperly manifested cars-tampered cars) (enr Aqaba to Hodeida-returned)
27. *TILIA* (CYPRUS)	18 Dec	N. RED SEA	USS MONTGOMERY (53 inaccessible containers-possibly cars) (enr Aqaba to Hodeida-diverted to Yanbu)
30. *RED SEA EUROPA* (GERMANY)	19 Dec	N. RED SEA	USS MISSISSIPPI SNS DIANA (2 containers not on manifest, chems, cars) (stainless sheets, tires, wool, tractors, meat) (enr Rotterdam to Aqaba-diverted no port yet)
31. *IBN KAHLDOON*	25 Dec	N. ARABIAN SEA	USS OLDENDORF USS FIFE USS TRENTON HMS BRAZEN HMAS SIDNEY (w/sugar, milk, spaghetti, tea) (enr Aden to Umm Qasar-diverted to Muscat)
32. *LEDENICE* (YUGOSLAVIA)	31 Dec	N. RED SEA	USS MISSISSIPPI (no original manifest-whiteout changes) (enr Sudan to Aqaba-divert to Djibouti)
34. *DMITRIY-FURMANOV* (RUSSIA)	04 Jan 1991	N. RED SEA	USS MISSISSIPPI SNS INFANTA-CHRISTINA (detonators, tank parts, rocket launchers) (w/o manifest/enr USSR to Aqaba)
	10 Jan	N. RED SEA	USS MISSISSIPPI SNS DIANA (reboarded-still unmanifested crates) (departed N. Red Sea through Suez Canal)
35. *PETR MASHEROV* (also *PYOTR*) (RUSSIA)	06 Jan	N. RED SEA	USS MISSISSIPPI (lead ingots without consignee) (enr Jeddah to Aqaba-layed to, proceeded)

DIVERTED SHIP (FLAG)	DATE	LOC	DIVERTING SHIP(S)
37. *RED SEA ENERGY* (GERMANY)	27 Jan	N. RED SEA (86 of 246 inaccessible railroad cars) (some cargo manifested to Jordan Export Co.) (enr Greece to Aqaba-diverted to Jeddah)	**USS S. B. ROBERTS**
39. *MAWASHI AL-GASSEEM* (SAUDI ARABIA)	02 Feb	N. RED SEA (30-40k sheep, no consignee on manifest) (enr Jeddah to Aqaba)	**USS BIDDLE**
40. *CLYMENE* (BAHAMAS)	02 Feb	N. RED SEA (50k mt wheat, no original manifest, only ltr) (enr Houston to Aqaba)	**USS S. B. ROBERTS**
41. *ARABIAN BREEZE* (JAPAN)	02 Feb	N. RED SEA (automobiles, no consignee on manifest) (enr Jeddah to Aqaba)	**USS S. B. ROBERTS** **USS HALYBURTON**
42. *RED SEA EUROPA* (GERMANY)	07 Feb	N. RED SEA (machine pts, tires, lunch meat, wheat, lube oil) (no original manifest, inaccessible containers) (enr Greece to Aqaba-diverted to Port Sudan)	**USS BIDDLE**
43. *RED SEA ENERGY* (GERMANY)	09 Feb	N. RED SEA (inaccessible cargo containers-no orig manifest) (enr Jeddah to Aqaba-no diverted port yet)	**USS THOMAS C. HART**
46. *FRIO CARIBIC* (PANAMA)	21 Feb	N. RED SEA (no original manifest) (enr Tampa to Aqaba-no divert port yet)	**USS SPRUANCE**
49. *LEDENICE* (YUGOSLAVIA)	26 Feb	N. RED SEA (metal shoes with KUWAIT stamp blocked out) (poison with no dangerous cargo manifest) (dimethyl phtalate & dichlorodifluoromethane) (altered manifest and cargo labels) (enr Port Sudan to Aqaba-divert to Yanbu)	**USS BIDDLE** **SNS VENCEDORA**
50. *SALAJ* (ROMANIA)	05 Mar	N. RED SEA (cargo - steel) (no original manifest and no consignee) (enr Bulgaria to Aqaba - diverted to Port Suez)	**USS S.B. ROBERTS**

51. *SALAJ*   07 Mar   N. RED SEA   **USS MOOSBRUGGER**
    (ROMANIA)
    (cargo - steel coils, nail wire)
    (no original manifest, improper bill of lading)
    (enr Bulgaria to Aqaba - rediverted)

52. *BRAHMS*   18 Mar   N. RED SEA   **USS NORMANDY**
    (MALTA)
    (cargo-fuel oil)
    (no manifest)
    (enr Syria to Aqaba-ordered to lay to)

53. *NOVMENCHU*   18 Mar   N. RED SEA   **USS NORMANDY**
    (CYPRUS)   **USS WILLIAM V. PRATT**
    (cargo-lube oil, tires)
    (28 inaccessible containers)
    (enr Bremen to Aqaba-diverted to Port Suez)

54. *RED SEA EUROPA*   27 Mar   N. RED SEA   **USS HALYBURTON**
    (GERMANY)
    (hazardous material, hsehold goods, baby food)
    (inaccessible conts, non-manifested material)
    (enr Greed to Aqaba-diverted to port)

55. *RIZE K*   28 Mar   N. RED SEA   **USS WILLIAM V. PRATT**
    (TURKEY)
    (determined to be humanitarian food)
    (manifest not indicating Aqaba-no consignee)
    (enr Turkey to Aqaba-humanitar. allowed to go)

60. *FORTUNE CELIA*   07 Apr   N. RED SEA   **USS HALYBURTON**
    (PANAMA)
    (coffee, sesame seeds, beans, rubber gloves)
    (inaccessable cargo)
    (enr Hodeida, YE to Aqaba-allowed to proceed)

62. *ARKADIY*   15 Apr   N. RED SEA   **USS CARON**
    SVERDLOV
    (RUSSIA)
    (auto parts, household goods, a/c parts)
    (inaccessible containers-no consignee)
    (enr USSR to Aqaba)

63. *WHITE NILE*   20 Apr   N. RED SEA   **USS CARON**
    (SUDAN)   **SNS VENCEDORA**
    (cargo-general containers)
    (75% containers inacces'ble-discreps on manifest)
    (enr Malta to Aqaba-divert to masters choice pt)

DIVERTED SHIP (FLAG)	DATE	LOC	DIVERTING SHIP(S)
64. *TIBOR SZAMUELY* (RUSSIA)	22 Apr	N. RED SEA (cargo-wood and rice) (lighters with intermed. manifests, inaccessible) (enr Viet Nam to Aqaba-diverted to Dvinsk)	USS CARON
65. *HUATUO* (CHINA)	23 Apr	N. RED SEA (cargo-machinery parts, containers) (inaccessible cargo, cargo not matching manifest) (enr Antwerp to Aqaba-lying to, awaiting instrut)	USS LEYTE GULF
66. *AURES* (ALGERIA)	29 Apr	N. RED SEA (cargo-milk, beans, medical supplies) (inacces'ible cargo for Iraq, manifst w/o consign) (enr Algeria to Aqaba-no divert port yet)	USS LEYTE GULF USS VREELAND
67. *TULCIDAC* (INDIA)	29 Apr	N. RED SEA (cargo-clothing, whiskey, electronics) (inacces'ble cargo for Iraq, manifst w/o consign) (enr England to Aqaba-no divert port yet)	USS VREELAND
68. *GREEN VALLEY* (UNITED STATES) (FIRST US SHIP DIVERTED)	02 May	N. RED SEA (cargo-office supp, motor vehicle, food, military) (inaccessible cargo) (enr Port Suez to Aqaba-no divert port yet)	USS HAWES
70. *AURES* (ALGERIA)	03 May	N. RED SEA (cargo-milk, beans, medical supplies-generators) (inacces'ble cargo, generators w/o UN perm) (enr Algeria to Aqaba-no divert port yet)	USS VREELAND

Numbers denote diversions by U. S. Navy ships only and/or with coalition ships, not total number of diversions.

APPENDIX K

SEALIFT

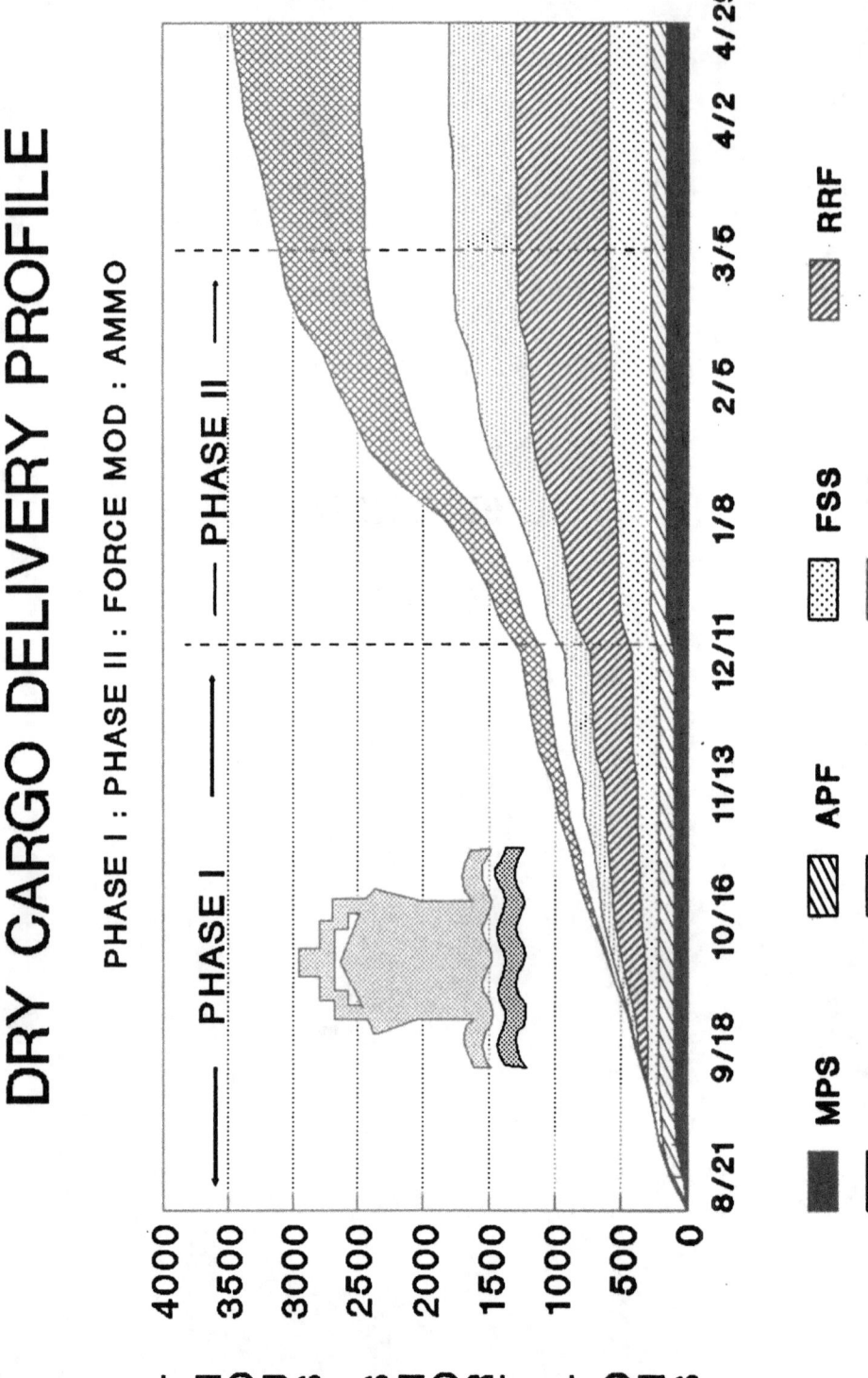

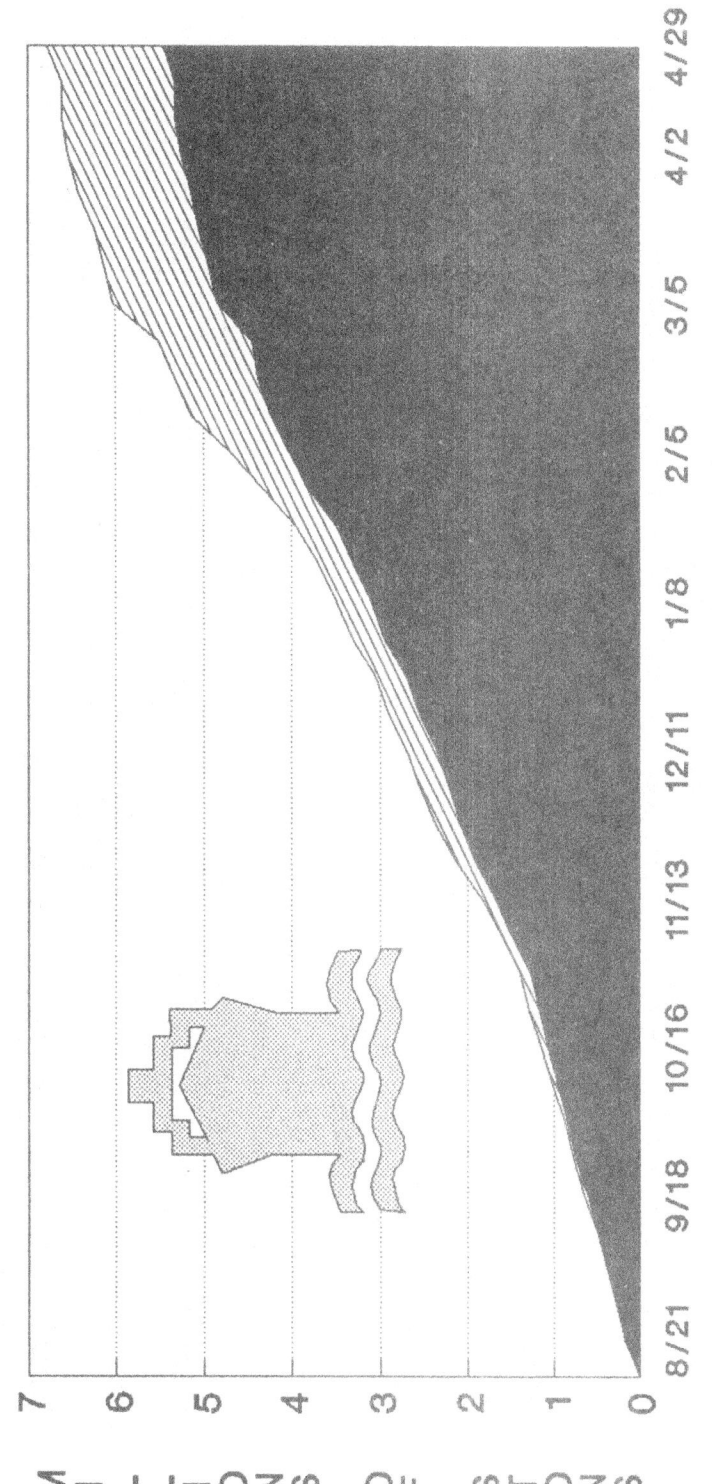

APPENDIX L

AIRLIFT

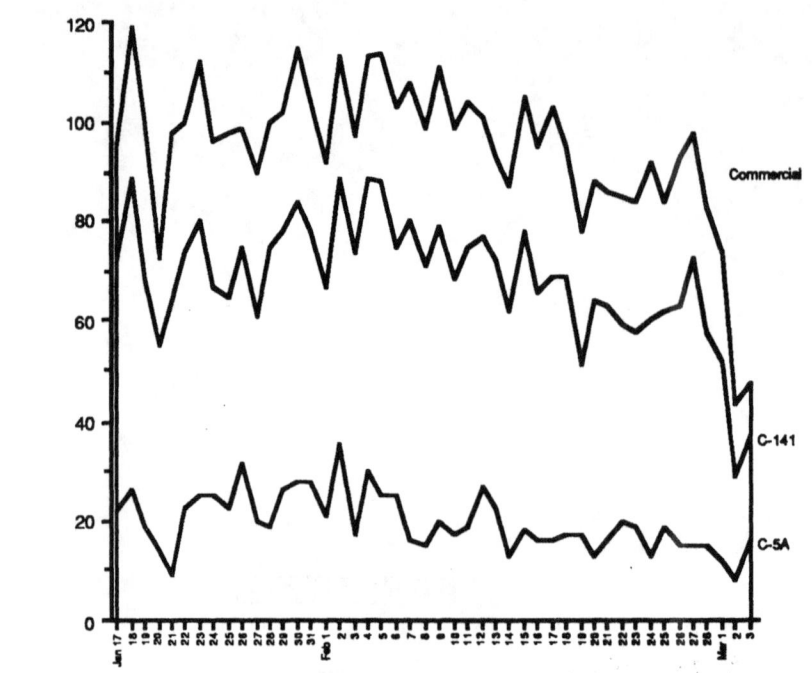

Date

Source: USCINCCENT SITREPS

Strat Air Data

Date	C-5	C-141	Commercial	Total	Cumulative
Jan 17	22	50	23	95	95
18	26	63	30	119	214
19	19	49	32	100	314
20	14	41	18	73	387
21	9	55	34	98	485
22	23	51	26	100	585
23	25	55	32	112	697
24	25	42	29	96	793
25	23	42	33	98	891
26	32	43	24	99	990
27	20	41	29	90	1080
28	19	56	25	100	1180
29	26	52	24	102	1282
30	28	56	31	115	1397
31	28	50	26	104	1501
Feb 1	21	46	25	99	1600
2	35	54	24	117	1717
3	17	57	23	97	1814
4	30	59	24	113	1927
5	25	63	26	114	2041
6	25	50	28	103	2144
7	16	64	28	108	2252
8	15	56	28	99	2351
9	20	59	32	111	2462
10	17	51	31	99	2561
11	19	56	29	104	2665
12	27	50	24	101	2766
13	23	49	21	93	2859
14	13	49	25	87	2946
15	18	60	27	105	3051
16	16	50	29	95	3146
17	16	53	34	103	3249
18	17	52	26	95	3344
19	17	34	27	78	3422
20	13	51	24	88	3510
21	16	47	23	86	3596
22	20	39	26	85	3681
23	19	39	26	84	3765
24	13	47	32	92	3857
25	19	43	22	84	
26	15	48	30	93	
27	15	58	25	98	
28	15	43	25	83	
Mar 1	12	40	22	74	
2	8	21	14	43	
3	16	21	11	49	

APPENDIX M

MISCELLANEOUS PERSONNEL DATA

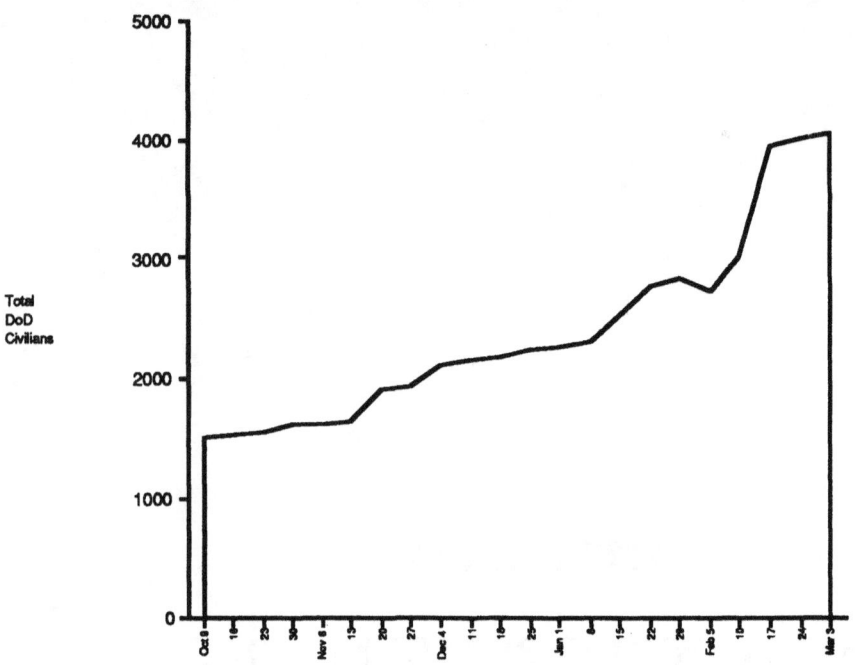

Date	Civilians
Oct 9	1488
16	1533
23	1547
30	1609
Nov 6	1613
13	1635
20	1902
27	1925
Dec 4	2107
11	2155
18	2181
25	2241
Jan 1	2244
8	2300
15	2520
22	2770
29	2835
Feb 5	2733
10	3027
17	3962
24	4012
Mar 3	4048

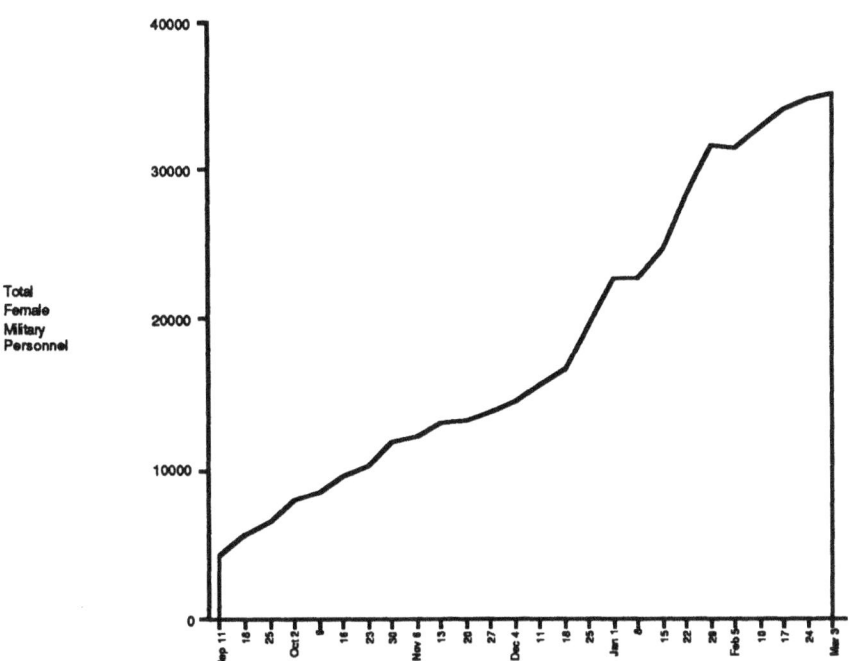

Date	Total
Sep 11	4323
18	5631
25	6662
Oct 2	8042
9	8543
16	9580
23	10420
30	11857
Nov 6	12268
13	13179
20	13462
27	13894
Dec 4	14463
11	15566
18	16758
25	19606
Jan 1	22799
8	22718
15	24743
22	28300
29	31602
Feb 5	31510
10	32915
17	34092
24	34838
Mar 3	35146

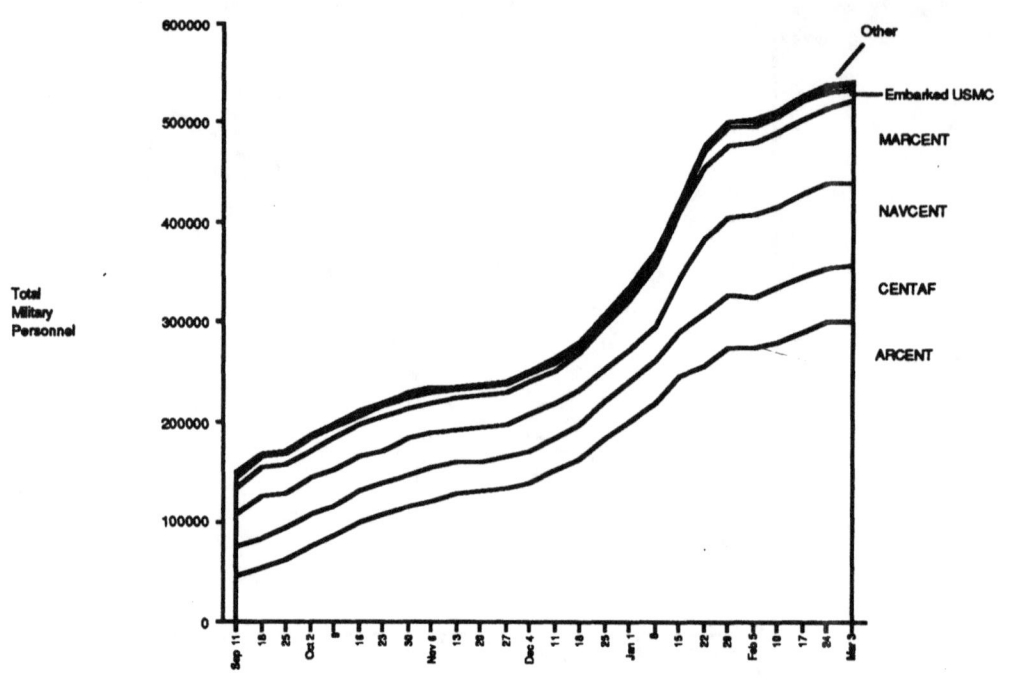

Mil Pers Data

Date	ARCENT	CENTAF	NAVCENT	MARCENT	Embarked	SOCCENT	HQ CENTCOM	JCSE	TOTAL
Sep 11	44632	29550	32143	26431	12165	2050	579	220	147770
18	53652	30179	40500	29172	10656	2707	694	219	167779
25	62427	31299	34125	29682	10669	3024	755	220	172201
Oct 2	74654	32445	35473	30166	10658	2942	635	215	187188
9	84573	32293	35733	30646	10629	2924	670	212	197680
16	99453	31500	34444	31343	10582	2919	687	211	211139
23	107070	31405	34510	31503	10479	2856	687	207	218717
30	115000	31520	36076	31391	10398	2912	722	182	228201
Nov 6	122288	30983	34978	31273	10197	2893	727	185	233524
13	128617	30981	32775	31151	7886	2883	741	181	235215
20	131195	30868	32721	31010	7953	2923	753	178	237601
27	133248	31194	33190	31148	7937	2940	768	174	240599
Dec 4	138481	32043	38428	31316	7925	2927	837	174	252131
11	151615	33717	33599	33182	7897	2925	859	190	263984
18	163644	34326	33443	38423	7885	2942	866	190	281719
25	184265	36443	32959	44541	7855	2994	899	187	310143
Jan 1	200414	39028	33165	50395	7852	2980	900	187	334921
8	218501	43139	35233	60514	7881	2975	931	184	367048
15	245290	46563	52160	65804	7858	3173	1007	186	419521
22	257064	50462	77189	71762	17048	3395	1047	209	478175
29	275793	51876	79119	72623	17059	3843	1080	207	501600
Feb 5	273863	53192	80303	73273	16799	4210	1109	292	503041
10	281347	54512	80876	74020	16875	4594	1111	306	513641
17	292177	54898	82514	74902	16867	4816	1132	307	527613
24	300952	54611	83042	75582	16921	5114	1146	307	537675
Mar 3	302879	54553	83599	83118	9684	5259	1148	325	540565

APPENDIX N

NAVAL RESERVE

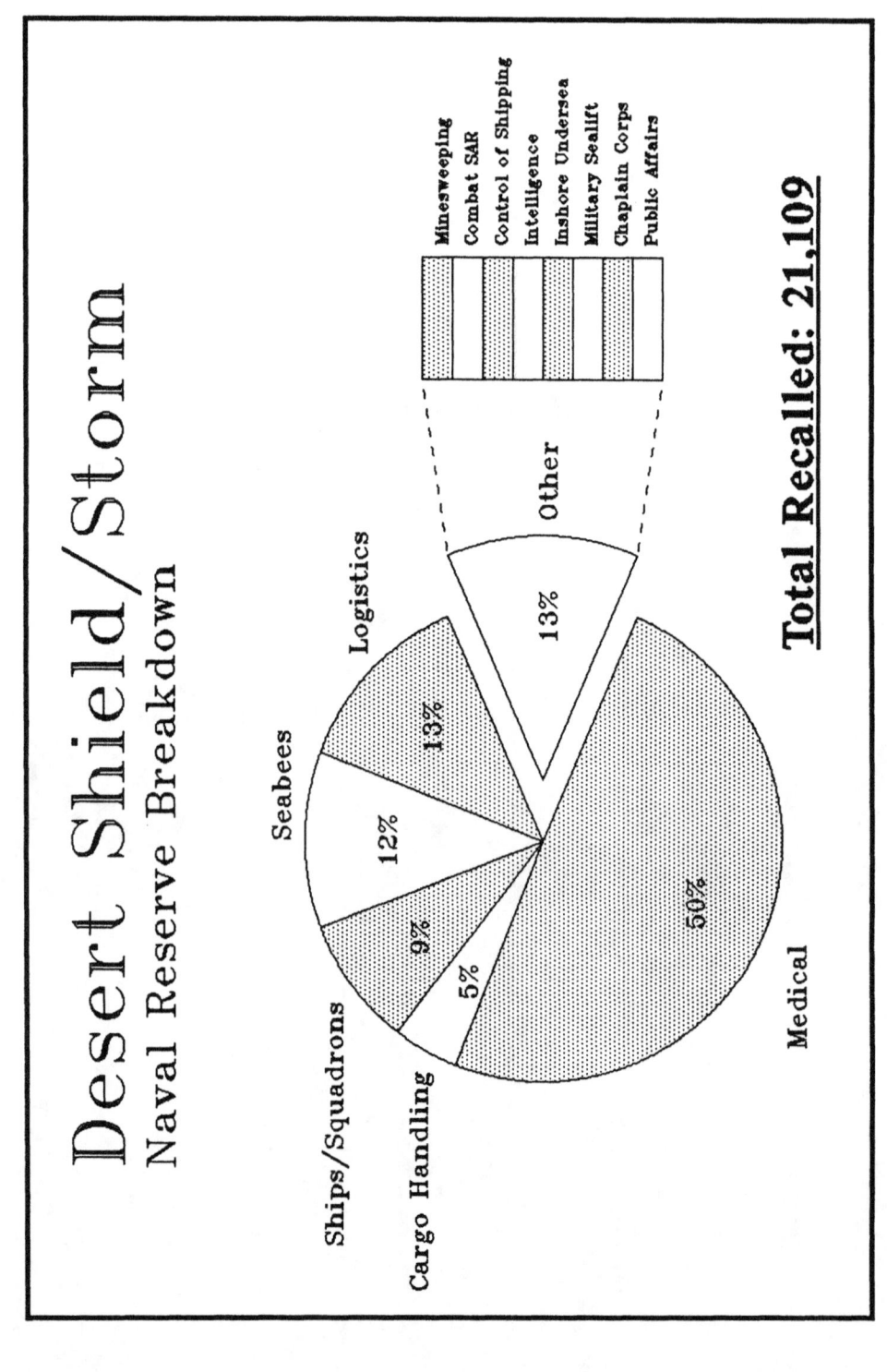

SELECTED NAVAL RESERVISTS ACTIVATED FOR DESERT SHIELD/STORM

MEDICAL	10,452
LOGISTICS SUPPORT	2,682
SEABEES	2,475
SHIP AUGMENT	1,838
CARGO HANDLING	961
MILITARY SEALIFT COMMAND	469
INTELLIGENCE	387
MOBILE INSHORE UNDERSEA WARFARE	354
NAVAL CONTROL OF SHIPPING	89
MINESWEEPERS	88
COMBAT SEARCH AND RESCUE	28
OTHER	<u>1,286</u>
TOTAL	**21,109**

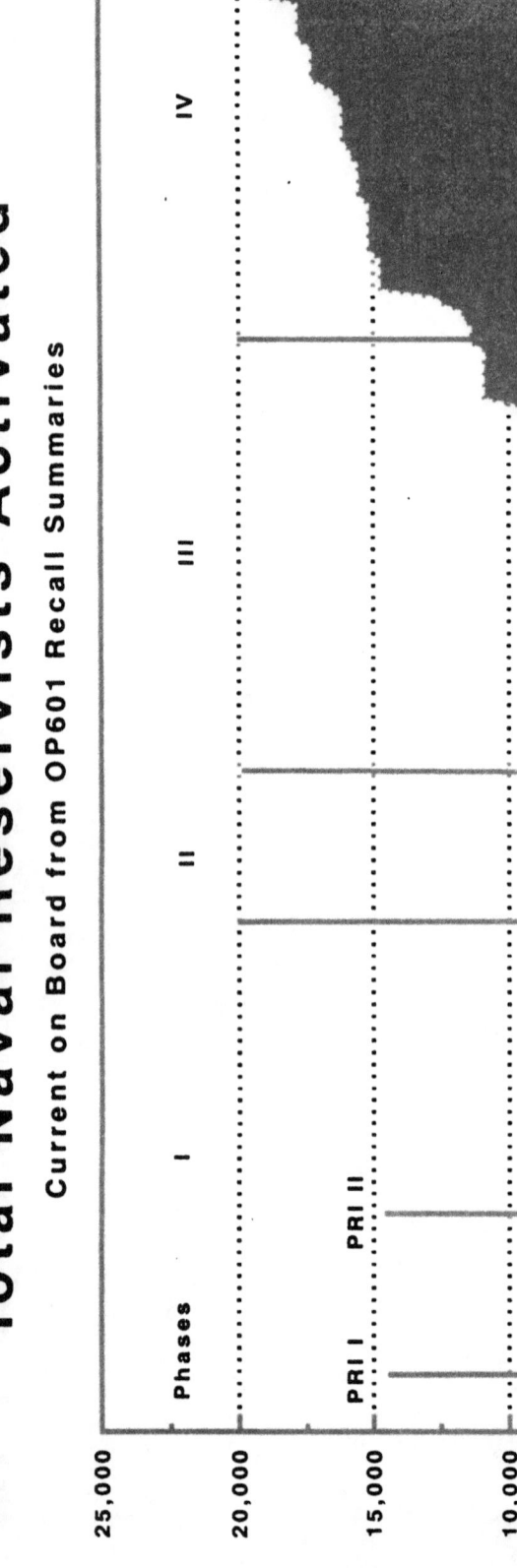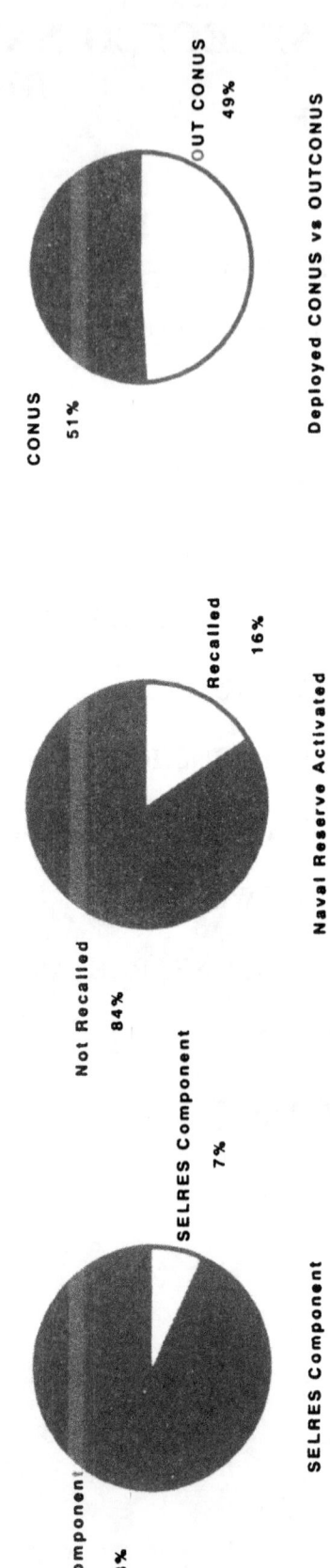

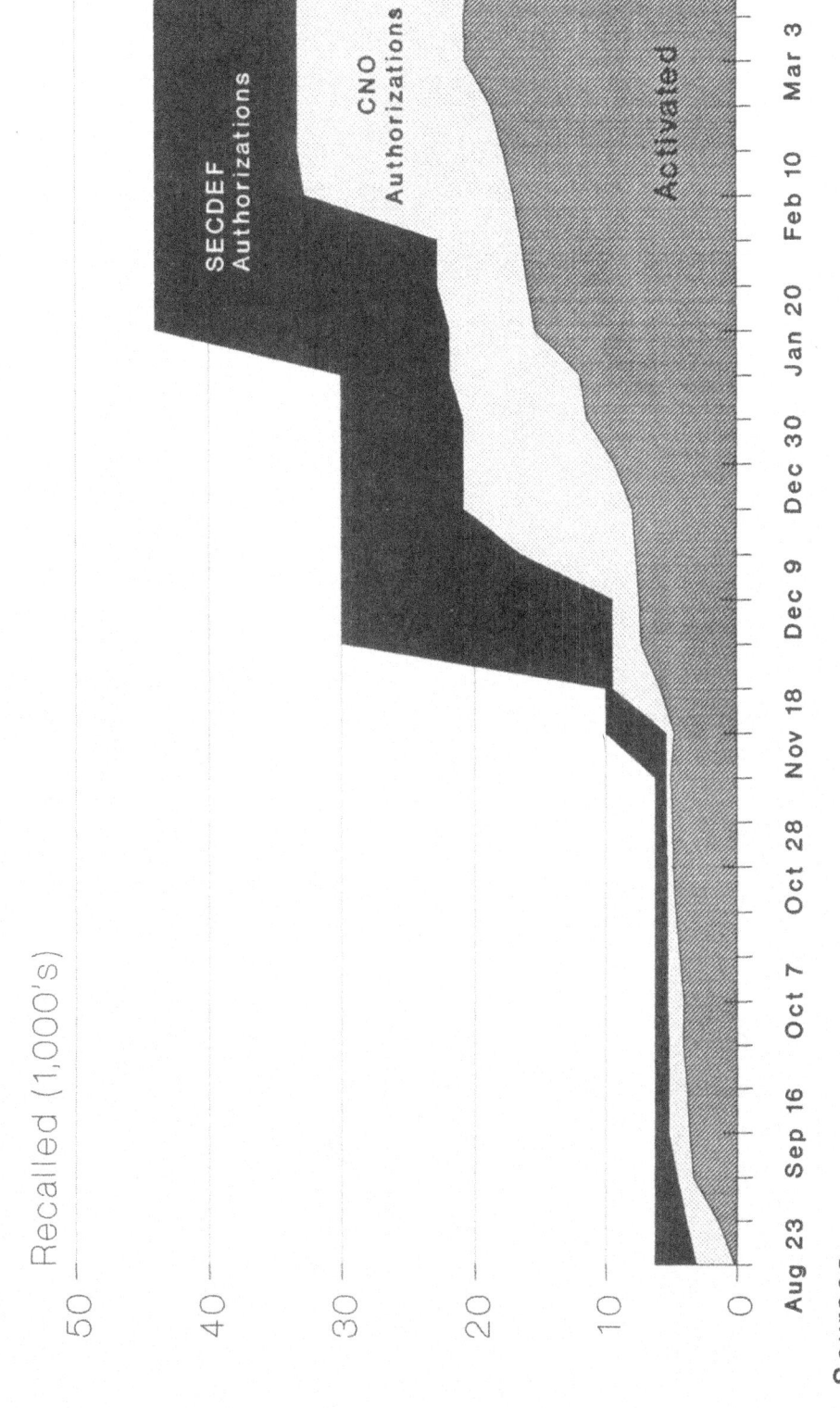

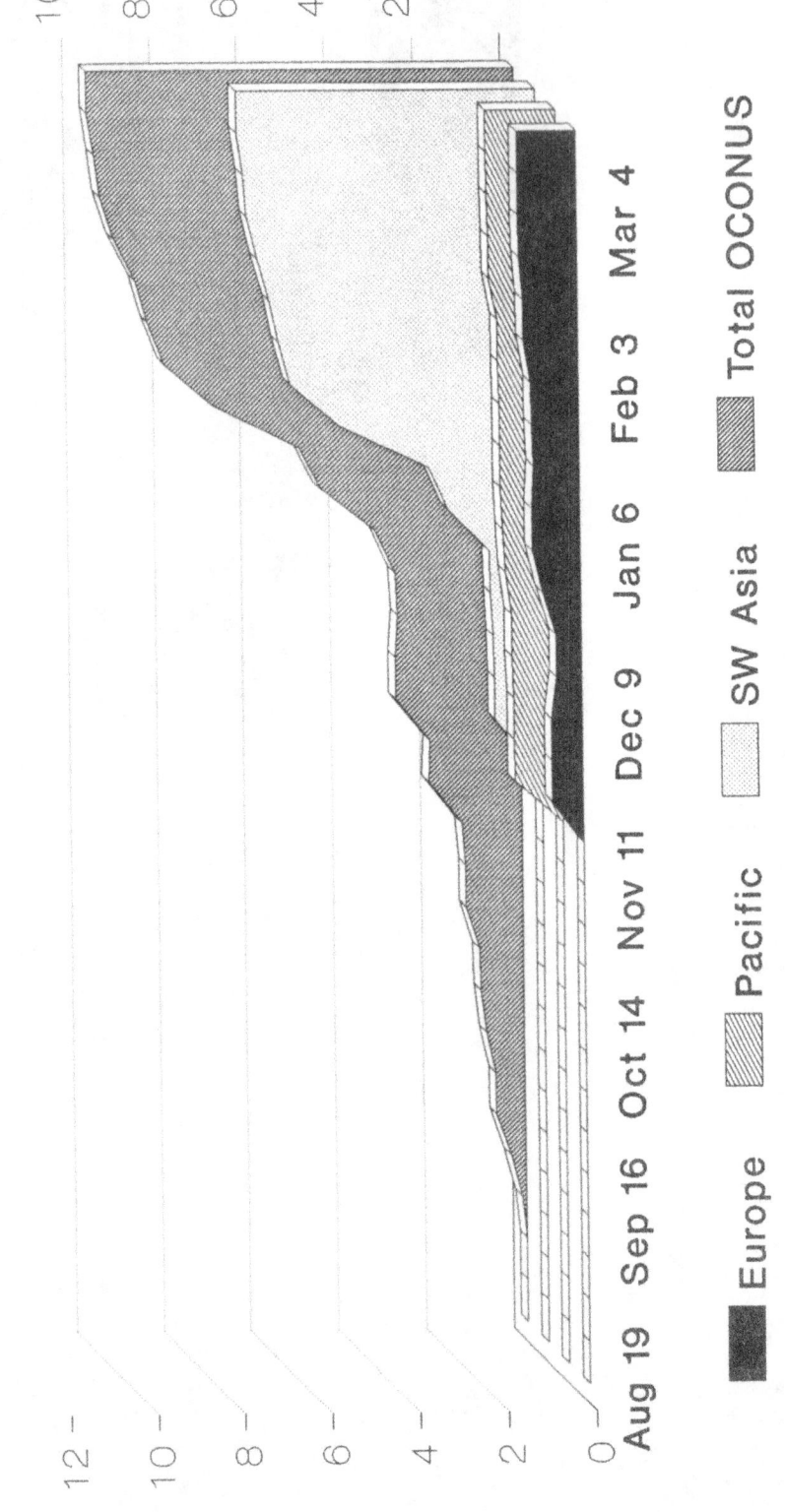

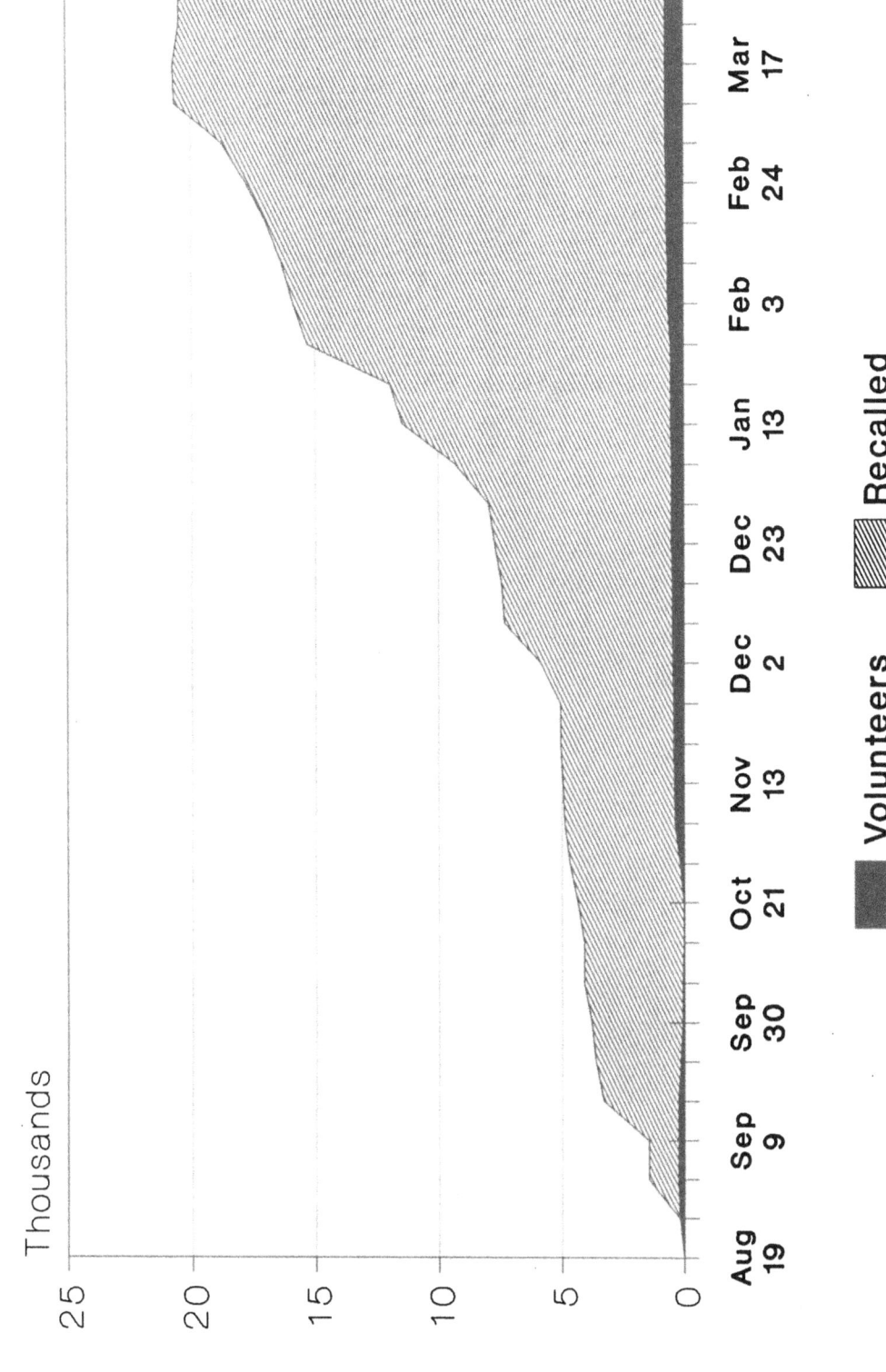

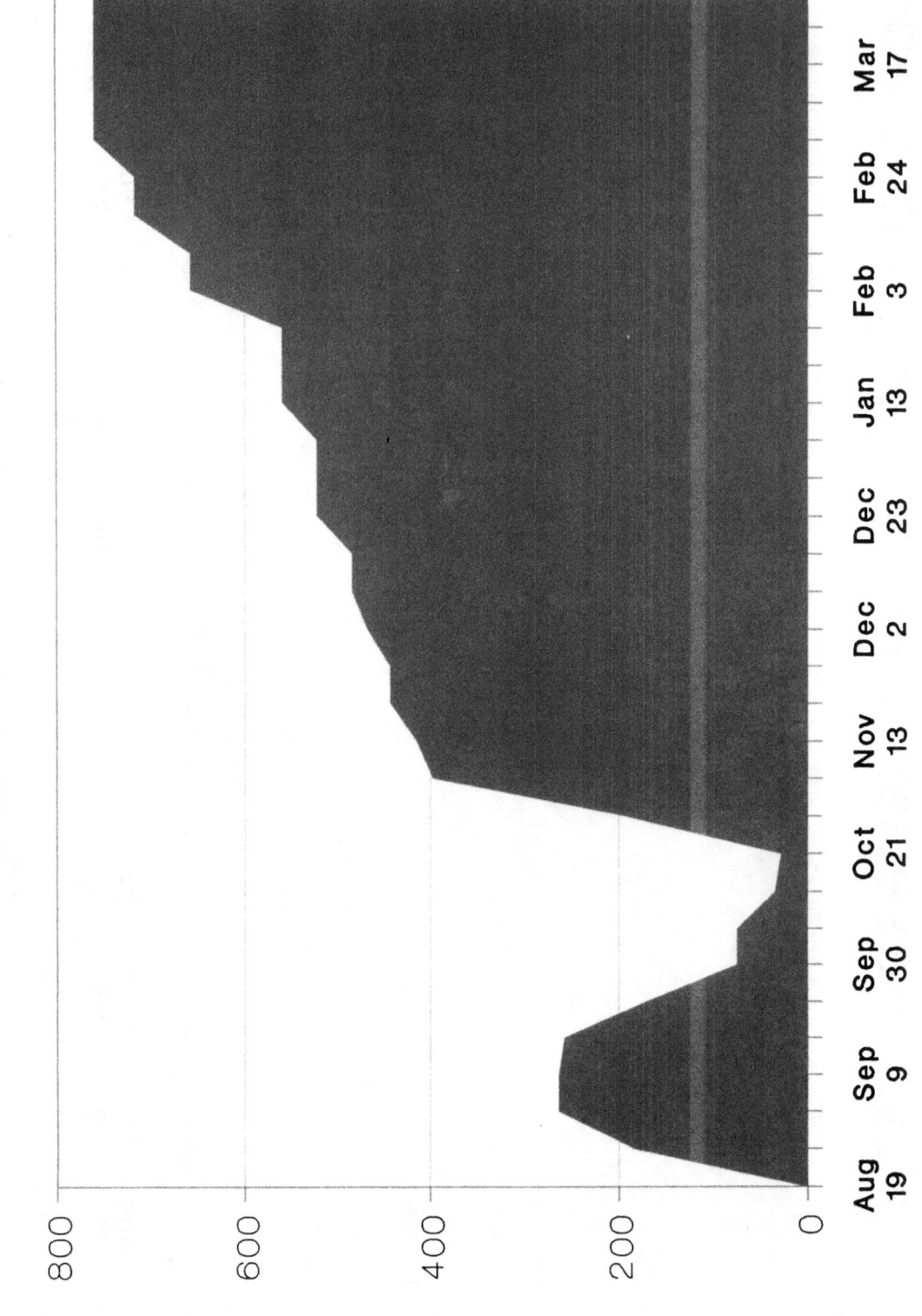

Naval Reserve Call-up Summary						
Date	Total Activated	Activated (673b/673)	Deployed OCONUS	Volunteers	IMA's	IRR's
23 Aug 90	183	0	0	183	0	-
27 Aug 90	1,443	1,179	0	264	0	-
9 Sep 90	3,324	3,066	98	258	1	-
16 Sep 90	3,644	3,473	346	171	1	-
23 Sep 90	3,810	3,736	660	74	1	-
30 Sep 90	4,105	4,031	660	74	1	-
7 Oct 90	4,097	4,063	860	34	1	-
14 Oct 90	4,370	4,342	982	28	1	-
21 Oct 90	4,681	4,488	1,000	193	1	-
28 Oct 90	4,892	4,495	1,300	397	1	-
4 Nov 90	4,945	4,530	1,300	415	1	-
13 Nov 90	5,056	4,613	1,375	443	1	-
18 Nov 90	4,800	4,617	2,114	183	1	-
25 Nov 90	5,884	5,417	2,086	467	1	-
2 Dec 90	7,333	6,850	2,095	484	1	-
9 Dec 90	7,464	6,980	2,487	484	1	-
16 Dec 90	7,720	7,198	2,778	522	1	-
23 Dec 90	7,961	7,439	2,829	522	1	-
30 Dec 90	9,303	8,781	3,267	522	1	-
1 Jan 91	11,446	10,887	4,491	559	1	-
13 Jan 91	11,949	11,390	4,963	559	24	-
20 Jan 91	15,333	14,774	6,926	559	24	-
27 Jan 91	15,895	15,237	8,055	658	57	-

Naval Reserve Call-up Summary						
Date	Total Activated	Activated (673b/673)	Deployed OCONUS	Volunteers	IMA's	IRR's
3 Feb 91	16,355	15,687	8,434	658	114	-
10 Feb 91	16,964	16,247	8,686	717	146	15
17 Feb 91	17,807	17,090	9,181	717	140	15
24 Feb 91	18,754	17,995	6,284	759	159	15
3 Mar 91	20,670	19,911	6,318	759	243	15
10 Mar 91	20,722	19,963	6,363	759	253	15
17 Mar 91	20,482	19,723	6,360	759	260	15

APPENDIX O

MEDICAL SUPPORT

AEROMEDICAL EVACUATION

DATE	STRATEGIC	TACTICAL	TOTAL
13-Jan	8	61	69
14-Jan	55	3	58
15-Jan	111	13	124
16-Jan	76	34	110
17-Jan	58	179	237
18-Jan	60	3	63
19-Jan	0	52	52
Avg. 13 Jan.-19 Jan	53	49	102
20-Jan	118	0	118
21-Jan	0	0	0
22-Jan	22	22	44
23-Jan	74	24	98
24-Jan	102	36	138
25-Jan	0	0	0
26-Jan	52	59	111
Avg. 20 Jan.-26 Jan	53	20	73
27-Jan	63	7	70
28-Jan	13	0	13
29-Jan	26	39	65
30-Jan	12	20	32
31-Jan	0	5	5
1-Feb	98	0	98
2-Feb	26	11	37
Avg. 27 Jan.-2 Feb	34	12	46
3-Feb	82	11	93
4-Feb	32	1	33
5-Feb	57	37	94
6-Feb	25	18	43
7-Feb	58	43	101
8-Feb	0	8	8
9-Feb	77	22	99
Avg. 3 Feb.-9 Feb	47	20	67
10-Feb	53	39	92
11-Feb	66	22	88
12-Feb	0	3	3
13-Feb	113	53	166
14-Feb	43	11	54
15-Feb	51	75	126
16-Feb	0	5	5
17-Feb	84	21	105
18-Feb	0	20	20
19-Feb	155	0	155
20-Feb	34	37	71
21-Feb	81	6	87
22-Feb	79	16	95
23-Feb	28	12	40

DATE	STRATEGIC (a)	TACTICAL (b)	TOTAL
Avg 13 Jan-19 Jan	53	49	102
Avg 20 Jan-26 Jan	53	20	73
Avg 27 Jan-02 Feb	34	12	46
Avg 03 Feb-09 Feb	47	20	67

AEROMEDICAL EVACUATION

Avg 10 Feb-16 Feb	47	30	76			
Avg 17 Feb-23 Feb	66	16	82			
24-Feb	94	36	130			
25-Feb	93	13	106			
26-Feb	0	66	66			
27-Feb	38	130	168			
28-Feb	107	42	149			
1-Mar	110	64	174			
2-Mar	23	209	232			
3-Mar	139	99	238			
4-Mar	196	165	361			

SOURCE: USCINCCENT MEDSTATS

NOTE:
a) Strategic = Evacuated from theatre.
b) Tactical = Evacuated within theatre.

NOTE: Information for 13, 17, and 19 January is incomplete due to nonreceipt of data from some units.

P.O.C. Amy Graham (703) 824-2432

OCCUPIED BEDS

DATE	ARMY	NAVY	USMC	USAF	ENEMY POW	U.S. CIVILIAN	OTHER CIV.	OTHER	TOTAL
13 Jan	363	33	23	32	0	0	4	2	457
14 Jan	435	51	115	45	0	0	0	5	651
15 Jan	392	47	108	53	0	0	4	4	608
16 Jan	362	57	103	50	0	0	0	1	573
17 Jan	301	45	11	47	0	0	0	4	408
18 Jan	414	37	69	37	0	1	0	5	563
19 Jan	396	16	11	43	0	1	6	1	474
Avg. 13 Jan-19 Jan.	380	41	63	44	0	0	2	3	533
20 Jan	254	27	58	66	0	18	86	154	663
21 Jan	317	27	54	50	0	0	149	50	647
22 Jan	367	20	61	94	0	0	165	14	721
23 Jan	310	28	46	57	7	0	227	19	694
24 Jan	289	24	34	56	7	2	235	45	692
25 Jan	262	26	46	48	7	1	274	72	736
26 Jan	249	30	55	49	7	0	125	182	697
Avg. 20 Jan- 26 Jan	293	26	51	60	4	3	180	77	693
27 Jan	264	30	57	49	7	0	96	203	706
28 Jan	275	38	62	52	7	0	89	101	624
29 Jan	315	41	55	57	4	5	174	78	729
30 Jan	341	57	90	63	5	0	226	80	862
31 Jan	306	69	86	61	4	0	113	93	732
01 Feb	322	63	102	55	10	0	103	110	765
02 Feb	352	64	87	62	30	1	103	121	820
Avg 27 Jan-02 Feb.	311	52	77	57	10	1	129	112	748
03 Feb	345	72	88	51	21	2	97	141	817
04 Feb	319	75	96	52	19	4	111	123	799
05 Feb	341	74	85	64	22	3	146	350	1085
06 Feb	517	74	61	46	21	0	243	143	1105
07 Feb	460	71	73	59	15	1	702	125	1506
08 Feb	460	84	80	63	12	2	709	131	1541
09 Feb	439	68	67	70	12	1	598	127	1382
Avg. 03 Feb- 09 Feb	412	74	79	58	17	2	372	163	1176
10-Feb	398	58	69	54	12	4	710	177	1482
11-Feb	409	47	74	47	13	5	739	139	1473
12-Feb	371	48	62	43	13	2	602	138	1279
13-Feb	315	55	78	46	13	2	614	154	1277
14-Feb	397	51	85	61	14	1	700	115	1424
15-Feb	397	43	27	51	13	0	681	111	1323
16 Feb	388	57	85	24	12	2	708	117	1393
Avg 10 Feb-16 Feb	382	51	69	47	13	2	679	136	1379
17-Feb	398	66	86	53	12	17	617	119	1368
18-Feb	424	62	78	72	13	1	719	150	1519
19-Feb	402	53	73	74	12	1	700	126	1441
20-Feb	406	60	80	69	14	1	729	86	1445
21-Feb	378	57	78	55	55	3	769	151	1507
22-Feb	472	60	89	47	11	14	754	105	1552
23-Feb	435	64	70	62	9	0	766	106	1512
DATE	ARMY	NAVY	USMC	USAF	ENEMY POW	U.S. CIVILIAN	OTHER CIV.	OTHER	TOTAL
Avg 13 Jan-19 Jan	380	41	63	44	0	0	2	3	533
Avg 20 Jan-26 Jan	293	26	51	60	4	3	180	77	693

OCCUPIED BEDS

Avg 27 Jan-02 Feb	311	52	77	57	10	1	129	112	748
Avg 03 Feb-09 Feb	412	74	79	58	17	2	372	163	1176
Avg 10 Feb-16 Feb	382	51	69	47	13	2	679	136	1379
Avg 17 Feb-23 Feb	416	60	79	62	12	5	722	120	1478
24-Feb	451	57	66	54	9	2	737	98	1474
25-Feb	433	47	58	45	29	2	735	113	1462
26-Feb	468	39	63	41	45	2	630	97	1385
27-Feb	578	37	76	43	69	1	655	188	1647
28-Feb	628	48	93	61	164	3	656	194	1847
1-Mar	618	43	86	49	360	5	660	182	2003
2-Mar	841	46	98	41	648	2	682	146	2504
3-Mar	487	36	67	35	821	3	717	154	2320
4-Mar	544	41	61	35	762	3	518	161	2125

SOURCE: USCINCCENT MEDSTATS

NOTE: Information for 13, 17, and 19 January is incomplete due to nonreceipt of data from some units.

P.O.C. Amy Graham (703) 824-2432

OUTPATIENT VISITS

DATE	ARMY	NAVY	USMC	USAF	ENEMY POW	U.S. CIVILIAN	OTHER CIV	OTHER	TOTAL
13-Jan	448	160	47	662	0	15	2	20	1353
14-Jan	644	149	126	601	0	2	16	20	1558
15-Jan	688	170	216	576	0	3	20	21	1694
16-Jan	933	190	250	675	0	3	2	15	2068
17-Jan	587	70	28	803	0	5	0	19	1512
18-Jan	433	106	199	472	0	9	0	26	1245
19-Jan	50	23	21	607	0	5	2	10	718
Avg. 13 Jan-19 Jan	540	124	127	628	0	6	6	19	1450
20-Jan	566	200	122	705	0	26	38	34	1691
21-Jan	539	64	80	691	0	2	4	45	1425
22-Jan	626	86	143	1028	0	6	48	78	2015
23-Jan	662	146	101	889	0	3	35	95	1931
24-Jan	723	397	96	824	0	12	109	30	2191
25-Jan	794	37	140	749	0	11	28	42	1801
26-Jan	634	146	107	786	0	13	15	47	1748
Avg. 20 Jan-26 Jan	649	154	113	810	0	10	40	53	1829
27-Jan	551	347	206	699	0	6	49	49	1907
28-Jan	525	253	174	629	0	5	31	103	1720
29-Jan	797	322	334	737	0	12	48	136	2386
30-Jan	721	401	166	777	50	134	8	37	2294
31-Jan	638	299	157	943	0	10	50	164	2261
1-Feb	666	317	105	813	0	7	35	60	2003
2-Feb	613	269	134	899	16	5	47	124	2107
Avg. 20 Jan-26 Jan	644	315	182	785	9	26	38	96	2097
3-Feb	572	305	129	751	0	10	54	173	1994
4-Feb	531	53	159	678	0	37	43	148	1649
5-Feb	657	177	133	829	3	11	38	169	2017
6-Feb	629	227	136	773	5	8	45	45	1868
7-Feb	743	213	89	780	5	5	57	140	2032
8-Feb	772	295	167	737	3	4	43	137	2158
9-Feb	721	188	129	747	2	8	40	131	1966
Avg. 3 Feb-9 Feb	661	208	135	756	3	12	46	135	1955
10-Feb	724	155	139	648	0	8	142	49	1865
11-Feb	518	344	119	681	5	4	36	165	1872
12-Feb	806	254	153	843	0	20	29	167	2272
13-Feb	901	298	179	744	5	26	35	163	2351
14-Feb	974	526	153	781	0	11	40	161	2646
15-Feb	889	417	133	785	0	20	37	121	2402
16-Feb	939	338	160	822	0	12	53	111	2435
Avg. 10 Feb-16 Feb	822	333	148	758	1	14	53	134	2263
17-Feb	884	303	132	749	0	22	45	285	2420
18-Feb	708	314	152	677	11	10	47	227	2146
19-Feb	981	326	150	740	7	17	48	218	2487
20-Feb	1002	332	181	805	0	14	57	227	2618
21-Feb	980	373	140	793	0	18	60	263	2627
22-Feb	1076	204	162	725	0	11	55	253	2486
23-Feb	1050	570	162	706	0	12	42	198	2740
DATE	ARMY	NAVY	USMC	USAF	ENEMY POW	U.S. CIVILIAN	OTHER CIV	OTHER	TOTAL
Avg 13 Jan-19 Jan	540	124	127	628	0	6	6	19	1450
Avg 20 Jan-26 Jan	649	154	113	810	0	10	40	53	1829

OUTPATIENT VISITS

Avg 27 Jan-02 Feb	644	315	182	785	9	26	38	96	2097
Avg 03 Feb-09 Feb	661	208	135	756	3	12	46	135	1955
Avg 10 Feb-16 Feb	822	333	148	758	1	14	53	134	2263
Avg 17 Feb-23 Feb	954	346	154	742	3	15	51	239	2503
24-Feb	905	491	111	578	0	12	75	218	2390
25-Feb	668	345	112	553	0	8	65	162	1913
26-Feb	908	372	129	687	0	15	46	155	2312
27-Feb	955	357	155	664	1	21	65	132	2350
28-Feb	800	201	102	656	23	7	31	184	2004
1-Mar	821	148	111	655	0	14	44	143	1936
2-Mar	811	281	105	671	0	19	63	197	2147
3-Mar	681	360	179	586	0	6	61	231	2104
4-Mar	625	215	98	480	90	10	107	204	1829

SOURCE: USCINCCENT MEDSTATS

NOTE: Information for 13, 17, and 19 January is incomplete due to nonreceipt of data from some units.

P.O.C. Amy Graham (703) 824-2432

APPENDIX P

MEDIA POOLS

TV & PRINT COVERAGE

DATE	MEDIA POOLS	AIRED TV COVERAGE	PRINT COVERAGE
JAN 16	BB		1:SARATOGA-Christian Science Monitor
17	FFG		1:WISCONSIN-Dallas Morning News
18	CV		
19	CV		
20	(A)		2:WISCONSIN-Balt.Sun/Dallas M.N.
21			2:NICHOLAS-Balt.Sun/Dallas M.N.
22	CG (D) LSD		2:JFK/GUNSTON HALL-A.P.
23		CNN-Amphib Deployment CBS-SLAM	3:JFK-Reuters/A.P./VA Pilot
24	(B)	CNN-JFK/UNREP	2:MOBILE BAY/VF-HDT/Dallas M.N.
25	(C)	ABC/CBS-RANGER ABC/NBC-AMERICA	1:MOBILE BAY-Harrison Daily Times
26		CNN-RANGER	1:MOBILE BAY-Harrison Daily Times
27	(E) CV	CNN-Hospital Ships	
28	AFS CG	CNN-Navy helo	2:JFK-Phila.Inquirer/VA Pilot
29	CVN	CNN/CBS-ROOSEVELT CNN-UNREP	1:VALLEY FORGE-Stars & Stripes
30		ABC-Ship Unrep	2:CURTS-AP/Detroit News
31		CNN-PUGET SOUND NBC-Flight Ops	4:CURTS/TR-DetN/DalTH/Dallas M.N.
FEB 1	AFS FFG	CNN/ABC-CURTS/POWs NBC-Helo	1:CURTS-L.A.Times
2	(G) LPH	CNN/ABC/CBS/NBC-Tomahawk Missiles Over Baghdad	
3			
4	(H) LCC (I)		1:CURTS-N.Y. News Day
5		CNN-Pilot Stress/USN Role in Gulf	
6			2:TR/SARA-Navy Times/Boston Herald
7	AFS LCC (K)		1:TR-Dallas Morning News
8	CVN BB	CNN-ROOSEVELT	
9	LCC (J)	CNN-WISCONSIN NBC-MISSOURI	2:WISCONSIN-DMN/Reuters
10	CG		7:WISC/TR-MS/BB/DMN/UPI/AP/Reuters
11	(L) MSO	CNN-NICHOLAS & ROOSEVELT	7:WISC/TR-WSJ/VAP/DMN/Hou/CPD/AP
12	(M) (N) LSD	CNN-ROOSEVELT & R.K.TURNER	4:WISC/MISS/CURTS-LAT/DetN/CTrib
13	(O)		1:WISCONSIN-L.A.Times
14	LCC AFS	ABC Prime Time Live - VADM Arthur	
15	(P)	CBS-TRIPOLI/Mine Ops	
16	(Q) LPH		
17			
18	(S) (T)	CNN-WISCONSIN/TRIPOLI/PRINCETON	5:TR/WISC/TRIP-DMN/VAP/New/MS/AP
19	(R) CV BB LST	CNN-VADM Mustin on Mines	5:TRIP/PRIN-DMN/KanGaz/DalTH/CPD/Re
20	LHA LSD CV (U)		5:PRIN/WISC/TRIP-CPD/Okla/Ark/New
21			4:NAS/GH/TRIP/PRIN-AP/CTrib/Miss
22	(V) (W) (X)		3:NASSAU/Amphib Ops-A.P.
23	DD	CBS-NASSAU CNN-GUNSTON HALL	6:NASSAU/MCM/Marines-CPD/AP/CTrib
24	M CV	CNN-MISSOURI/FLT HOSP/AMPHIB Ops/ Air Support	5:NASSAU/GUN HALL/Grnd Ops-AP/USNW/NW
25	BB CG		4:WISC/AMPHIB-SDU/WT/AP/USNW/NW
26	CV CV (BB)		2:GUN HALL/MISS-VA Pilot
27	CV (DD) (Z) (AA)		1:GUNSTON HALL-Christian Science Mon.
28	(CC) (EE)		

P-2

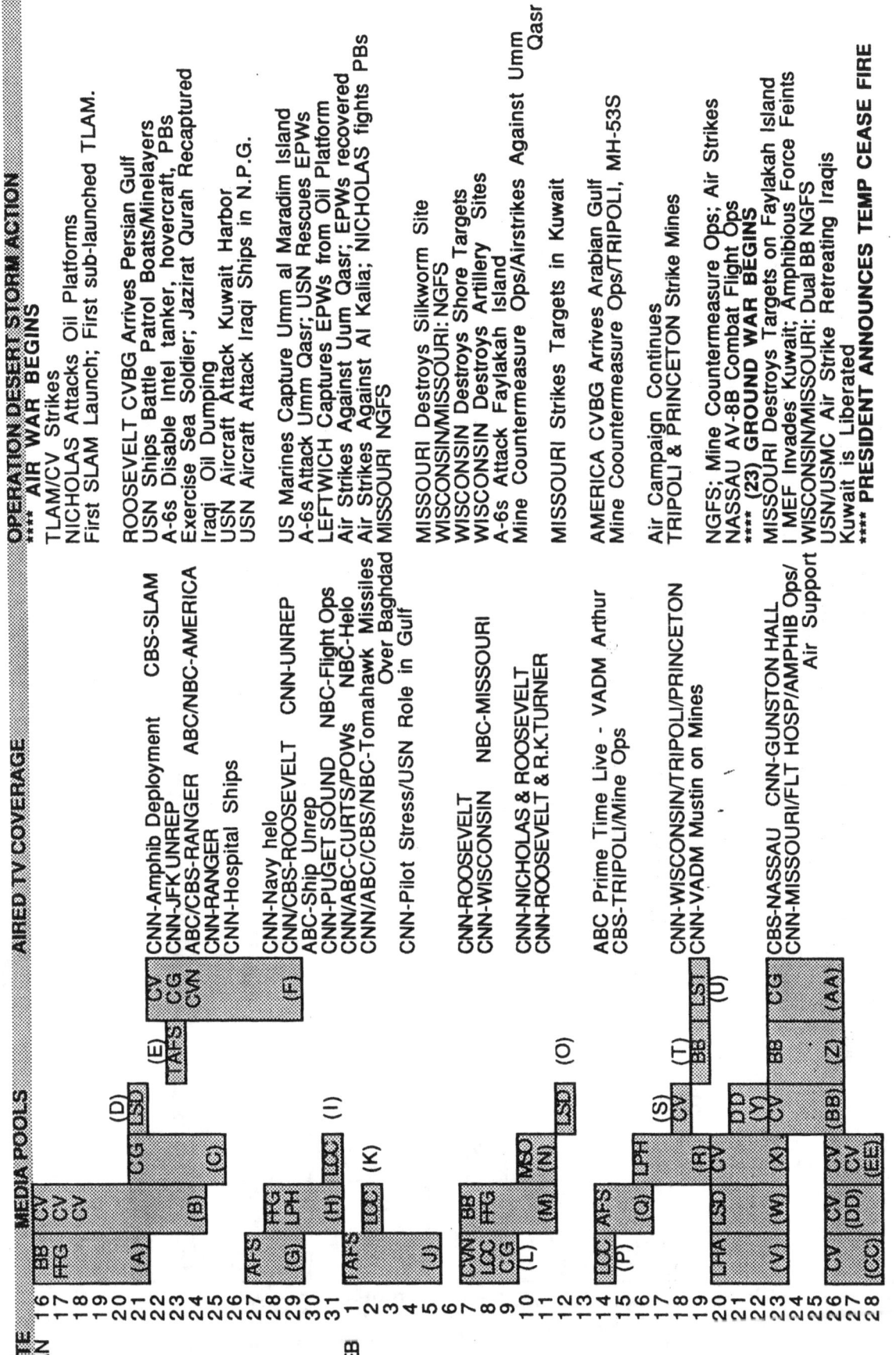

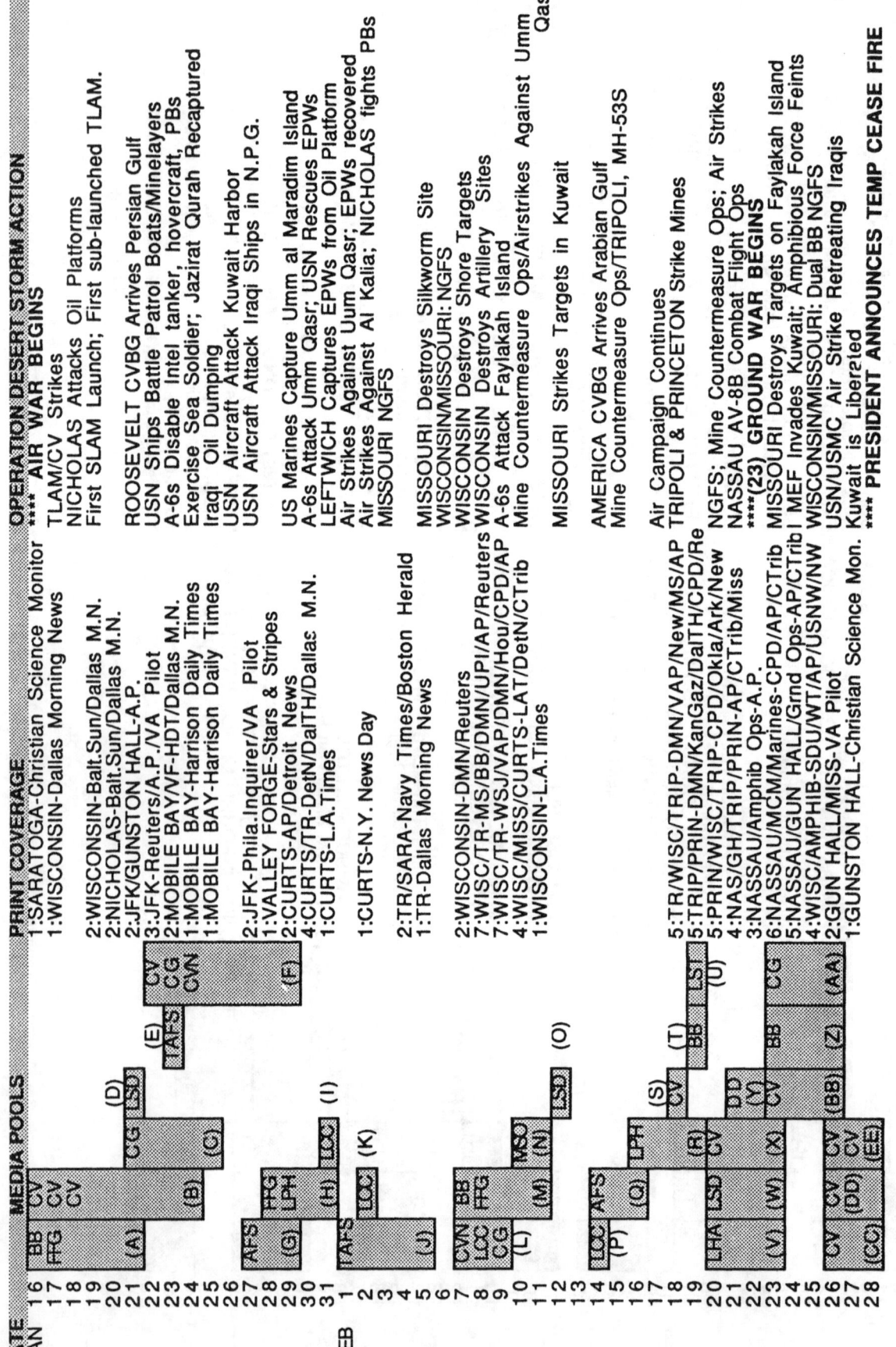

MEDIA EMBARKS/PRINT COVERAGE

DESERT STORM
Media Embarks/TV & Print Coverage

Media Pool (M.P.) Embarks

A	MP#5	USS Wisconsin/Nicholas	13-21 Jan
B	MP#7	USS JFK/Saratoga/America	15-24 Jan
C	MP#4	USS Mobile Bay	21-25 Jan
D	MP#7	USS Gunston Hall	21 Jan
E	MP#7	USS Spica	23 Jan
F	MP#7	USS Ranger/Valley Forge/Roosevelt	22-29 Jan
G	MP#5	USS Niagara Falls	27-29 Jan
H	MP#5	USS Curts/Okinawa	28-31 Jan
I	MP#1	USS Blue Ridge	31 Jan
J	MP#7	USS Spica	1-5 Feb
K	MP#2	USS Blue Ridge	2 Feb
L	MP#7	USS Blue Ridge/TR/R.K.Turner	7-9 Feb
M	MP#5	USS Wisconsin/Nicholas	7-11 Feb
N	MP#4	USS Adroit	10-11 Feb
O	MP#7	USS Portland	12 Feb
P	MP#4	USS Blue Ridge	14 Feb
Q	MP#5	USS San Jose	14-16 Feb
R	MP#9	USS Tripoli	16-19 Feb
S	MP#6	USS Midway	18 Feb
T	MP#0	USS Wisconsin	19 Feb
U	MP#5	USS Barbour County	19 Feb
V	MP#5	USS Nassau	20-23 Feb
W	MP#8	USS Gunston Hall	20-23 Feb
X	MP#8	USS America	20-23 Feb
Y	MP#5	USS Leftwich	21-22 Feb
Z	MP#5	USS Missouri	23-26 Feb
AA	MP#5	USS Valley Forge	23-26 Feb
BB	MP#8	USS Midway	23-26 Feb
CC	MP#8	USS Ranger	26-28 Feb
DD	MP#7	USS America	26-28 Feb
EE	MP#7	USS JFK/Saratoga	26-28 Feb

DESERT STORM
Media Embarks/TV & Print Coverage Abbreviations for Chart

Ships

GUN HALL/GH	USS Gunston Hall
JFK	USS John Fitzgerald Kennedy
MISS	USS Mississippi
NAS	USS Nassau
PRIN	USS Princeton
SARA	USS Saratoga
TR	USS Theodore Roosevelt
TRIP	USS Tripoli
WISC	USS Wisconsin

Other

Amphib Ops	Amphibious Operations
VF	Fighter Squadron
Grnd Ops	Ground Operations

DESERT STORM
Media Embarks/TV & Print Coverage
Abbreviations for Chart

Newspapers

Ark	Arkansas Gazette
A.P./AP	Associated Press
BaltSun	Baltimore Sun
BaxtBull/BB	Baxter Bulletin
Christian Science Mon	Christian Science Monitor
CPD	Cleveland Plain Dealer
CTrib	Chicago Tribune
Dallas M.N./DMN	Dallas Morning News
DalTH	Dallas Times Herald
DetN	Detroit News
HDT	Harrison Daily Times
Hou	Houston Tribune
KanGaz	Kansas Gazette
LAT/L.A.Times	Los Angeles Times
MilwSen/MS	Milwaukee Sentinel
Miss	Mississippi Press
New	Newark Star-Ledger
NW	Newsweek
N.Y. Times	New York Times
Okla	Oklahoma Tribune
Re	Reuters
SDU	San Diego Union
USNW	U.S. News & World Report
VA Pilot/VAP	Virginia Pilot
Wash Times/WT	Washington Times
WSJ	Wisconsin State Journal

www.ingramcontent.com/pod-product-compliance
Lightning Source LLC
Chambersburg PA
CBHW082118230426
43671CB00015B/2731